John Muir

ERS OF

BY

WILLIAM FREDERIC BADÈ

VOLUME II

TOVT
BIEN OV
RIEN

BOSTON AND NEW YORK

HOUGHTON MIFFLIN COMPANY

The Riberside Press Cambridge

1924

The Riverside Press
CAMBRIDGE · MASSACHUSETTS
PRINTED IN THE U.S.A.

CONTENTS

THE LIFE AND LETTERS OF
JOHN MUIR
VOLUME II

THE LIFE AND LETTERS OF
JOHN MUIR

. .

CHAPTER XI

ON WIDENING CURRENTS

1873–1875

THE ten months' interval of Muir's Oakland
sojourn made a complete break in his accustomed activities. It was a storm and stress
period to which he refers afterward as "the
strange Oakland epoch," and we are left to infer that the strangeness consisted chiefly in the
fact that he was housebound — by his own
choice, to be sure, but nevertheless shut away
from the free life of the mountains. It is not
surprising, perhaps, that this period is marked
by an almost complete stoppage of his correspondence, though he never was more continuously busy with his pen than during these
months.

Easily the foremost literary journal of the
Pacific Coast at that time was the "Overland
Monthly." It had been founded in 1868, and
Bret Harte was the man to whom it owed both

its beginning and the fame it achieved under his editorship. The magazine, however, was not a profit-yielding enterprise, for John H. Carmany, its owner, professed to have lost thirty thousand dollars in his endeavor to make it pay. In a sheaf of reminiscences written years afterward, he reveals the double reason why the magazine proved expensive and why so many distinguished names, such as those of Mark Twain, Joaquin Miller, Ambrose Bierce, Edward Rowland Sill, Bret Harte, and John Muir, appear on its roll of contributors. "They have reason to remember me," he wrote, "for never have such prices been paid for poems, stories, and articles as I paid to the writers of the old 'Overland.'"

Bret Harte, balking at a contract designed to correct his dilatory literary habits, left the magazine in 1871, and, after several unsatisfactory attempts to supply his place, Benjamin P. Avery became editor of the "Overland." In March, 1874, he wrote a letter acknowledging the first number of Muir's notable series of "Studies in the Sierra," thereby disclosing what the latter had been doing during the winter months. "I am delighted," he tells Muir, "with your very original and clearly written paper on 'Mountain Sculpture' which reveals the law beneath the beauty of moun-

4

tain and rock forms." This article, accompanied by numerous illustrative line drawings, appeared as the leading contribution in May and was followed in monthly succession by six others, in the order given in an earlier chapter.[1]

Not many weeks after the receipt of this initial article, Mr. Avery accepted an appointment as Minister to China. "Not ambition for honors," he wrote to Muir, "but the compulsion of broken health made me risk a foreign appointment, and I especially regret that the opportunity to share in the publication of your valuable papers, and to know you most intimately, is to be lost to me." To the deep regret of his friends, Avery died in China the following year. Mr. Carmany, despairing of the "Overland" as a financial venture, let it come to an end in 1875, and Muir, when his current engagements were discharged, formed new literary connections.

There can be no doubt that during the closing years of the magazine, 1874–75, Muir's articles constituted by far the most significant contribution. It was in good measure due to Mrs. Carr that he was finally induced to write this series of "Sierra Studies." She had even suggested suspension of correspondence in order to enable him to accomplish the task.

[1] Vol. i, p. 358.

"You told me I ought to abandon letter writing," he wrote to her on Christmas day, 1872, "and I see plainly enough that you are right in this, because my correspondence has gone on increasing year by year and has become far too bulky and miscellaneous in its character, and consumes too much of my time. Therefore I mean to take your advice and allow broad acres of silence to spread between my letters, however much of self-denial may be demanded."

In the same letter, which a strange combination of circumstances has just brought to light again after fifty-two years, he expresses pungently that distaste for the mechanics of writing which undoubtedly accounts in part for the relative smallness of his formal literary output.

Book-making frightens me [he declares], because it demands so much artificialness and retrograding. Somehow, up here in these fountain skies [of Yosemite] I feel like a flake of glass through which light passes, but which, conscious of the inexhaustibleness of its sun fountain, cares not whether its passing light coins itself into other forms or goes unchanged — neither charcoaled nor diamonded! Moreover, I find that though I have a few thoughts entangled in the fibres of my mind, I possess no words into which I can shape them. You tell me that I must be patient and reach out and grope in lexicon gran-

6

aries for the words I want. But if some loquacious
angel were to touch my lips with literary fire, be-
stowing every word of Webster, I would scarce
thank him for the gift, because most of the words of
the English language are made of mud, for muddy
purposes, while those invented to contain spiritual
matter are doubtful and unfixed in capacity and
form, as wind-ridden mist-rags.

These mountain fires that glow in one's blood are
free to all, but I cannot find the chemistry that may
press them unimpaired into booksellers' bricks.
True, with that august instrument, the English language, in the manufacture of which so many brains
have been broken, I can proclaim to you that moon-
shine is glorious, and sunshine more glorious, that
winds rage, and waters roar, and that in 'terrible
times' glaciers guttered the mountains with their
hard cold snouts. This is about the limit of what I
feel capable of doing for the public — the moiling,
squirming, fog-breathing public. But for my few
friends I can do more because they already know
the mountain harmonies and can catch the tones I
gather for them, though written in a few harsh and
gravelly sentences.

There was another aspect of writing that
Muir found irksome and that was its solitariness. Being a fluent and vivid conversational-
ist, accustomed to the excitation of eager hear-
ers, he missed the give-and-take of conversation when he sat down with no company but
that of his pen. Even the writing of a letter to
a friend had something of the conversational

about it. But to write between four walls for the "Babylonish mobs" that hived past his window was another matter. Fresh from Cassiope, the heather of the High Sierra, aglow with enthusiasm for the beauty that had burned itself into his soul, he could but wonder and grow indignant at the stolid self-sufficiency of "the metallic, money-clinking crowds," among whom he felt himself as alien as any Hebrew psalmist or prophet by the waters of Babylon.

It is not to be wondered at, therefore, that this first sojourn in the San Francisco Bay region was for Muir a kind of exile under which he evidently chafed a good deal. His human environment was so unblushingly materialistic that, in spite of a few sympathetic friends, it seemed to him well-nigh impossible to obtain a hearing on behalf of Nature from any other standpoint than that of commercial utility. On this point he differed trenchantly with his contemporaries and doubtless engaged in a good many arguments, for his frankness and downright sincerity did not permit him to compromise the supremacy of values which by his own standard far exceeded those of commercialism. It is by reference to such verbal passages of arms that we must explain his allusion, in the following letter, to "all the morbidness that has been hooted at me."

ON WIDENING CURRENTS

The issue was one which, in his own mind, he had settled fundamentally on his thousand-mile walk to the Gulf, but which challenged him again at every street corner in Oakland, and he was not the man to retire from combat in such a cause. He was, in fact, an eager and formidable opponent. "No one who did not know Muir in those days," remarked one of his old friends to me, "can have any conception of Muir's brilliance as a conversational antagonist in an argument." The world made especially for the uses of man? "Certainly not," said Muir. "No dogma taught by the present civilization forms so insuperable an obstacle to a right understanding of the relations which human culture sustains to wildness. Every animal, plant, and crystal controverts it in the plainest terms. Yet it is taught from century to century as something ever new and precious, and in the resulting darkness the enormous conceit is allowed to go unchallenged!"

Though grilling in his very blood over this huckster appraisement of Nature, Muir labored hard and continuously with his pen throughout the winter and the following spring and summer. When autumn came he had completed not only his seven "Studies in the Sierra," but had also written a paper entitled "Studies in the

Formation of Mountains in the Sierra Nevada"
for the American Association for the Advancement of Science, and articles on "Wild Sheep
of California" and "Byways of Yosemite
Travel." About this time his health had begun
to suffer from excessive confinement and irregular diet at restaurants, so, yielding with
sudden resolution to an overpowering longing
for the mountains, he set out again for Yosemite. The following letter in which his correspondence with Mrs. Carr reaches its highest
level and, in a sense, its conclusion, celebrates
his escape from an uncongenial environment.

To Mrs. Ezra S. Carr

YOSEMITE VALLEY, [*September*, 1874]

DEAR MRS. CARR:

Here again are pine trees, and the wind, and
living rock and water! I've met two of my
ouzels on one of the pebble ripples of the river
where I used to be with them. Most of the
meadow gardens are disenchanted and dead,
yet I found a few mint spikes and asters and
brave, sunful goldenrods and a patch of the
tiny Mimulus that has two spots on each
lip. The fragrance and the color and the
form, and the whole spiritual expression of
goldenrods are hopeful and strength-giving
beyond any other flowers that I know. A

single spike is sufficient to heal unbelief and melancholy.

On leaving Oakland I was so excited over my escape that, of course, I forgot and left all the accounts I was to collect. No wonder, and no matter. I'm beneath that grand old pine that I have heard so often in storms both at night and in the day. It sings grandly now, every needle sun-thrilled and shining and responding tunefully to the azure wind.

When I left I was in a dreamy exhausted daze. Yet from mere habit or instinct I tried to observe and study. From the car window I watched the gradual transitions from muddy water, spongy tule, marsh and level field as we shot up the San Jose Valley, and marked as best I could the forms of the stream cañons as they opened to the plain and the outlines of the undulating hillocks and headlands between. Interest increased at every mile, until it seemed unbearable to be thrust so flyingly onward even towards the blessed Sierras. I will study them yet, free from time and wheels. When we turned suddenly and dashed into the narrow mouth of the Livermore pass I was looking out of the right side of the car. The window was closed on account of the cinders and smoke from the locomotive. All at once my eyes clasped a big hard rock not a hundred yards away, every line of which is as strictly and out-spokenly glacial as any of the most alphabetic of the high and young Sierra. That one sure glacial word thrilled and overjoyed me more than you will ever believe. Town smokes and shadows had not dimmed my vision, for I had passed this glacial rock twice before without reading its meaning.

As we proceeded, the general glacialness of the range became more and more apparent, until we reached Pleasanton where once there was a grand *mer de glace.* Here the red sun went down in a cloudless glow and I leaned back, happy and weary and possessed with a lifeful of noble problems.

At Lathrop we suppered and changed cars. The last of the daylight had long faded and I sauntered away from the din while the baggage was being transferred. The young moon hung like a sickle above the shorn wheat fields, Ursa Major pictured the northern sky, the Milky Way curved sublimely through the broadcast stars like some grand celestial moraine with planets for boulders, and the whole night shone resplendent, adorned with that calm imperishable beauty which it has worn unchanged from the beginning.

I slept at Turlock and next morning faced the Sierra and set out through the sand afoot.

ON WIDENING CURRENTS

The freedom I felt was exhilarating, and the burning heat and thirst and faintness could not make it less. Before I had walked ten miles I was wearied and footsore, but it was real earnest work and I liked it. Any kind of simple natural destruction is preferable to the numb, dumb, apathetic deaths of a town.

Before I was out of sight of Turlock I found a handful of the glorious *Hemizonia virgata* and a few of the patient, steadfast eriogonums that I learned to love around the slopes of Twenty-Hill Hollow. While I stood with these old dear friends we were joined by a lark, and in a few seconds more Harry Edwards [1] came flapping by with spotted wings. Just think of the completeness of that reunion! — Twenty-Hill Hollow, Hemizonia, Eriogonum, Lark, Butterfly, and I, and lavish outflows of genuine Twenty-Hill Hollow sun gold. I threw down my coat and one shirt in the sand, forgetting Hopeton and heedless that the sun was becoming hotter every minute. I was wild once more and let my watch warn and point as it pleased.

Heavy wagon loads of wheat had been hauled along the road and the wheels had sunk deep and left smooth beveled furrows in the sand. Upon the smooth slopes of these sand furrows I soon observed a most beautiful and

[1] For the meaning of this allusion see vol. I, p. 263.

varied embroidery, evidently tracks of some kind. At first I thought of mice, but soon saw they were too light and delicate for mice. Then a tiny lizard darted into the stubble ahead of me, and I carefully examined the track he made, but it was entirely unlike the fine print embroidery I was studying. However I knew that he might make very different tracks if walking leisurely. Therefore I determined to catch one and experiment. I found out in Florida that lizards, however swift, are short-winded, so I gave chase and soon captured a tiny gray fellow and carried him to a smooth sand-bed where he could embroider without getting away into grass tufts or holes. He was so wearied that he couldn't skim and was compelled to walk, and I was excited with delight in seeing an exquisitely beautiful strip of embroidery about five-eighths of an inch wide, drawn out in flowing curves behind him as from a loom. The riddle was solved. I knew that mountain boulders moved in music; so also do lizards, and their written music, printed by their feet, moved so swiftly as to be invisible, covers the hot sands with beauty wherever they go.

But my sand embroidery lesson was by no means done. I speedily discovered a yet more delicate pattern on the sands, woven into that

14

of the lizard. I examined the strange combination of bars and dots. No five-toed lizard had printed that music. I watched narrowly down on my knees, following the strange and beautiful pattern along the wheel furrows and out into the stubble. Occasionally the pattern would suddenly end in a shallow pit half an inch across and an eighth of an inch deep. I was fairly puzzled, picked up my bundle, and trudged discontentedly away, but my eyes were hungrily awake and I watched all the ground. At length a gray grasshopper rattled and flew up, and the truth flashed upon me that he was the complementary embroiderer of the lizard. Then followed long careful observation, but I never could see the grasshopper until he jumped, and after he alighted he invariably stood watching me with his legs set ready for another jump in case of danger. Nevertheless I soon made sure that he was my man, for I found that in jumping he made the shallow pits I had observed at the termination of the pattern I was studying. But no matter how patiently I waited he wouldn't *walk* while I was sufficiently near to observe. They are so nearly the color of the sand. I therefore caught one and lifted his wing covers and cut off about half of each wing with my penknife, and carried him to a favorable place on the sand. At

15

first he did nothing but jump and make dimples, but soon became weary and *walked* in common rhythm with all his six legs, and my interest you may guess while I watched the embroidery — the written music laid down in a beautiful ribbon-like strip behind. I glowed with wild joy as if I had found a new glacier — copied specimens of the precious fabric into my notebook, and strode away with my own feet sinking with a dull craunch, craunch, craunch in the hot gray sand, glad to believe that the dark and cloudy vicissitudes of the Oakland period had not dimmed my vision in the least. Surely Mother Nature pitied the poor boy and showed him pictures.

Happen what would, fever, thirst, or sunstroke, my joy for that day was complete. Yet I was to receive still more. A train of curving tracks with a line in the middle next fixed my attention, and almost before I had time to make a guess concerning their author, a small hawk came shooting down vertically out of the sky a few steps ahead of me and picked up something in his talons. After rising thirty or forty feet overhead, he dropped it by the roadside as if to show me what it was. I ran forward and found a little bunchy field mouse and at once suspected him of being embroiderer number three. After an exciting chase through

16

stubble heaps and weed thickets I wearied and captured him without being bitten and turned him free to make his mark in a favorable sand bed. He also embroidered better than he knew, and at once claimed the authorship of the new track work.

I soon learned to distinguish the pretty sparrow track from that of the magpie and lark with their three delicate branches and the straight scratch behind made by the back-curving claw, dragged loosely like a spur of a Mexican vaquero. The cushioned elastic feet of the hare frequently were seen mixed with the pattering scratchy prints of the squirrels. I was now wholly trackful. I fancied I could see the air whirling in dimpled eddies from sparrow and lark wings. Earthquake boulders descending in a song of curves, snowflakes glinting songfully hither and thither. "The water in music the oar forsakes." The air in music the wing forsakes. All things move in music and write it. The mouse, lizard, and grasshopper sing together on the Turlock sands, sing with the morning stars.

Scarce had I begun to catch the eternal harmonies of Nature when I heard the hearty god-damning din of the mule driver, dust whirled in the sun gold, and I could see the sweltering mules leaning forward, dragging the heavily piled wheat wagons, deep sunk in the sand. My embroidery perished by the mile, but grasshoppers never wearied nor the gray lizards nor the larks, and the coarse confusion of man was speedily healed.

About noon I found a family of grangers feeding, and remembering your admonitions anent my health requested leave to join them. My head ached with fever and sunshine, and I couldn't dare the ancient brown bacon, nor the beans and cakes, but water and splendid buttermilk came in perfect affinity, and made me strong.

Towards evening, after passing through miles of blooming Hemizonia, I reached Hopeton on the edge of the oak fringe of the Merced. Here all were yellow and woebegone with malarious fever. I rested one day, spending the time in examining the remarkably flat water-eroded valley of the Merced and the geological sections which it offers. In going across to the river I had a suggestive time breaking my way through tangles of blackberry and brier-rose and willow. I admire delicate plants that are well prickled and therefore took my scratched face and hands patiently. I bathed in the sacred stream, seeming to catch all its mountain tones while it softly mumbled and rippled over the shallows of brown pebbles. The whole river back to its icy sources seemed to rise in clear vision, with its countless cascades and falls and blooming meadows and gardens. Its pine groves, too, and the winds that play them, all appeared and sounded.

In the cool of the evening I caught Browny and cantered across to the Tuolumne, the whole way being fragrant and golden with Hemizonia. A breeze swept in from your Golden Gate regions over the passes and across the plains, fanning the hot ground and drooping plants and refreshing every beast and tired and weary, plodding man.

It was dark ere I reached my old frien 1 Delaney, but was instantly recognized by my voice, and welcomed in the old good uncivilized way, not to be misunderstood.

All the region adjacent to the Tuolumne River where it sweeps out into the plain after its long eventful journey in the mountains, is exceedingly picturesque. Round terraced hills, brown and yellow with grasses and compositæ and adorned with open groves of darkly foliaged live oak are grouped in a most open tranquil manner and laid upon a smooth level base of purple plain, while the river bank is lined with nooks of great beauty and variety in which the river has swept and curled, shifting from side to side, retreating and returning, as determined

19

by floods and the gradual erosion and removal of drift beds formerly laid down. A few miles above here at the village of La Grange the wild river has made some astonishing deposits in its young days, through which it now flows with the manners of stately old age, apparently disclaiming all knowledge of them. But a thousand, thousand boulders gathered from many a moraine, swashed and ground in pot-holes, record their history and tell of white floods of a grandeur not easily conceived. Noble sections nearly a hundred feet deep are laid bare, like a book, by the mining company. Water is drawn from the river several miles above and conducted by ditches and pipes and made to play upon these deposits for the gold they contain. Thus the Tuolumne of to-day is compelled to unravel and lay bare its own ancient history which is a thousandfold more important than the handfuls of gold sand it chances to contain.

I mean to return to these magnificent records in a week or two and turn the gold disease of the La Grangers to account in learning the grand old story of the Sierra flood period. If these hundred laborious hydraulickers were under my employ they could not do me better service, and all along the Sierra flank thousands of strong arms are working for me, incited by the small golden bait. Who shall say that I am not rich?

Up through the purple foothills to Coulterville, where I met many hearty, shaggy mountaineers glad to see me. Strange to say the "Overland" studies have been read and discussed in the most unlikely places. Some numbers have found their way through the Bloody Cañon pass to Mono.

In the evening Black and I rode together up into the sugar pine forests and on to his old ranch in the moonlight. The grand priest-like pines held their arms above us in blessing. The wind sang songs of welcome. The cool glaciers and the running crystal fountains were in it. I was no longer *on* but *in* the mountains — home again, and my pulses were filled. On and on in white moonlight-spangles on the streams, shadows in rock hollows and briery ravines, tree architecture on the sky more divine than ever stars in their spires, leafy mosaic in meadow and bank. Never had the Sierra seemed so inexhaustible — mile on mile onward in the forest through groves old and young, pine tassels overarching and brushing both cheeks at once. The chirping of crickets only deepened the stillness.

About eight o'clock a strange mass of tones came surging and waving through the pines.

"That's the death song," said Black, as he reined up his horse to listen. "Some Indian is dead." Soon two glaring watch-fires shone red through the forest, marking the place of congregation. The fire glare and the wild wailing came with indescribable impressiveness through the still dark woods. I listened eagerly as the weird curves of woe swelled and cadenced, now rising steep like glacial precipices, now swooping low in polished slopes. Falling boulders and rushing streams and wind tones caught from rock and tree were in it. As we at length rode away and the heaviest notes were lost in distance, I wondered that so much of mountain nature should well out from such a source. Miles away we met Indian groups slipping through the shadows on their way to join the death wail.

Farther on, a harsh grunting and growling seemed to come from the opposite bank of a hazelly brook along which we rode. "What? Hush! That's a bear," ejaculated Black in a gruff bearish undertone. "Yes," said [I], "some rough old bruin is sauntering this fine night, seeking some wayside sheep lost from migrating flocks." Of course all night-sounds otherwise unaccountable are accredited to bears. On ascending a sloping hillock less than a mile from the first we heard another grunting bear, but whether or no daylight would transform our bears to pigs may well be counted into the story.

Past Bower Cave and along a narrow winding trail in deep shadow — so dark, had to throw the reins on Browny's neck and trust to his skill, for I could not see the ground and the hillside was steep. A fine, bright tributary of the Merced sang far beneath us as we climbed higher, higher through the hazels and dogwoods that fringed the rough black boles of spruces and pines. We were now nearing the old camping ground of the Pilot Peak region where I learned to know the large nodding lilies (*L. pardalinum*) so abundant along these streams, and the groups of alder-shaded cataracts so characteristic of the North Merced Fork. Moonlight whitened all the long fluted slopes of the opposite bank, but we rode in continuous shadow. The rush and gurgle and prolonged *Aaaaaah* of the stream coming up, sifting into the wind, was very solemnly impressive. It was here that you first seemed to join me. I reached up as Browny carried me underneath a big Douglas spruce and plucked one of its long plumy sprays, which brought you from the Oakland dead in a moment. You are more spruce than pine, though I never definitely knew it till now.

23

Miles and miles of tree scripture along the sky, a bible that will one day be read! The beauty of its letters and sentences have burned me like fire through all these Sierra seasons. Yet I cannot interpret their hidden thoughts. They are terrestrial expressions of the sun, pure as water and snow. Heavens! listen to the wind song! I'm still writing beneath that grand old pine in Black's yard and that other companion, scarcely less noble, back of which I sheltered during the earthquake, is just a few yards beyond. The shadows of their boles lie like charred logs on the gray sand, while half the yard is embroidered with their branches and leaves. There goes a woodpecker with an acorn to drive into its thick bark for winter, and well it may gather its stores, for I can myself detect winter in the wind.

Few nights of my mountain life have been more eventful than that of my ride in the woods from Coulterville, where I made my reunion with the winds and pines. It was eleven o'clock when we reached Black's ranch. I was weary and soon died in sleep. How cool and vital and recreative was the hale young mountain air. On higher, higher up into the holy of holies of the woods! Pure white lustrous clouds overshadowed the massive congregations of silver fir and pine. We entered, and a thousand living arms were waved in solemn blessing. An infinity of mountain life. How complete is the absorption of one's life into the spirit of mountain woods. No one can love or hate an enemy here, for no one can conceive of such a creature as an enemy. Nor can one have any distinctive love of friends. The dearest and best of you all seemed of no special account, mere trifles.

Hazel Green water, famous among mountaineers, distilled from the pores of an ancient moraine, spiced and toned in a maze of fragrant roots, winter nor summer warm or cool it! Shadows over shadows keep its fountains ever cool. Moss and felted leaves guard from spring and autumn frosts, while a woolly robe of snow protects from the intenser cold of winter. Bears, deer, birds, and Indians love the water and nuts of Hazel Green alike, while the pine squirrel reigns supreme and haunts its incomparable groves like a spirit. Here a grand old glacier swept over from the Tuolumne ice fountains into the basin of the Merced, leaving the Hazel Green moraine for the food of her coming trees and fountains of her predestined waters.

Along the Merced divide to the ancient glacial lake-bowl of Crane's Flat, was ever fir or pine more perfect? What groves! What combinations of green and silver gray and glowing white of glinting sunbeams. Where is leaf or limb awanting, and is this the upshot of the so-called "mountain glooms" and mountain storms? If so, is Sierra forestry aught beside an outflow of Divine Love? These round-bottomed grooves sweeping across the divide, and down whose sides our horses canter with accelerated speed, are the pathways of ancient ice-currents, and it is just where these crushing glaciers have borne down most heavily that the greatest loveliness of grove and forest appears.

A deep cañon filled with blue air now comes in view on the right. That is the valley of the Merced, and the highest rocks visible through the trees belong to the Yosemite Valley. More miles of glorious forest, then out into free light and down, down, down into the groves and meadows of Yosemite. Sierra sculpture in its entirety without the same study on the spot. No one of the rocks seems to call me now, nor any of the distant mountains. Surely this Merced and Tuolumne chapter of my life is done.

I have been out on the river bank with your letters. How good and wise they seem to be! You wrote better than you knew. Altogether they form a precious volume whose sentences are more intimately connected with my mountain work than any one will ever be able to appreciate. An ouzel came as I sat reading, alighting in the water with a delicate and graceful glint on his bosom. How pure is the morning light on the great gray wall, and how marvelous the subdued lights of the moon! The nights are wholly enchanting.

I will not try [to] tell the Valley. Yet I feel that I am a stranger here. I have been gathering you a handful of leaves. Show them to dear Keith and give some to Mrs. McChesney. They are probably the last of Yosemite that I will ever give you. I will go out in a day or so. Farewell! I seem to be more really leaving you here than there. Keep these long pages, for they are a kind of memorandum of my walk after the strange Oakland epoch, and I may want to copy some of them when I have leisure.

Remember me to my friends. I trust you are not now so sorely overladen. Good-night. Keep the goldenrod and yarrow. They are auld lang syne.

Ever lovingly yours
JOHN MUIR

To take leave of Yosemite was harder than he anticipated. Days grew into weeks as in leisurely succession he visited his favorite haunts — places to which during the preceding summer he had taken on a camping trip [1] a group of his closest friends, including Emily Pelton and Mrs. Carr. It was on this outing that bears raided the provisions cached by the party during an excursion into the Tuolumne Cañon and Muir saved his companions from hardship by fetching a new supply of food from Yosemite, making the arduous trip of forty miles without pause and in an amazingly short time.

YOSEMITE VALLEY, *October 7th,* 1874

DEAR MRS. CARR:

I expected to have been among the foothill drift long ago, but the mountains fairly seized me, and ere I knew I was up the Merced Cañon where we were last year, past Shadow and Merced Lakes and our Soda Springs. I returned last night. Had a glorious storm, and a thousand sacred beauties that seemed yet more and more divine. I camped four nights at Shadow Lake [2] at the old place in the pine thicket. I have ouzel tales to tell. I was alone and during the whole excursion, or period rather, was in a kind of calm incurable ecstasy. I am hopelessly and forever a mountaineer.

How glorious my studies seem, and how simple. I found out a noble truth concerning

[1] See vol. I, p. 322.   [2] Now called Merced Lake.

the Merced moraines that escaped me hitherto. Civilization and fever and all the morbidness that has been hooted at me have not dimmed my glacial eye, and I care to live only to entice people to look at Nature's loveliness. My own special self is nothing. My feet have recovered their cunning. I feel myself again.

Tell Keith the colors are coming to the groves. I leave Yosemite for over the mountains to Mono and Lake Tahoe. Will be in Tahoe in a week, thence anywhere Shastaward, etc. I think I may be at Brownsville, Yuba County, where I may get a letter from you. I promised to call on Emily Pelton there. Mrs. Black has fairly mothered me. She will be down in a few weeks. Farewell.

JOHN MUIR

Having worked the Yosemite problem out of his blood he was faced with the question of the next step in his career. Apparently while debating with others the character of the relation which Nature should sustain to man he had found his calling, one in which his glacial studies in Yosemite formed only an incident, though a large one. Hereafter his supreme purpose in life must be "to entice people to look at Nature's loveliness" — understandingly, of course.

In the seventies, before lumber companies, fires, and the fumes from copper smelters had laid a blight upon the Shasta landscapes, the environs of the great mountain were a veritable garden of the Lord. Its famous mineral springs and abundant fish and game, no less than its snowy grandeur, attracted a steady stream of visitors. Clarence King had discovered glaciers on its flanks and many parts of the mountain were still imperfectly explored. The year was waning into late October when Muir, seeking new treasuries of Nature's loveliness, turned his face Shastaward.

In going to Mount Shasta, Muir walked along the main Oregon and California stage-road from Redding to Sisson's. Unable to find any one willing to make the ascent of the mountain with him so late in the season, he secured the aid of Jerome Fay, a local resident, to take blankets and a week's supply of food as far as a pack-horse could break through the snow. Selecting a sheltered spot for a camp in the upper edge of the timber belt, he made his adventurous ascent alone from there on the 2d of November, and returned to his camp before dark. Realizing that a storm was brewing, he hastily made a "storm-nest" and snugged himself in with firewood to enjoy the novel sensation of a Shasta storm at an altitude of nine thousand feet. The elements broke loose violently the next morning, and continued for nearly a week, while Muir, his trusty notebook in hand, watched the deposition of snow upon the trees, studied the individual crystals with a lens, observed a squirrel finding her stores under the drifts, and made friends with wild sheep that sought shelter near his camp. He was much disappointed when Mr. Sisson, concerned for his safety, sent two horses through the blinding snowstorm and brought him down on the fifth day from the timber-line to his house. The following letter was written just before he began the first stage of the ascent:

To Mrs. Ezra S. Carr

SISSON'S STATION, *November 1st,* 1874

DEAR MRS. CARR:

Here is icy Shasta fifteen miles away, yet at the very door. It is all close-wrapt in clean young snow down to the very base — one mass of white from the dense black forest-girdle at an elevation of five or six thousand feet to the very summit. The extent of its individuality is perfectly wonderful. When I first caught sight of it over the braided folds of the Sacramento Valley I was fifty miles away and afoot, alone and weary. Yet all my blood turned to wine, and I have not been weary since.

Stone was to have accompanied me, but has failed of course. The last storm was severe and all the mountaineers shake their heads and say impossible, etc., but you know that I will meet all its icy snows lovingly.

I set out in a few minutes for the edge of the timber-line. Then upwards, if unstormy, in the early morning. If the snow proves to be mealy and loose it is barely possible that I may be unable to urge my way through so many upward miles, as there is no intermediate camping ground. Yet I am feverless and strong now, and can spend two days with their intermediate night in one deliberate unstrained effort.

I am the more eager to ascend to study the mechanical conditions of the fresh snow at so great an elevation; also to obtain clear views of the comparative quantities of lava denudation northward and southward; also general views of the channels of the ancient Shasta glaciers, and many other lesser problems besides — the fountains of the rivers here, and the living glaciers. I would like to remain a week or two, and may have to return next year in summer.

I wrote a short letter [1] a few days ago which was printed in the Evening Bulletin, and I suppose you have seen it. I wonder how you all

[1] "Salmon Breeding on the McCloud River," *San Francisco Evening Bulletin*, Oct. 29, 1874.

are faring in your wildernesses, educational, departmental, institutional, etc. Write me a line here in care of Sisson. I think it will reach me on my return from icy Shasta. Love to all — Keith and the boys and the McChesneys. Don't forward any letters from the Oakland office. I want only mountains until my return to civilization. Farewell.

Ever cordially yours

JOHN MUIR

One of Muir's endearing traits was his genuine fondness for children, who rewarded his sympathy with touching confidence and devotion. The following letter, written to his admiring little chum[1] in the McChesney household, sheds additional light upon his Shasta rambles and the mood, so different from mere adventure-seeking, in which he went questing for knowledge of Nature.

To Alice McChesney

SISSON'S STATION
FOOT OF MOUNT SHASTA
November 8th, 1874

MY DEAR HIGHLAND LASSIE ALICE:

It is a stormy day here at the foot of the big snowy Shasta and so I am in Sisson's house

_____

[1] See vol. I, p. 372.

where it is cozy and warm. There are four lassies here — one is bonnie, one is bonnier, and one is far bonniest, but I don't know them yet and I am a little lonesome and wish Alice McChesney were here. I can never help thinking that you were a little unkind in sending me off to the mountains without a kiss and you must make that up when I get back.

I was up on the top of Mount Shasta, and it is very high and all deep-buried in snow, and I am tired with the hard climbing and wading and wallowing. When I was coming up here on purposè to climb Mount Shasta people would often say to me, "Where are you going?" and I would say, "To Shasta," and they would say, "Shasta City?" and I would say, "Oh, no, I mean *Mount* Shasta!" Then they would laugh and say, "*Mount Shasta!!* Why man, you can't go on Mount Shasta *now*. You're two months too late. The snow is ten feet deep on it, and you would be all buried up in the snow, and freeze to death." And then I would say, "But I like snow, and I like frost and ice, and I'm used to climbing and wallowing in it." And they would say, "Oh, that's all right enough to talk about or sing about, but I'm a mountaineer myself, and know all about that Shasta Butte and you just can't go noway and nohow." But I did go, because I loved snow

34

and mountains better than they did. Some places I had to creep, and some places to slide, and some places to scramble, but most places I had to climb, climb, climb deep in the frosty snow.

I started at half-past two in the morning, all alone, and it stormed wildly and beautifully before I got back here and they thought that poor, crazy mountain climber must be frozen solid and lost below the drifts, but I found a place at the foot of a low bunch of trees and made a hollow and gathered wood and built a cheery fire and soon was warm; and though the wind and the snow swept wildly past, I was snug-bug-rug, and in three days I came down here. But I liked the storm and wanted to stay longer.

The weather is stormy yet, and most of the robins are getting ready to go away to a warmer place, and so they are gathering into big flocks. I saw them getting their breakfast this morning on cherries. Some hunters are here and so we get plenty of wild venison to eat, and they killed two bears and nailed their skins on the side of the barn to dry. There are lots of both bears and deer on Shasta, and three kinds of squirrels.

Shasta snowflakes are very beautiful, and I saw them finely under my magnifying glass.

Here are some bonnie Cratægus leaves I
gathered for you. Fare ye well, my lassie. I'm
going to-morrow with some hunters to see if I
can find out something more about bears or
wild sheep.

Give my love to your mother and father and
Carrie, and tell your mother to keep my letters
until I come back, for I don't want to know
anything just now except mountains. But I
want your papa to write to me, for I will be up
here, hanging about the snowy skirts of Shasta,
for one or two or three weeks.

It is a dark, wild night, and the Shasta
squirrels are curled up cozily in their nests, and
the grouse have feather pantlets on and are all
roosting under the broad, shaggy branches of
the fir trees. Good-night, my lassie, and may
you nest well and sleep well — as the Shasta
squirrels and grouse.   JOHN MUIR

During the following weeks he circled the
base of the mountain, visited the Black Butte
and the foot of the Whitney Glacier, as well as
Rhett and Klamath lakes, and gathered into
his notebook a rich harvest of observations to
be made into magazine articles later. Some of
the material, however, he utilized at once in a
series of letters to the "Evening Bulletin" of
San Francisco.

ON WIDENING CURRENTS

In explanation of various allusions in some of the following letters to Mrs. Carr, it should be added that she and her husband had in view, and later acquired, a tract of land in what was then the outskirts of Pasadena. Both had been very active in organizing the farmers of California into a State Grange in 1873. Two years later Dr. Carr was elected State Superintendent of Public Instruction, and during his incumbency Mrs. Carr served as deputy Superintendent, discharging most of the routine work of the office in Sacramento, besides lecturing before granges and teachers' institutes throughout the State. There were many quarreling political factions in California, and the Grangers' movement and the Department of Public Instruction were never far from the center of the political storms.

To Mrs. Ezra S. Carr

SISSON'S STATION, *December 9th*, 1874

DEAR MRS. CARR:

Coming in for a sleep and rest I was glad to receive your card. I seem to be more than married to icy Shasta. One yellow, mellow morning six days ago, when Shasta's snows were looming and blooming, I stepped outside the door to gaze, and was instantly drawn up over the meadows, over the forests to the main

Shasta glacier in one rushing, cometic whiz, then, swooping to Shasta Valley, whirled off around the base like a satellite of the grand icy sun. I have just completed my first revolution. Length of orbit, one hundred miles; time, one Shasta day.

For two days and a half I had nothing in the way of food, yet suffered nothing, and was finely nerved for the most delicate work of mountaineering, both among crevasses and lava cliffs. Now I am sleeping and *eating*. I found some geological facts that are perfectly glorious, and botanical ones, too.

I wish I could make the public be kind to Keith and his paint.

And so you contemplate vines and oranges among the warm California angels! I wish you would all go a-granging among oranges and bananas and all such blazing red-hot fruits, for you are a species of Hindoo sun fruit yourself. For me, I like better the huckleberries of cool glacial bogs, and acid currants, and benevolent, rosy, beaming apples, and common Indian summer pumpkins.

I wish you could see the holy morning alpenglow of Shasta.

Farewell. I'll be down into gray Oakland some time. I am glad you are essentially independent of those commonplace plotters that

have so marred your peace. Eat oranges and
hear the larks and wait on the sun.

Ever cordially

JOHN MUIR

To Mrs. Ezra S. Carr

SISSON'S STATION, *December 21st,* 1874

DEAR MRS. CARR:

I have just returned from a fourth Shasta excursion, and find your [letter] of the 17th. I
wish you could have been with me on Shasta's
shoulder last eve in the sun-glow. I was over
on the head-waters of the McCloud, and what
a head! Think of a spring giving rise to a
river! I fairly quiver with joyous exultation
when I think of it. The infinity of Nature's
glory in rock, cloud, and water! As soon as I
beheld the McCloud upon its lower course I
knew there must be something extraordinary
in its alpine fountains, and I shouted, "O
where, my glorious river, do you come from?"
Think of a spring fifty yards wide at the mouth,
issuing from the base of a lava bluff with wild
songs — not gloomily from a dark cavey
mouth, but from a world of ferns and mosses
gold and green! I broke my way through chaparral and all kinds of river-bank tangle in
eager vigor, utterly unweariable.

The dark blue stream sang solemnly with a

39

deep voice, pooling and boulder-dashing and *aha-a-a-ing* in white flashing rapids, when suddenly I heard water notes I never had heard before. They came from that mysterious spring; and then the Elk forest, and the alpine-glow, and the sunset! Poor pen cannot tell it.

The sun this morning is at work with its blessings as if it had never blessed before. He never wearies of revealing himself on Shasta. But in a few hours I leave this altar and all its — Well, to my Father I say thank you, and go willingly.

I go by stage and rail to Brownsville to see Emily [Pelton] and the rocks there and the Yuba. Then perhaps a few days among the auriferous drifts on the Tuolumne, and then to Oakland and that book, walking across the Coast Range on the way, either through one of the passes or over Mount Diablo. I feel a sort of nervous fear of another period of town dark, but I don't want to be silly about it. The sun glow will all fade out of me, and I will be deathly as Shasta in the dark. But mornings will come, dawnings of some kind, and if not, I have lived more than a common eternity already.

Farewell. Don't overwork — that is not the work your Father wants. I wish you could

come a-beeing in the Shasta honey lands. Love
to the boys.   [JOHN MUIR]

On one of the excursions to which he refers
in the preceding letter, Muir accompanied four
hunters, three of them Scotchmen,[1] who were
in search of wild sheep. The party went to
Sheep Rock, twenty miles north of Sisson's,
and from there fifty miles farther to Mount
Bremer, then one of the most noted strongholds
of wild game in the Shasta region. This expedition afforded Muir a new opportunity to study
wild sheep and his observations were charmingly utilized in the little essay "Wild Wool,"
one of his last contributions to the "Overland"
in 1875, republished afterwards in "Steep
Trails."

A week after writing the above letter he was
at Knoxville, also known as Brownsville, on
the divide between the Yuba and Feather
Rivers. It was a mild, but tempestuous, December, and during a gale that sprang up while
he was exploring a valley tributary to the
Yuba, he climbed a Douglas spruce in order to

[1] Among these Scots was G. Buchanan Hepburn, of Had-
dingdonshire, on one of whose letters Muir made the memorandum, "Lord Hepburn, killed in Mexico or Lower California." Twenty years later, during his visit to Scotland,
Muir was by chance enabled to communicate the details of
the man's unhappy fate to his relatives.

be able to enjoy the better the wild music of the storm. The experience afterwards bore fruit in one of his finest descriptions — an article entitled "A Wind Storm in the Forests of the Yuba," which appeared in "Scribner's Monthly" in November, 1878, and later as a chapter in "The Mountains of California." With the possible exception of his dog story, "Stickeen," no article drew more enthusiastic comments from readers who felt moved to write their appreciation.

From his earliest youth Muir had derived keen enjoyment from storms, but he had never tried to give a reason for the joy that was in him. The reaction he got from the reading public showed that they regarded his enthusiasm for storms as admirable, but also as singular. The latter was a surprise to Muir, who regarded all the manifestations of Nature as coming within the range of his interest, and saw no reason why men should *fear* storms. Reflecting upon the fact, he reached the conclusion that such fear is due to a wrong attitude toward nature, to imaginary or grossly exaggerated notions of danger, or, in short, to a "lack of faith in the Scriptures of Nature," as, he averred, was the case with Ruskin. As for himself, a great storm was nothing but "a cordial outpouring of Nature's love."

ON WIDENING CURRENTS

By what he regarded as a fortunate coincidence, he was still on the headwaters of the Feather and the Yuba rivers on the date of the memorable Marysville flood, January 19, 1875. A driving warm rainstorm suddenly melted the heavy snows that filled the drainage basins of these rivers and sent an unprecedented flood down into the lowlands, submerging many homesteads and a good part of Marysville. One can almost sense the haste with which he dashed off the lines of the following letter on the morning of the day of the flood — impatient to heed the call of the storm.

To Mrs. Ezra S. Carr

BROWNSVILLE, YUBA COUNTY
January 19th, 1875

MY DEAR MOTHER CARR:

Here are some of the dearest and bonniest of our Father's bairns — the little ones that so few care to see. I never saw such enthusiasm in the care and breeding of mosses as Nature manifests among these northern Sierras. I have studied a big fruitful week among the cañons and ridges of the Feather and another among the Yuba rivers, living and dead.

I have seen a dead river — a sight worth going round the world to see. The dead rivers and dead gravels wherein lies the gold form mag-

43

nificent problems, and I feel wild and unmanageable with the intense interest they excite, but I *will* choke myself off and finish my glacial work and that little book of studies. I have been spending a few fine social days with Emily [Pelton], but now work.

How gloriously it storms! The pines are in ecstasy, and I feel it and must go out to them. I must borrow a big coat and mingle in the storm and make some studies. Farewell. Love to all.

M.

P.S. How are Ned and Keith? I wish Keith had been with me these Shasta and Feather River days. I have gained a thousandfold more than I hoped. Heaven send you Light and the good blessings of wildness. How the rains plash and roar, and how the pines wave and pray!

Tradition still tells of his return to the Knox House after the storm, dripping and bedraggled; of the pity and solicitude of his friends over his condition, and their surprise when he in turn pitied them for having missed "a storm of exalted beauty and riches." The account of his experience was his final contribution to the "Overland Monthly" in June, 1875, under the title, "A Flood-Storm in the Sierra." Nowhere has he revealed his fervid enjoyment of storms more unreservedly than in this article.[1] "How terribly downright," he observes, "must be the utterances of storms and earthquakes to those accustomed to the soft hypocrisies of society. Man's control is being extended over the forces of nature, but it is well, at least for the present, that storms can still make themselves heard through our thickest walls. . . . Some were made to think."

There was a new note in his discourses, written and spoken, when he emerged from the forests of the Yuba. Fear and utilitarianism, he was convinced, are a crippling equipment for one who wishes to understand and appreciate the beauty of the world about him. But meanness of soul is even worse. Herded in cities, where the struggle for gain sweeps along with the crowd even the exceptional individual, men rarely come in sight of their better selves. There is more hope for those who live in the country. But instead of listening to the earnest and varied voices of nature, the country resident, also, is too often of the shepherd type who can only hear "baa." "Even the howls and

---

[1] It was incorporated in part only as the chapter on "The River Floods" in *The Mountains of California*. The omitted portions are important to a student of Muir's personality.

45

ki-yis of coyotes might be blessings if well heard, but he hears them only through a blur of mutton and wool, and they do him no good."

Despite these abnormalities, Muir insisted, we must live in close contact with nature if we are to keep fresh and clean the fountains of moral sanity. "The world needs the woods and is beginning to come to them," he asserts in his flood-storm article. "But it is not yet ready ... for storms. ... Nevertheless the world moves onward, and 'it is coming yet, for a' that,' that the beauty of storms will be as visible as that of calms."

CHAPTER XII

" THE WORLD NEEDS THE WOODS "

1875–1878

WHEN out of doors, Muir was scarcely conscious of the passage of time, so completely was he absorbed, almost physically absorbed, in the natural objects about him. The mountains, the stars, the trees, and sweet-belled Cassiope recked not of time! Why should he? Nor was he at such periods burdened with thoughts of a calling. On the contrary, he rejoiced in his freedom and, like Thoreau, sought by honest labor of any sort only means enough to preserve it intact.

But when he came out of the forests, or down from the mountains, and had to take account, in letters and personal contacts, of the lives, loves, and occupations of relatives and friends, he sometimes was brought up sharply against the fact that he had reached middle age and yet had neither a home nor what most men in those days would have recognized as a profession. Then, as in the following letter, one catches a note of apology for the life he is leading. He can only say, and say it triumphantly,

47

that the course of his bark is controlled by other stars than theirs, that he must be free to live by the laws of his own life.

To Sarah Muir Galloway

OAKLAND, [*February 26th,*] 1875

MY DEAR SISTER SARAH:

I have just returned from a long train of excursions in the Sierras and find yours and many other letters waiting, all that accumulated for five months. I spent my holidays on the Yuba and Feather rivers exploring. I have, of course, worked hard and enjoyed hard, ascending mountains, crossing cañons, rambling ceaselessly over hill and dale, plain and lava bed.

I thought of you all gathered with your little ones enjoying the sweet and simple pleasures that belong to your lives and loves. I have not yet in all my wanderings found a single person so free as myself. Yet I am bound to my studies, and the laws of my own life. At times I feel as if driven with whips, and ridden upon. When in the woods I sit at times for hours watching birds or squirrels or looking down into the faces of flowers without suffering any feeling of haste. Yet I am swept onward in a general current that bears on irresistibly. When, therefore, I shall be allowed to float homeward, I dinna, dinna ken, but I hope.

48

THE WORLD NEEDS THE WOODS

The world, as well as the mountains, is good to me, and my studies flow on in a wider and wider current by the incoming of many a noble tributary. Probably if I were living amongst you all you would follow me in my scientific work, but as it is, you will do so imperfectly. However, when I visit you, you will all have to submit to numerous lectures. . . .

Give my love to David and to Mrs. Galloway and all your little ones, and remember me as ever lovingly your brother,

JOHN

On the 28th of April he led a party to the summit of Mount Shasta for the purpose of finding a proper place to locate the monument of the Coast and Geodetic Survey. Two days later he made another ascent with Jerome Fay in order to complete some barometrical observations. While engaged in this task a fierce storm arose, enveloping them, with great suddenness, in inky darkness through which roared a blast of snow and hail. His companion deemed it impossible under the circumstances to regain their camp at timber-line, so the two made their way as best they could to the sputtering fumaroles or "Hot Springs" on the summit. The perils of that stormy night, described at some length in "Steep Trails," were of a

49

much more serious nature than one might infer from the casual reference to the adventure in the following letter.

To Mrs. Ezra S. Carr

1419 TAYLOR ST., *May 4th*, 1875

DEAR MRS. CARR:

Here I am safe in the arms of Daddy Swett — home again from icy Shasta and richer than ever in dead river gravel and in snowstorms and snow. The upper end of the main Sacramento Valley is entirely covered with ancient river drift and I wandered over many square miles of it. In every pebble I could hear the sounds of running water. The whole deposit is a poem whose many books and chapters form the geological Vedas of our glorious state.

I discovered a new species of hail on the summit of Shasta and experienced one of the most beautiful and most violent snowstorms imaginable. I would have been with you ere this to tell you about it and to give you some lilies and pine tassels that I brought for you and Mrs. McChesney and Ina Coolbrith, but alack! I am battered and scarred like a log that has come down the Tuolumne in flood-time, and I am also lame with frost nipping. Nothing serious, however, and I will be well and better than before in a few days.

THE WORLD NEEDS THE WOODS

I was caught in a violent snowstorm and held upon the summit of the mountain all night in my shirt sleeves. The intense cold and the want of food and sleep made the fire of life smoulder and burn low. Nevertheless in company with another strong mountaineer [Jerome Fay] I broke through six miles of frosty snow down into the timber and reached fire and food and sleep and am better than ever, with all the valuable experiences. Altogether I have had a very instructive and delightful trip.

The Bryanthus you wanted was snow-buried, and I was too lame to dig it out for you, but I will probably go back ere long. I'll be over in a few days or so.   [JOHN MUIR]

With the approach of summer, Muir returned to the Yosemite and Mount Whitney region, taking with him his friends William Keith, J. B. McChesney, and John Swett. In the letters he wrote from there to the "San Francisco Evening Bulletin" one feels that the forest trees of the Sierra Nevada are getting a deepening hold upon his imagination. "Throughout all this glorious region," he writes, "there is nothing that so constantly interests and challenges the admiration of the traveller as the belts of forest through which he passes."

Of all the trees of the forest the dearest to

51

him was the sugar pine (*Pinus Lambertiana*),
and he frequently refers to it as the "King
of the pines." "Many a volume," he declares
in one of the letters written on this outing,
"might be filled with the history of its development from the brown whirling-winged seed-nut
to its ripe and Godlike old age; the quantity
and range of its individuality, its gestures in
storms or while sleeping in summer light, the
quality of its sugar and nut, and the glossy
fragrant wood" — all are distinctive. But, as
his notebooks and some of the following letters
show, he now begins to make an intensive study
of all the trees of the Pacific Coast, particularly
of the redwood. Thus, quite unconsciously, he
was in training to become the leading defender
of the Sierra forests during critical emergencies
that arose in the nineties.

To Mrs. Ezra S. Carr

YOSEMITE VALLEY, *June 3d*, 1875

DEAR MRS. CARR:

Where are you? Lost in conventions, elec-
tions, women's rights and fights, and buried
beneath many a load of musty granger hay.
You always seem inaccessible to me, as if you
were in a crowd, and even when I write, my
written words seem to be heard by many that I
do not like.

THE WORLD NEEDS THE WOODS

I wish some of your predictions given in your last may come true, like the first you made long ago. Yet somehow it seems hardly likely that you will ever be sufficiently free, for your labors multiply from year to year. Yet who knows.

I found poor Lamon's[1] grave, as you directed. The upper end of the Valley seems fairly silent and empty without him.

Keith got fine sketches, and I found new beauties and truths of all kinds. Mack [McChesney] and Swett will tell you all. I send you my buttonhole plume.

Farewell.

JOHN MUIR

To Mrs. Ezra S. Carr

BLACK'S HOTEL
YOSEMITE, CALIFORNIA
July 31*st*, 1875

DEAR MRS. CARR:

I have just arrived from our long excursion to Mount Whitney, all hale and happy, and find your weary plodding letter, containing things that from this rocky standpoint seem strangely mixed — things celestial and terrestrial, cultivated and wild. Your letters set one

[1] James C. Lamon, pioneer settler of Yosemite Valley, who died May 22, 1875. See characterization of him in Muir's *The Yosemite.*

a-thinking, and yet somehow they never seem to make those problems of life clear, and I always feel glad that they do not form any part of my work, but that my lessons are simple rocks and waters and plants and humble beasts, all pure and in their places, the Man beast with all his complications being laid upon stronger shoulders.

I did not bring you down any Sedum roots or Cassiope sprays because I had not then received your letter, not that I forgot you as I passed the blessed Sierra heathers, or the primulas, or the pines laden with fragrant, nutty cones. But I am more and more made to feel that my gardens and herbariums and woods are all in their places as they grow, and I know them there, and can find them when I will. Yet I ought to carry their poor dead or dying forms to those who can have no better.

The Valley is lovely, scarce more than a whit the worse for the flower-crushing feet that every summer brings. . . . I am not decided about my summer. I want to go with the Sequoias a month or two into all their homes from north to south, learning what I can of their conditions and prospects, their age, stature, the area they occupy, etc. But John Swett, who is brother now, papa then, orders me home to booking. Bless me, what an awful thing town duty is! I was once free as any pine-playing wind, and feel that I have still a good length of line, but alack! there seems to be a hook or two of civilization in me that I would fain pull out, yet *would not pull out* — O, O, O!!!

I suppose you are weary of saying book, book, book, and perhaps when you fear me lost in rocks and Mono deserts I will, with Scotch perverseness, do all you ask and more. All this letter is about myself, and why not when I'm the only person in all the wide world that I know anything about — Keith, the cascade, not excepted.

Fare ye well, mother quail, good betide your brood and be they and you saved from the hawks and the big ugly buzzards and cormorants — grangeal, political, right and wrongical, — and I will be

Ever truly

JOHN MUIR

"Only that and nothing more."

To Sarah Muir Galloway

YOSEMITE VALLEY, *November 2nd,* 1875

DEAR SISTER SARAH:

Here is your letter with the Dalles in it. I'm glad you have escaped so long from the cows and sewing and baking to God's green wild

Dalles and dells, for I know you were young again and that the natural love of beauty you possess had free, fair play. I shall never forget the big happy day I spent there on the rocky, gorgey Wisconsin above Kilbourn City. What lanes full of purple orchids and ferns! *Aspidium fragrans* I found there for the first time, and what hillsides of huckleberries and rare asters and goldenrods. Don't you wish you were wild like me and as free to satisfy your love for whatever is pure and beautiful?

I returned last night from a two and a half months' excursion through the grandest portion of the Sierra Nevada forests. You remember reading of the big trees of Calaveras County, discovered fifteen or twenty years ago. Well, I have been studying the species (*Sequoia gigantea*) and have been all this time wandering amid those giants. They extend in a broken, interrupted belt along the western flank of the range a distance of one hundred and eighty miles. But I will not attempt to describe them here. I have written about them and will send you printed descriptions.

I fancy your little flock is growing fast towards prime. Yet how short seems the time when you occupied your family place on Hickory Hill. Our lives go on and close like a day — morning, noon, night. Yet how full of pure happiness these life days may be, and how worthy of the God that plans them and suns them!

The book you speak of is not yet commenced, but I must go into winter quarters at once and go to work. While in the field I can only observe — take in, but give nothing out. The first winter snow is just now falling on Yosemite rocks. The domes are whitened, and ere long avalanches will rush with loud boom and roar, like new-made waterfalls. The November number of "Harper's Monthly" contains "Living Glaciers of California." The illustrations are from my pencil sketches, some of which were made when my fingers were so benumbed with frost I could scarcely hold my pencil.

Give my love to David and the children and Mrs. Galloway, and I will hope yet to see you all. But now, once more, Farewell.

[JOHN MUIR]

In tracing out the main forest belt of the Sierra Nevada, as Muir did during these years, he became appalled by the destructive forces at work therein. No less than five sawmills were found operating in the edge of the Big Tree belt. On account of the size of the trees and the difficulty of felling them, they were blasted down with dynamite, a proceeding that added a new element of criminal waste to the

terrible destruction. The noble Fresno grove
of Big Trees and the one situated on the north
fork of the Kaweah already were fearfully
ravaged. The wonderful grove on the north
fork of the Kings River still was intact, but a
man by the name of Charles Converse had just
formed a company to reduce it to cheap lumber
in the usual wasteful manner.

Hoping to arouse California legislators to at
least the economic importance of checking this
destruction he sent to the "Sacramento Record-
Union" a communication entitled "God's
First Temples," with the sub-heading, "How
Shall we Preserve our Forests?" It appeared
on February 5, 1876, and while it made little
impression upon legislators it made Muir the
center around which conservation sentiment
began to crystallize. Few at this time had
pointed out, as he did, the practical importance
of conserving the forests on account of their
relation to climate, soil, and water-flow in the
streams. The deadliest enemies of the forests
and the public good, he declared, were not the
sawmills in spite of their slash fires and waste-
fulness. That unsavory distinction belonged
to the "sheep-men," as they were called, and
Muir's indictment of them in the above-
mentioned article, based upon careful observation, ran as follows:

THE WORLD NEEDS THE WOODS

Incredible numbers of sheep are driven to the mountain pastures every summer, and in order to make easy paths and to improve the pastures, running fires are set everywhere to burn off the old logs and underbrush. These fires are far more universal and destructive than would be guessed. They sweep through nearly the entire forest belt of the range from one extremity to the other, and in the dry weather, before the coming on of winter storms, are very destructive to all kinds of young trees, and especially to sequoia, whose loose, fibrous bark catches and burns at once. Excepting the Calaveras, I, last summer, examined every sequoia grove in the range, together with the main belt extending across the basins of Kaweah and Tule, and found everywhere the most deplorable waste from this cause. Indians burn off underbrush to facilitate deer-hunting. Campers of all kinds often permit fires to run, so also do mill-men, but the fires of "sheep-men" probably form more than ninety per cent of all destructive fires that sweep the woods. ... Whether our loose-jointed Government is really able or willing to do anything in the matter remains to be seen. If our law-makers were to discover and enforce any method tending to lessen even in a small degree the destruction going on, they would thus cover a multitude of legislative sins in the eyes of every tree lover. I am satisfied, however, that the question can be intelligently discussed only after a careful survey of our forests has been made, together with studies of the forces now acting upon them.

The concluding suggestion bore fruit years

afterward when President Cleveland, in 1896, appointed a commission to report upon the condition of the national forest areas.

To Sarah Muir Galloway

1419 TAYLOR ST., SAN FRANCISCO
April 17th, 1876

DEAR SISTER SARAH:

I was glad the other day to have the hard continuous toil of book writing interrupted by the postman handing in your letter. It is full of news, but I can think of little to put in the letter you ask for.

My life these days is like the life of a glacier, one eternal grind, and the top of my head suffers a weariness at times that you know nothing about. I'm glad to see by the hills across the bay, all yellow and purple with buttercups and gilias, that spring is blending fast into summer, and soon I'll throw down my pen, and take up my heels to go mountaineering once more.

My first book is taking shape now, and is mostly written, but still far from complete. I hope to see it in print, rubbed, and scrubbed, and elaborated, some time next year.

Among the unlooked-for burdens fate is loading upon my toil-doomed shoulders, is this literature and lecture tour. I suppose I will be called upon for two more addresses in San

Francisco ere I make my annual hegira to the woods. A few weeks ago I lectured at San Jose and Oakland.

I'm glad to hear of the general good health and welfare of our scattered and multiplied family, of Katie's returning health, and Joanna's. Remember me warmly to Mrs. Galloway, tell her I will be in Wisconsin in two or three years, and hope to see her, still surrounded by her many affectionate friends. I was pleasantly surprised to notice the enclosed clipping to-day in the "N.Y. Tribune." I also read a notice of a book by Professor James Law of Cornell University, whom I used to play with. I met one of his scholars a short time ago. Give my love to David and all your little big ones.

Ever very affectionately yours

JOHN MUIR

To Sarah Muir Galloway

1419 TAYLOR ST., SAN FRANCISCO
January 12th, [1877]

DEAR SISTER SARAH:

I received your welcome letter to-day. I was beginning to think you were neglecting me. The sad news of dear old Mrs. Galloway, though not unexpected, makes me feel that I have lost a friend. Few lives are so beautiful and complete as hers, and few could have had the glorious satisfaction, in dying, to know that so few words spoken were other than kind, and so few deeds that did anything more than augment the happiness of others. How many really good people waste, and worse than waste, their short lives in mean bickerings, when they might lovingly, in broad Christian charity, enjoy the glorious privilege of doing plain, simple, every-day good. Mrs. Galloway's character was one of the most beautiful and perfect I ever knew.

How delightful it is for you all to gather on the holidays, and what a grand multitude you must make when you are all mustered. Little did I think when I used to be, and am now, fonder of home and still domestic life than any one of the boys, that I only should be a bachelor and doomed to roam always far outside the family circle. But we are governed more than we know and are driven with whips we know not where. Your pleasures, and the happiness of your lives in general, are far greater than you know, being clustered together, yet independent, and living in one of the most beautiful regions under the sun. Long may you all live to enjoy your blessings and to learn to love one another and make sacrifices for one another's good.

You inquire about [my] books. The others

I spoke of are a book of excursions, another on Yosemite and the adjacent mountains, and another "Studies in the Sierra" (scientific). The present volume will be descriptive of the Sierra animals, birds, forests, falls, glaciers, etc., which, if I live, you will see next fall or winter. I have not written enough to compose with much facility, and as I am also very careful and have but a limited vocabulary, I make slow progress. Still, although I never meant to write the results of my explorations, now I have begun I rather enjoy it and the public do me the credit of reading all I write, and paying me for it, which is some satisfaction, and I will not probably fail in my first effort on the book, inasmuch as I always make out to accomplish in some way what I undertake.

I don't write regularly for anything, although I'm said to be a regular correspondent of the [San Francisco] "Evening Bulletin," and have the privilege of writing for it when I like. Harper's have two unpublished illustrated articles of mine, but after they pay for them they keep them as long as they like, sometimes a year or more, before publishing.

Love to David and George, and all your fine lassies, and love, dear Sarah, to yourself.

From your wandering brother

[JOHN MUIR]

The following letter invites comment. Until far into the later years of his life Muir wrote by preference with quills which he cut himself. Over against his bantering remark, that the pen he sends her may be a goose quill after all, should be set the fact that among the mementos preserved by his sister Sarah is a quill-pen wrapped with a cutting from one of John's letters which reads, "Your letter about the first book recalls old happy days on the mountains. The pen you speak of was made of a wing-feather of an eagle, picked up on Mount Hoffman, back a few miles from Yosemite." The book he wrote with it did not see the light of day, at least in the form which he then gave it, and it is not certain what it contained beyond glowing descriptions of Sierra forests and scenery, and appeals for their preservation. That "the world needs the woods" has now become more than a sentimental conviction with him; the moral and economic aspects of the question begin to emerge strongly. One likes to think it a fact of more than poetic significance that such a book by such a man was written with a quill from an eagle's wing, and that the most patriotic service ever rendered by an American eagle was that of the one who contributed a wing pinion to John Muir for the defense of the western forests.

THE WORLD NEEDS THE WOODS

To Sarah Muir Galloway

SAN FRANCISCO, *April 23rd,* 1877

MY DEAR SISTER SARAH:

To thee I give and bequeath this old gray quill with which I have written every word of my first book, knowing, as I do, your predilection for curiosities.

I can hardly remember its origin, but I think it is one that I picked up on the mountains, fallen from the wing of a golden eagle; but, possibly, it may be only a pinion feather of some tame old gray goose, and my love of truth compels me to make this unpoetical statement. The book that has grown from its whittled nib is, however, as wild as any that has ever appeared in these tame, civilized days. Perhaps I should have waited until the book was in print, for it is not absolutely certain that it will be accepted by the publishing houses. It has first to be submitted to the tasting critics, but as everything in the way of magazine and newspaper articles that the old pen has ever traced has been accepted and paid for, I reasonably hope I shall have no difficulties in obtaining a publisher. The manuscript has just been sent to New York, and will be reported on in a few weeks. I leave for the mountains of Utah to-day.

The frayed upper end of the pen was pro-

duced by nervous gnawing when some inter-
ruption in my logic or rhetoric occurred from
stupidity or weariness. I gnawed the upper end
to send the thoughts below and out at the other.

Love to all your happy family and to thee
and David. The circumstances of my life since
I last bade you farewell have wrought many
changes in me, but my love for you all has only
grown greater from year to year, and whatsoever befalls I shall ever be,

Yours affectionately

JOHN MUIR

The statement, in the preceding letter, that
he is leaving for the mountains of Utah, the
reader familiar with Muir's writings will at
once connect with the vivid Utah sketches that
have appeared in the volume entitled "Steep
Trails." In the same book are found the two
articles on "The San Gabriel Valley" and
"The San Gabriel Mountains," which grew out
of an excursion he made into southern California soon after his return from Utah.

Mrs. Carr, who in 1877 had suffered the loss
of another of her sons, was at this time preparing to carry out her long cherished plan to retire from public life to her new home in the
South. With her for a magnet, Carmelita, as
she called it, became for a time the literary

center of southern California. There Helen Hunt Jackson wrote the greater part of her novel "Ramona," and numerous other literary folk, both East and West, made it at one time or another the goal of their pilgrimages. In her spacious garden she indulged to the full her passion for bringing together a great variety of unusual plants, shrubs, and trees, many of them contributed by John Muir. Dr. E. M. Congar, mentioned in one of the following letters, had been a fellow student of Muir at the University of Wisconsin.

To Mrs. Ezra S. Carr

SWETT HOME, *July* 23rd, [1877]

DEAR MRS. CARR:

I made only a short dash into the dear old Highlands above Yosemite, but all was so full of everything I love, every day seemed a measureless period. I never enjoyed the Tuolumne cataracts so much; coming out of the sun lands, the gray salt deserts of Utah, these wild ice waters sang themselves into my soul more enthusiastically than ever, and the forests' breath was sweeter, and Cassiope fairer than in all my first fresh contacts.

But I am not going to tell it here. I only write now to say that next Saturday I will sail to Los Angeles and spend a few weeks in getting some general views of the adjacent region, then work northward and begin a careful study of the Redwood. I will at least have time this season for the lower portion of the belt, that is for all south of here. If you have any messages, you may have time to write me (I sail at 10 A.M.), or if not, you may direct to Los Angeles. I hope to see Congar, and also the spot you have elected for home. I wish you could be there in your grown, fruitful groves, all rooted and grounded in the fine garden nook that I know you will make. It must be a great consolation, in the midst of the fires you are compassed with, to look forward to a tranquil seclusion in the South of which you are so fond.

John [Swett] says he may not move to Berkeley, and if not I may be here this winter, though I still feel some tendency towards another winter in some mountain den.

It is long indeed since I had anything like a quiet talk with you. You have been going like an avalanche for many a year, and I sometimes fear you will not be able to settle into rest even in the orange groves. I'm glad to know that the Doctor is so well. You must be pained by the shameful attacks made upon your tried friend LaGrange. Farewell.

Ever cordially yours

JOHN MUIR

THE WORLD NEEDS THE WOODS

To Mrs. Ezra S. Carr

PICO HOUSE
LOS ANGELES, CALIFORNIA
August 12th, 1877

DEAR MRS. CARR:

I've seen your sunny Pasadena and the patch called yours. Everything about here pleases me and I felt sorely tempted to take Dr. Congar's advice and invest in an orange patch myself. I feel sure you will be happy here with the Doctor and Allie among so rich a luxuriance of sunny vegetation. How you will dig and dibble in that mellow loam! I cannot think of you standing erect for a single moment, unless it be in looking away out into the dreamy West.

I made a fine shaggy little five days' excursion back in the heart of the San Gabriel Mountains, and then a week of real pleasure with Congar resurrecting the past about Madison. He has a fine little farm, fine little family, and fine cozy home. I felt at home with Congar and at once took possession of his premises and all that in them is. We drove down through the settlements eastward and saw the best orange groves and vineyards, but the mountains I, as usual, met alone. Although so gray and silent and unpromising they are full of wild gardens and ferneries. Lilyries! — some specimens ten feet high with twenty lilies, big enough for bonnets! The main results I will tell you some other time, should you ever have an hour's leisure.

I go North to-day, by rail to Newhall, thence by stage to Soledad and on to Monterey, where I will take to the woods and feel my way in free study to San Francisco. May reach the City about the middle of next month. . . .

Ever cordially

J. M.

To Mrs. Ezra S. Carr

1419 TAYLOR ST., SAN FRANCISCO
September 3d, [1877]

DEAR MRS. CARR:

I have just been over at Alameda with poor dear old Gibbons.[1] You have seen him, and I need give no particulars. "The only thing I'm afraid of, John," he said, looking up with his old child face, "is that I shall never be able to climb the Oakland hills again." But he is so healthy and so well cared for, we will be strong to hope that he will. He spoke for an hour with characteristic unselfishness on the injustice done Dr. [Albert] Kellogg in failing to recognize his long-continued devotion to science at the botanical love feast held here the other

---

[1] W. P. Gibbons, M.D., an able amateur botanist and early member of the California Academy of Sciences.

night. He threatens to write up the whole dis-creditable affair, and is very anxious to obtain from you a copy of that Gray letter to Kellogg which was not delivered.

I had a glorious ramble in the Santa Cruz woods, and have found out one very interesting and picturesque fact concerning the growth of this Sequoia. I mean to devote many a long week to its study. What the upshot may be I cannot guess, but you know I am never sent empty away.

I made an excursion to the summit of Mt. Hamilton in extraordinary style, accompanied by Allen, Norton, Brawley, and all the lady professors and their friends — a curious con-trast to my ordinary *still hunting*. Spent a week at San Jose, enjoyed my visit with Allen very much. Lectured to the faculty on methods of study without undergoing any very great scare.

I believe I wrote you from Los Angeles about my Pasadena week. Have sent a couple of letters to the "Bulletin" from there — not yet published.

I have no inflexible plans as yet for the re-maining months of the season, but Yosemite seems to place itself as a most persistent candi-date for my winter. I shall soon be in flight to the Sierras, or Oregon.

I seem to give up hope of ever seeing you calm again. Don't grind too hard at these Sacramento mills. Remember me to the Doctor and Allie.

Ever yours cordially
JOHN MUIR

One of the earliest and most distinguished pioneer settlers of California was General John Bidwell, of Chico, at whose extensive and beautiful ranch distinguished travelers and scientists often were hospitably entertained. In 1877, Sir Joseph Hooker and Asa Gray were among the guests of Rancho Chico, when they returned from a botanical trip to Mount Shasta, whither they had gone under the guidance of John Muir. This excursion, of which more later, drew Muir also into the friendly circle of the Bidwell family, and the following letter was written after a prolonged visit at Rancho Chico. "Lize in Jackets," wrote the late Mrs. Annie E. K. Bidwell in kindly transmitting a copy of this letter, "refers to my sister's mule, which, when attacked by yellow jackets whose nests we trod upon, would rise almost perpendicularly, then plunge forward frantically, kicking and twisting her tail with a rapidity that elicited uproarious laughter from Mr. Muir. Each of our riding animals had characteristic movements on this occasion, which Mr. Muir classified with much merriment." Just before his departure, on October 2, Muir expressed the wish that he might be able to descend the Sacramento River in a skiff, whereupon General Bidwell had his ranch carpenter hastily construct a kind of boat in which Muir made the trip described in the following letter.

To General John Bidwell, Mrs. Bidwell, and Miss Sallie Kennedy

SACRAMENTO, *October* 10*th*, 1877

FRIENDS THREE:

The Chico flagship and I are safely arrived in Sacramento, unwrecked, unsnagged, and the whole winding way was one glorious strip of enjoyment. When I bade you good-bye, on the bank I was benumbed and bent down with your lavish kindnesses like one of your vine-laden willows. It is seldom that I experience much difficulty in leaving civilization for God's wilds, but I was loath indeed to leave you three that day after our long free ramble in the mountain woods and that five weeks' rest in your cool fruity home. The last I saw of you was Miss Kennedy white among the leaves like a fleck of mist, then sweeping around a bend you were all gone — the old wildness came back, and I began to observe, and enjoy, and be myself again.

My first camp was made on a little oval island some ten or twelve miles down, where a clump of arching willows formed a fine nest-like shelter; and where I spread my quilt on the gravel and opened the box so daintily and thoughtfully stored for my comfort. I began to reflect again on your real goodness to me from first to last, and said, "I'll not forget those Chico three as long as I live."

I placed the two flags at the head of my bed, one on each side, and as the campfire shone upon them the effect was very imposing and patriotic. The night came on full of strange sounds from birds and insects new to me, but the starry sky was clear and came arching over my lowland nest seemingly as bright and familiar with its glorious constellations as when beheld through the thin crisp atmosphere of the mountain-tops.

On the second day the Spoonbill sprang a bad leak from the swelling of the bottom timbers; two of them crumpled out thus [sketch] [1] at a point where they were badly nailed, and I had to run her ashore for repairs. I turned her

[1] After Mrs. Bidwell's death, the writer unfortunately was unable to obtain from her relatives the loan of this letter for the reproduction of the two included sketches.

upside down on a pebbly bar, took out one of the timbers, whittled it carefully down to the right dimensions, replaced it, and nailed it tight and fast with a stone for a hammer; then calked the new joint, shoved her back into the current, and rechristened her "The Snag-Jumper." She afterwards behaved splendidly in the most trying places, and leaked only at the rate of fifteen tincupfuls per hour.

Her performances in the way of snag-jumping are truly wonderful. Most snags are covered with slimy algæ and lean downstream and the sloping bows of the Jumper enabled her to glance gracefully up and over them, when not too high above the water, while her lightness prevented any strain sufficient to crush her bottom. [Sketch of boat.] On one occasion she took a firm slippery snag a little obliquely and was nearly rolled upside down, as a sod is turned by a plow. Then I charged myself to be more careful, and while rowing often looked well ahead for snag ripples — but soon I came to a long glassy reach, and my vigilance not being eternal, my thoughts wandered upstream back to those grand spring fountains on the head of the McCloud and Pitt. Then I tried to picture those hidden tributaries that flow beneath the lava tablelands, and recognized in them a capital illustration of the fact that in their farthest fountains all rivers are lost to mortal eye, that the sources of all are hidden as those of the Nile, and so, also, that in this respect every river of knowledge is a Nile. Thus I was philosophizing, rowing with a steady stroke, and as the current was rapid, the Jumper was making fine headway, when with a tremendous bump she reared like "Lize in Jackets," swung around stern downstream, and remained fast on her beam ends, erect like a coffin against a wall. She managed, however, to get out of even this scrape without disaster to herself or to me.

I usually sailed from sunrise to sunset, rowing one third of the time, paddling one third, and drifting the other third in restful comfort, landing now and then to examine a section of the bank or some bush or tree. Under these conditions the voyage to this port was five days in length. On the morning of the third day I hid my craft in the bank vines and set off crosslots for the highest of the Marysville Buttes, reached the summit, made my observations, and got back to the river and Jumper by two o'clock. The distance to the nearest foothill of the group is about three miles, but to the base of the southmost and highest butte is six miles, and its elevation is about eighteen hundred feet above its base, or in round numbers two

thousand feet above tidewater. The whole
group is volcanic, taking sharp basaltic forms
near the summit, and with stratified conglom-
erates of finely polished quartz and metamorphic pebbles tilted against their flanks. There
is a sparse growth of live oak and laurel on the
southern slopes, the latter predominating, and
on the north quite a close tangle of dwarf oak
forming a chaparral. I noticed the white
mountain spiræa also, and madroña, with a
few willows, and three ferns toward the summit. *Pellæa andromedæfolia, Gymnogramma
triangularis*, and *Cheilanthes gracillima;* and
many a fine flower — penstemons, gilias, and
our brave eriogonums of blessed memory. The
summit of this highest southmost butte is a
coast survey station.

The river is very crooked, becoming more
and more so in its lower course, flowing in
grand lingering deliberation, now south, now
north, east and west with fine un-American in-
directness. The upper portion down as far as
Colusa is full of rapids, but below this point
the current is beautifully calm and lake-like,
with innumerable reaches of most surpassing
loveliness. How you would have enjoyed it!
The bank vines all the way down are of the
same species as those that festoon your beautiful Chico Creek (*Vitis californica*), but nowhere

77

do they reach such glorious exuberance of development as with you.

The temperature of the water varies only about two and a half degrees between Chico and Sacramento, a distance by the river of nearly two hundred miles — the upper temperature 64°, the lower 66½°. I found the temperature of the Feather [River] waters at their confluence one degree colder than those of the Sacramento, 65° and 66° respectively, which is a difference in exactly the opposite direction from what I anticipated. All the brown discoloring mud of the lower Sacramento, thus far, is derived from the Feather, and it is curious to observe how completely the two currents keep themselves apart for three or four miles. I never landed to talk to any one, or ask questions, but was frequently cheered from the bank and challenged by old sailors "Ship ahoy," etc., and while seated in the stern reading a magazine and drifting noiselessly with the current, I overheard a deck hand on one of the steamers say, "Now that's what I call taking it aisy."

I am still at a loss to know what there is in the rig or model of the Jumper that excited such universal curiosity. Even the birds of the river, and the animals that came to drink, though paying little or no heed to the passing steamers with all their plash and outroar, at once fixed their attention on my little flagship, some taking flight with loud screams, others waiting with outstretched necks until I nearly touched them, while others circled overhead. The domestic animals usually dashed up the bank in extravagant haste, one crowding on the heels of the other as if suffering extreme terror. I placed one flag, the smaller, on the highest pinnacle of the Butte, where I trust it may long wave to your memory; the other I have still. Watching the thousand land birds — linnets, orioles, sparrows, flickers, quails, etc. — Nature's darlings, taking their morning baths, was no small part of my enjoyments.

I was greatly interested in the fine bank sections shown to extraordinary advantage at the present low water, because they cast so much light upon the formation of this grand valley, but I cannot tell my results here.

This letter is already far too long, and I will hasten to a close. I will rest here a day or so, and then push off again to the mouth of the river a hundred miles or so farther, chiefly to study the deposition of the sediment at the head of the bay, then push for the mountains. I would row up the San Joaquin, but two weeks or more would be required for the trip, and I fear snow on the mountains.

I am glad to know that you are really interested in science, and I might almost venture another lecture upon you, but in the mean time forbear. Looking backward I see you three in your leafy home, and while I wave my hand, I will only wait to thank you all over and over again for the thousand kind things you have done and said — drives, and grapes, and rest, "a' that and a' that."

And now, once more, farewell.

Ever cordially your friend

JOHN MUIR

During this same summer of 1877, and previous to the experiences narrated in the preceding letter, the great English botanist Sir Joseph Dalton Hooker had accepted an invitation from Dr. F. V. Hayden, then in charge of the United States Geological and Geographical Survey of the Territories, to visit under his conduct the Rocky Mountain region, with the object of contributing to the records of the Survey a report on the botany of the western states. Professor Asa Gray was also of the party. After gathering some special botanical collections in Colorado, New Mexico, and Utah, they came to California and persuaded John Muir, on account of his familiarity with the region, to go with them to Mount Shasta. One September evening, as they were en-

camped on its flanks in a forest of silver firs,
Muir built a big fire, whose glow stimulated
an abundant flow of interesting conversation.
Gray recounted reminiscences of his collecting tours in the Alleghanies; Hooker told of
his travels in the Himalayas and of his work
with Tyndall, Huxley, and Darwin. "And of
course," notes Muir, "we talked of trees, ar-
gued the relationship of varying species, etc.;
and I remember that Sir Joseph, who in his
long active life had traveled through all the
great forests of the world, admitted, in reply to
a question of mine, that in grandeur, variety,
and beauty, no forest on the globe rivaled the
great coniferous forests of my much loved
Sierra."

But the most memorable incident of that
night on the flanks of Shasta grew out of the
mention of *Linnæa borealis* — the charming
little evergreen trailer whose name perpetuates
the memory of the illustrious Linnæus. "Muir,
why have you not found *Linnæa* in California?" said Gray suddenly during a pause in the
conversation. "It must be here, or hereabouts,
on the northern boundary of the Sierra. I have
heard of it, and have specimens from Washington and Oregon all through these northern
woods, and you should have found it here."
The camp fire sank into heaps of glowing coals,

the conversation ceased, and all fell asleep with *Linnœa* uppermost in their minds.

The next morning Gray continued his work alone, while Hooker and Muir made an excursion westward across one of the upper tributaries of the Sacramento. In crossing a small stream, they noticed a green bank carpeted with what Hooker at once recognized as *Linnœa* — the first discovery of the plant within the bounds of California. "It would seem," said Muir, "that Gray had felt its presence the night before on the mountain ten miles away. That was a great night, the like of which was never to be enjoyed by us again, for we soon separated and Gray died." [1] The impression Muir made upon Hooker is reflected in his letters. In one of them, written twenty-five years after the event, Hooker declares, "My memory of you is very strong and durable, and that of our days in the forests is inextinguishable."

In the following letter to his sister Muir gives some additional details of the Shasta excursion, and makes reference to an exceedingly strenuous exploring trip up the Middle Fork of the Kings River, from which he had just returned.

[1] Muir's article on Linnæus in *Library of the World's Best Literature*, vol. 16 (1897).

THE WORLD NEEDS THE WOODS

To Sarah Muir Galloway

THANKSGIVING EVENING
AT OLD 1419 TAYLOR ST.
[*November* 29, 1877]

MY DEAR SISTER SARAH:

I find an unanswered letter of yours dated September 23d, and though I have been very hungry on the mountains a few weeks ago, and have just been making bountiful amends at a regular turkey thank-feast of the old New England type, I must make an effort to answer it, however incapacitated by "stuffing," for, depend upon it, this Turkish method of thanks does make the simplest kind of literary effort hard; one's brains go heavily along the easiest lines like a laden wagon in a bog.

But I can at least answer your questions. The Professor Gray I was with on Shasta is the writer of the school botanies, the most distinguished botanist in America, and Sir Joseph Hooker is the leading botanist of England. We had a fine rare time together in the Shasta forests, discussing the botanical characters of the grandest coniferous trees in the world, camping out, and enjoying ourselves in pure freedom. Gray is an old friend that I led around Yosemite years ago, and with whom I have corresponded for a long time. Sir Joseph I never met before. He is a fine cordial Eng-

lishman, President of the Royal Scientific
Society, and has charge of the Kew Botanic
Gardens. He is a great traveler, but perfectly
free from all chilling airs of superiority. He
told me a great deal about the Himalayas, the
deodar forests there, and the gorgeous rhododendrons that cover their flanks with lavish
bloom for miles and miles, and about the
cedars of Lebanon that he visited and the distribution of the species in different parts of
Syria, and its relation to the deodar so widely
extended over the mountains of India. And
besides this scientific talk he told many a story
and kept the camp in fine lively humor. On
taking his leave he gave me a hearty invitation
to London, and promised to show me through
the famous government gardens at Kew, and
all round, etc., etc. When I shall be able to
avail myself of this and similar advantages I
don't know. I have met a good many of Nature's noblemen one way and another out here,
and hope to see some of them at their homes,
but my own researches seem to hold me fast to
this comparatively solitary life.

Next you speak of my storm night on Shasta.
Terrible as it would appear from the account
printed, the half was not told, but I will not
likely be caught in the same experience again,
though as I have said, I have just been very

hungry — one meal in four days, coupled with the most difficult, nerve-trying cliff work. This was on Kings River a few weeks ago. Still, strange to say, I did not feel it much, and there seems to be scarce any limit to my endurance.

I am far from being friendless here, and on this particular day I might have eaten a score of prodigious thank dinners if I could have been in as many places at the same time, but the more I learn of the world the happier seems to me the life you live. You speak of your family gatherings, of a week's visit at Mother's and here and there. Make the most of your privileges to trust and love and live in near, unjealous, generous sympathy with one another, for I assure you these are blessings scarce at all recognized in their real divine greatness. . . .

We had a company of fourteen at dinner tonight, and we had what is called a grand time, but these big eating parties never seem to me to pay for the trouble they make, though all seem to enjoy them immensely. A crust by a brookside out on the mountains with God is more to me than all, beyond comparison. Nevertheless these poor legs in their weariness do enjoy a soft bed at times and plenty of nourishment. I had another grand turkey feast a week ago. Coming home here I left my boat at Martinez, thirty miles up the bay, and walked to Oakland across the top of Mount Diablo, and on the way called at my friends, the Strentzels, who have eighty acres of choice orchards and vineyards, where I rested two days, my first rest in six weeks. They pitied my weary looks, and made me eat and sleep, stuffing me with turkey, chicken, beef, fruits, and jellies in the most extravagant manner imaginable, and begged me to stay a month. Last eve dined at a French friend's in the city, and you would have been surprised to see so temperate a Scotchman doing such justice to French dishes. The fact is I've been hungry ever since starving in the mountain cañons.

This evening the guests would ask me how I felt while starving? Why I did not die like other people? How many bears I had seen, and deer, etc.? How deep the snow is now and where the snow line is located, etc.? Then upstairs we chat and sing and play piano, etc., and then I slip off from the company and write this. Now it [is] near midnight, and I must slip from thee also, wishing you and David and all your dear family good-night. With love,

[JOHN MUIR]

THE WORLD NEEDS THE WOODS

To General John Bidwell

1419 TAYLOR ST., SAN FRANCISCO
December 3, 1877

MY DEAR GENERAL:

I arrived in my old winter quarters here a week ago, my season's field work done, and I was just sitting down to write to Mrs. Bidwell when your letter of November 29th came in. The tardiness of my Kings River postal is easily explained. I committed it to the care of a mountaineer who was about to descend to the lowlands, and he probably carried it for a month or so in his breeches' pocket in accordance with the well-known business habits of that class of men. And now since you are so kindly interested in my welfare I must give you here a sketch of my explorations since I wrote you from Sacramento.

I left Snag-Jumper at Sacramento in charge of a man whose name I have forgotten. He has boats of his own, and I tied Snag to one of his stakes in a snug out-of-the-way nook above the railroad bridge. I met this pilot a mile up the river on his way home from hunting. He kindly led me into port, and then conducted me in the dark up the Barbary Coast into the town; and on taking leave he volunteered the information that he was always kindly disposed towards strangers, but that most people met under such circumstances would have robbed and made away with me, etc. I think, therefore, that leaving Snag in his care will form an interesting experiment on human nature.

I fully intended to sail on down into the bay and up the San Joaquin as far as Millerton, but when I came to examine a map of the river deltas and found that the distance was upwards of three hundred miles, and learned also that the upper San Joaquin was not navigable this dry year even for my craft, and when I also took into consideration the approach of winter and danger of snowstorms on the Kings River summits, I concluded to urge my way into the mountains at once, and leave the San Joaquin studies until my return.

Accordingly I took the steamer to San Francisco, where I remained one day, leaving extra baggage, and getting some changes of clothing. Then went direct by rail to Visalia, thence pushed up the mountains to Hyde's Mill on the Kaweah, where I obtained some flour, which, together with the tea Mrs. Bidwell supplied me with, and that piece of dried beef, and a little sugar, constituted my stock of provisions. From here I crossed the divide, going northward through fine Sequoia woods to Converse's on Kings River. Here I spent two days making some studies on the Big Trees, chiefly with reference to their age. Then I turned eastward and pushed off into the glorious wilderness, following the general direction of the South Fork a few miles back from the brink until I had crossed three tributary cañons from 1500 to 2000 feet deep. In the eastmost and middle one of the three I was delighted to discover some four or five square miles of Sequoia, where I had long guessed the existence of these grand old tree kings.

After this capital discovery I made my way to the bottom of the main South Fork Cañon down a rugged side gorge, having a descent of more than four thousand feet. This was at a point about two miles above the confluence of Boulder Creek. From here I pushed slowly on up the bottom of the cañon, through brush and avalanche boulders, past many a charming fall and garden sacred to nature, and at length reached the grand yosemite at the head, where I stopped two days to make some measurements of the cliffs and cascades. This done, I crossed over the divide to the Middle Fork by a pass 12,200 feet high, and struck the head of a small tributary that conducted me to the head of the main Middle Fork Cañon, which I followed down through its entire length, though it has hitherto been regarded as absolutely inaccessible in its lower reaches. This accomplished, and all my necessary sketches and measurements made, I climbed the cañon wall below the confluence of the Middle and South Forks and came out at Converse's again; then back to Hyde's Mill, Visalia, and thence to Merced City by rail, thence by stage to Snelling, and thence to Hopeton afoot.

Here I built a little unpretentious successor to Snag out of some gnarled, sun-twisted fencing, launched it in the Merced opposite the village, and rowed down into the San Joaquin — thence down the San Joaquin past Stockton and through the tule region into the bay near Martinez. There I abandoned my boat and set off cross lots for Mount Diablo, spent a night on the summit, and walked the next day into Oakland. And here my fine summer's wanderings came to an end. And now I find that this mere skeleton finger board indication of my excursion has filled at least the space of a long letter, while I have told you nothing of my gains. If you were nearer I would take a day or two and come and report, and talk inveterately in and out of season until you would be glad to have me once more in the cañons and silence. But Chico is far, and I can only finish with a catalogue of my new riches, setting them down one after the other like words in a spelling book.

THE WORLD NEEDS THE WOODS

1. Four or five square miles of Sequoias.
2. The ages of twenty-six specimen Sequoias.
3. A fine fact about bears.
4. A sure measurement of the deepest of all the ancient glaciers yet traced in the Sierra.
5. Two waterfalls of the first order, and cascades innumerable.
6. *A new Yosemite valley!!!*
7. Grand facts concerning the formation of the central plain of California.
8. A picturesque cluster of facts concerning the river birds and animals.
9. A glorious series of new landscapes, with mountain furniture and garniture of the most ravishing grandeur and beauty.

Here, Mrs. Bidwell, is a rose leaf from a wild briar on Mount Diablo whose leaves are more flowery than its petals. Isn't it beautiful? That new Yosemite Valley is located in the heart of the Middle Fork Cañon, the most remote, and inaccessible, and one of the very grandest of all the mountain temples of the range. It is still sacred to Nature, its gardens untrodden, and every nook and rejoicing cataract wears the bloom and glad sun-beauty of primeval wildness — ferns and lilies and grasses over one's head. I saw a flock of five deer in one of its open meadows, and a grizzly bear quietly munching acorns under a tree within a few steps.

The cold was keen and searching the night I spent on the summit by the edge of a glacier lake twenty-two degrees below the freezing point, and a storm wind blowing in fine hearty surges among the shattered cliffs overhead, and, to crown all, snow flowers began to fly a few minutes after midnight, causing me to fold that quilt of yours and fly to avoid a serious snowbound. By daylight I was down in the main Middle Fork in a milder climate and safer position at an elevation of only seventy-five hundred feet. All the summit peaks were quickly clad in close unbroken white.

I was terribly hungry ere I got out of this wild cañon — had less than sufficient for one meal in the last four days, and this, coupled with very hard nerve-trying cliff work was sufficiently exhausting for any mountaineer. Yet strange to say, I did not suffer much. Crystal water, and air, and honey sucked from the scarlet flowers of Zauschneria, about one tenth as much as would suffice for a humming bird, was my last breakfast — a very temperate meal, was it not? — wholly ungross and very nearly spiritual. The last effort before reaching food was a climb up out of the main cañon of five thousand feet. Still I made it in fair time — only a little faint, no giddiness, want of spirit, or incapacity to observe and enjoy, or any nonsense of this kind. How I should have liked to have then tumbled into your care for a day or two!

My sail down the Merced and San Joaquin was about two hundred and fifty miles in length and took two weeks, a far more difficult and less interesting [trip], as far as scenery is concerned, than my memorable first voyage down the Sacramento. Sandbars and gravelly riffles, as well as snags gave me much trouble, and in the Tule wilderness I had to tether my tiny craft to a bunch of rushes and sleep cold in her bottom with the seat for a pillow. I have gotten past most of the weariness but am hungry yet notwithstanding friends have been stuffing me here ever since. I may go hungry through life and into the very grave and beyond unless you effect a cure, and I'm sure I should like to try Rancho Chico — would have tried it ere this were you not so far off.

I slept in your quilt all through the excursion, and brought it here tolerably clean and whole. The flag I left tied to the bush-top in the bottom of the third F Cañon. I have not yet written to Gray, have you? Remember me to your sister, I mean to write to her soon. I must close. With lively remembrances of your rare kindness, I am

Ever very cordially yours

JOHN MUIR

*To Dr. and Mrs. John Strentzel, and
Miss Strentzel*

1419 TAYLOR ST., SAN FRANCISCO
December 5th, 1877

FRIENDS THREE:

I made a capital little excursion over your Mount Diablo and arrived in good order in San Francisco after that fine rest in your wee white house.

I sauntered on leisurely after bidding you good-bye, enjoying the landscape as it was gradually unrolled in the evening light. One charming bit of picture after another came into view at every turn of the road, and while the sunset fires were burning brightest I had attained an elevation sufficient for a grand comprehensive feast.

I reached the summit a little after dark and selected a sheltered nook in the chaparral to rest for the night and await the coming of the sun. The wind blew a gale, but I did not suffer much from the cold. The night was keen and crisp and the stars shone out with better brilliancy than one could hope for in these lowland atmospheres.

The sunrise was truly glorious. After lingering an hour or so, observing and feasting and making a few notes, I went down to that halfway hotel for breakfast. I was the only guest, while the family numbered four, well attired and intellectual looking persons, who for a time kept up a solemn, quakerish silence which I tried in vain to break up. But at length all four began a hearty, spontaneous discussion upon the art of cat killing, solemnly and decently relating in turn all their experience in this delightful business in bygone time, embracing everything with grave fervor in the whole scale of cat, all the way up from sackfuls of purblind kittens to tigerish Toms. Then I knew that such knowledge was attainable only by intellectual New Englanders.

My walk down the mountain-side across the valleys and through the Oakland hills was very delightful, and I feasted on many a bit of pure picture in purple and gold, Nature's best, and beheld the most ravishingly beautiful sunset on the Bay I ever yet enjoyed in the lowlands.

I shall not soon forget the rest I enjoyed in your pure white bed, or the feast on your fruity table. Seldom have I been so deeply weary, and as for hunger, I've been hungry still in spite of it all, and for aught I see in the signs of the stomach may go hungry on through life and into the grave and beyond

Heaven forbid a dry year! May wheat grow!

With lively remembrances of your rare kindness, I am,

Very cordially your friend

JOHN MUIR

The winter and the spring months passed swiftly in the effort to correlate and put into literary form his study of the forests. There were additional "tree days," too, and other visits with the congenial three on the Strentzel ranch. But when the Swetts, with whom he made his home, departed for the summer, taking their little daughter with them, he furloughed himself to the woods again without ceremony. "Helen Swett," he wrote to the Strentzels on May 5th, "left this morning, and the house is in every way most dolefully dull, and I won't stay in it. Will go into the woods, perhaps about Mendocino — will see more trees."

CHAPTER XIII

NEVADA, ALASKA, AND A HOME

1878–1880

DURING the summer of 1878 the United States Coast and Geodetic Survey made a reconnaissance along the 39th parallel of latitude in order to effect the primary triangulation of Nevada and Utah. The survey party was in charge of Assistant August F. Rodgers, and was making preparations to set out from Sacramento in June, when Muir returned from a trip to the headwaters of the north and middle forks of the American River. He decided immediately to accept an invitation to join the party, although some of his friends, notably the Strentzels, sought to dissuade him on account of the Indian disturbances which had made Nevada unsafe territory for a number of years. Idaho was then actually in the throes of an Indian war that entailed the destruction and abandonment of the Malheur Reservation across the boundary in Oregon.

But the perils of the situation were in Muir's view outweighed by the exceptional opportunity to explore numerous detached mountain ranges and valleys of Nevada about which little

97

was known at the time. "If an explorer of God's fine wildernesses should wait until every danger be removed," he wrote to Mrs. Strentzel, "then he would wait until the sun set. The war country lies to the north of our line of work, some two or three hundred miles. Some of the Pah Utes have gone north to join the Bannocks, and those left behind are not to be trusted, but we shall be well armed, and they will not dare to attack a party like ours unless they mean to declare war, however gladly they might seize the opportunity of killing a lonely and unknown explorer. In any case we will never be more than two hundred miles from the railroad."

Unfortunately Muir, becoming absorbed the following year in the wonders of Alaska, never found time to reduce his Nevada explorations to writing in the form of well-considered articles. He did, however, write for the "San Francisco Evening Bulletin" a number of sketches during the progress of the expedition, and these, published in "Steep Trails," can now be supplemented with the following letters to the Strentzels — the only extant series written during that expedition.

Since Muir ultimately married into the Strentzel family, its antecedents are of interest to the reader and may be sketched briefly in this connection. John Strentzel, born in Lublin, Poland, was a participant in the unsuccessful Polish revolution of 1830. To escape the bitter fate of being drafted into the victorious Russian army he fled to Upper Hungary where he obtained a practical knowledge of viticulture, and later was trained as a physician at the University of Buda-Pesth. Coming to the United States in 1840, he joined at Louisville, Kentucky, a party of pioneers known as Peters' Colonization Company, and went with them to the Trinity River in Texas, where he built a cabin on the present site of the city of Dallas, then a wild Comanche country. When the colony failed and dispersed he removed to Lamar County in the same state, was married at Honeygrove to Louisiana Erwin, a native of Tennessee, and in 1849, with his wife and baby daughter, came across the plains from Texas to California as medical adviser to the Clarkesville "train" of pioneer immigrants. Not long afterwards he settled in the Alhambra [1] Valley

[1] According to the journal of Dr. Strentzel, this was not the original name of the valley. A company of Spanish soldiers, sent to chastise some Indians, was unable to obtain provisions there, and so named it, "Cañada de la Hambre," or Valley of Hunger. "Mrs. Strentzel, on arriving here," writes her husband, "was displeased with the name, and, remembering Irving's glowing description of the Moorish paradise, decided to re-christen our home Alhambra." Ever since then the valley has borne this modification of the original name.

near Martinez, and became one of the earliest and most successful horticulturists of California.

Miss Louie Wanda Strentzel, now arrived at mature womanhood, was not only the pride of the family, but was known widely for the grace with which she dispensed the generous hospitality of the Strentzel household. She had received her education in the Atkins Seminary for Young Ladies at Benicia and, according to her father, was "passionately fond of flowers and music." Among her admiring friends was Mrs. Carr, who at various times had vainly tried to bring about a meeting between Miss Strentzel and Mr. Muir. "You see how I am snubbed in trying to get John Muir to accompany me to your house this week," wrote Mrs. Carr in April, 1875. Mount Shasta was in opposition at the time, and easily won the choice.

But so many roads and interests met at the Strentzel ranch, so many friends had the two in common, that sooner or later an acquaintanceship was bound to result. In 1878 Muir began to be a frequent and fondly expected guest in the Strentzel household, and he was to discover ere long that the most beautiful adventures are not those one deliberately goes to seek.

Meantime, despite the dissuasion of his solicitous friends, he was off to the wildernesses of Nevada. Since the Survey had adopted for triangulation purposes a pentagon whose angles met at Genoa Peak, the party first made its way to the town of the same name in its vicinity, where the first of the following letters was written.

To Dr. and Mrs. John Strentzel
GENOA, NEVADA, *July* 6, 1878

DEAR STRENTZELS:

We rode our horses from Sacramento to this little village via Placerville and Lake Tahoe. The plains and foothills were terribly hot, the upper Sierra along the south fork of the American River cool and picturesque, and the Lake region almost cold. Spent three delightful days at the Lake — steamed around it, and visited Cascade Lake a mile beyond the western shore of Tahoo.

We are now making up our train ready to push off into the Great Basin. Am well mounted, and with the fine brave old garden desert before me, fear no ill. We will probably reach Austin, Nevada, in about a month. Write to me there, care Captain A. F. Rodgers.

Your fruity hollow wears a most beautiful and benignant aspect from this alkaline stand-

101

point, and so does the memory of your extravagant kindness.

Farewell

JOHN MUIR

To Dr. and Mrs. Strentzel

WEST WALKER RIVER
NEAR WELLINGTON'S STATION
July 11*th,* 1878

DEAR STRENTZELS:

We are now fairly free in the sunny basin of the grand old sea that stretched from the Wasatch to the Sierra. There is something perfectly enchanting to me in this young desert with its stranded island ranges. How bravely they rejoice in the flooding sunshine and endure the heat and drought.

All goes well in camp. All the Indians we meet are harmless as sagebushes, though perhaps about as bitter at heart. The river here goes brawling out into the plain after breaking through a range of basaltic lava.

In three days we shall be on top of Mount Grant, the highest peak of the Wassuck Range, to the west of Walker Lake.

I send you some Nevada prunes, or peaches rather. They are very handsome and have a fine wild flavor. The bushes are from three to six feet high, growing among the sage. It is a

102

true *Prunus*. Whether cultivation could ever make it soft enough and big enough for civilized teeth I dinna ken, but guess so. Plant it and see. It will not be ashamed of any pampered "free" or "cling," or even your oranges.

The wild brier roses are in full bloom, sweeter and bonnier far than Louie's best, bonnie though they be.

I can see no post-office ahead nearer than Austin, Nevada, which we may reach in three weeks. The packs are afloat.

Good-morning.

[JOHN MUIR]

To Dr. John Strentzel

AUSTIN, NEVADA
August 5th, 1878

DEAR DOCTOR:

Your kind note of the 24th was received the other day and your discussion of fruits and the fineness in general of civilized things takes me at some little disadvantage.

From the "Switch" we rode to the old Fort Churchill on the Carson and at the "Upper" lower end of Mason Valley were delighted to find the ancient outlet of Walker Lake down through a very picturesque cañon to its confluence with the Carson. It appears therefore that not only the Humboldt and Carson, but

103

the Walker River also poured its waters into
the Great Sink towards the end of the glacial
period. From Fort Churchill we pushed eastward between Carson Lake and the Sink.
Boo! how hot it was riding in the solemn, silent
glare, shadeless, waterless. Here is what the
early emigrants called the forty-mile desert,
well marked with bones and broken wagons.
Strange how the very sunshine may become
dreary. How strange a spell this region casts
over poor mortals accustomed to shade and
coolness and green fertility. Yet there is no
real cause, that I could see, for reasonable beings losing their wits and becoming frightened.
There are the lovely tender abronias blooming
in the fervid sand and sun, and a species of sun-
flower, and a curious leguminous bush crowded
with purple blossoms, and a green saltwort,
and four or five species of artemisia, really
beautiful, and three or four handsome grasses.

Lizards reveled in the grateful heat and a
brave little tamias that carries his tail forward
over his back, and here and there a hare. Immense areas, however, are smooth and hard
and plantless, reflecting light like water. How
eloquently they tell of the period, just gone by,
when this region was as remarkable for its lavish abundance of lake water as now for its
aridity. The same grand geological story is in-

scribed on the mountain flanks, old beach lines that seem to have been drawn with a ruler, registering the successive levels at which the grand lake stood, corresponding most significantly with the fluctuations of the glaciers as marked by the terraced lateral moraines and successively higher terminal moraines.

After crossing the Sink we ascended the mountain range that bounds it on the East, eight thousand to ten thousand feet high. How treeless and barren it seemed. Yet how full of small charming gardens, with mints, primroses, brier-roses, penstemons, spiræas, etc., watered by trickling streams too small to sing audibly. How glorious a view of the Sink from the mountain-top. The colors are ineffably lovely, as if here Nature were doing her very best painting.

But a letter tells little. We next ascended the Augusta Range, crossed the Desetoya and Shoshone ranges, then crossed Reese River valley and ascended the Toyabe Range, eleven thousand feet high. Lovely gardens in all. Discovered here the true *Pinus flexilis* at ten thousand feet. It enters the Sierra in one or two places on the south extremity of the Sierra, east flank. Saw only one rattlesnake. No hostile Indians. Had a visit at my tent yesterday from Captain Bob, one of the Pah

Ute plenipotentiaries who lately visited Mc-
Dowell at San Francisco. Next address for two
weeks from this date, Eureka, Nevada.

I'm sure I showed my appreciation of good
things. That's a fine suggestion about the
grapes. Try me, Doctor, on tame, tame
Tokays.

Cordially yours

JOHN MUIR

To Dr. and Mrs. John Strentzel

IN CAMP NEAR BELMONT, NEVADA
August 28th, 1878

DEAR STRENTZELS:

I sent you a note from Austin. Thence we
traveled southward down the Big Smoky
Valley, crossing and recrossing it between the
Toyabe and Toquima Ranges, the dominating
summits of which we ascended. Thence still
southward towards Death Valley to Lone
Mountain; thence northeastward to this little
mining town.

From the summit of a huge volcanic table
mountain of the Toquima Range I observed
a truly glorious spectacle — a dozen "cloud-
bursts" falling at once while we were cordially
pelted with hail. The falling water cloud-
drapery, thunder tones, lightning, and tranquil
blue sky windows between made one of the

most impressive pictures I ever beheld. One
of these cloud-bursts fell upon Austin, another
upon Eureka. But still more glorious to me
was the big significant fact I found here, fresh,
telling glacial phenomena — a whole series.
Moraines, *roches moutonnées*, glacial sculptures,
and even feeble specimens of glacier meadows
and glacier lakes. I also observed less manifest
glaciation on several other ranges. I have long
guessed that this Great Basin was loaded with
ice during the last cold period; but the rocks
are as unresisting and the water spouts to
which all the ranges have been exposed have
not simply obscured the glacial scriptures
here, but nearly buried and obliterated them,
so that only the skilled observer would detect
a single word, and he would probably be called
a glaciated monomaniac. Now it is clear that
this fiery inland region was icy prior to the
lake period.

I have also been so fortunate as to settle that
pine species we discussed, and found the nest
and young of the Alpine sparrow. What do you
think of all this — "A' that and a' that"? The
sun heat has been intense. What a triangle of
noses! — Captain Rodgers', Eimbeck's, and
mine — mine sore, Eimbeck's sorer, Captain's
sorest — scaled and dry as the backs of lizards,
and divided into sections all over the surface

and turned up on the edges like the surface layers of the desiccated sections of adobe flats.

On Lone Mountain we were *thirsty*. How we thought of the cool singing streams of the Sierra while our blood fevered and boiled and throbbed! Three of us ascended the mountain against my counsel and remonstrances while forty miles from any known water. Two of the three nearly lost their lives. I suffered least, though I suffered as never before, and was the only one strong enough to ascend a sandy cañon to find and fetch the animals after descending the mountain. Then I had to find my two companions. One I found death-like, lying in the hot sand, scarcely conscious and unable to speak above a frightful whisper. I managed, however, to get him on his horse. The other I found in a kind of delirious stupor, voiceless, in the sagebrush. It was a fearfully exciting search, and I forgot my own exhaustion in it, though I never for a moment lost my will and wits, or doubted our ability to endure and escape. We reached water at daybreak of the second day — two days and nights in this fire without water! A lesson has been learned that will last, and we will not suffer so again. Of course we could not eat or sleep all this time, for we could not swallow food and the fever prevented sleep. To-morrow we set out for the White Pine region.

Cordially yours

J. MUIR

To Mrs. John Strentzel

BELMONT, NEVADA
August 31st, 1878

DEAR MRS. STRENTZEL:

I wrote you a note the other day before receiving your letter of the 14th which reached me this morning. The men are packing up and I have only a moment. We have been engaged so long southward that we may not go to Eureka. If not we will make direct to Hamilton and the box the Doctor so kindly sent I will have forwarded.

The fiery sun is pouring his first beams across the gray Belmont hills, but so long as there is anything like a fair supply of any kind of water to keep my blood thin and flowing, it affects me but little. We are all well again, or nearly so — I quite. Our leader still shows traces of fever. The difference between wet and dry bulb thermometer here is often 40° or more, causing excessive waste from lungs and skin, and, unless water be constantly supplied, one's blood seems to thicken to such an extent that if Shylock should ask, "If you prick him, will

he bleed?" I should answer, "I dinna ken."
Heavens! if the juicy grapes had come manna-
like from the sky that last thirst-night!

Farewell. We go.

Cordially and thankfully yours

JOHN MUIR

[The following note was written, probably
the evening of the same day, on the reverse of
the letter-sheet.]

The very finest, softest, most ethereal purple
hue tinges, permeates, covers, glorifies the
mountains and the level. How lovely then,
how suggestive of the best heaven, how unlike
a desert now! While the little garden, the
hurrying moths, the opening flowers, and the
cool evening wind that now begins to flow and
lave down the gray slopes above heighten the
peacefulness and loveliness of the scene.

To Dr. and Mrs. John Strentzel

HAMILTON, NEVADA
September 11, 1878

DEAR STRENTZELS:

All goes well in camp save that box of grapes
you so kindly sent. I telegraphed for it, on arriving at this place, to be sent by Wells Fargo,
but it has not come, and we leave here to-
morrow. We had hoped to have been in Eureka

by the middle of last month, but the unknown factors so abundant in our work have pushed us so far southward we will not now be likely to go there at all. Nevertheless I have enjoyed your kindness even in this last grape expression of it, but you must not try to send any more, because we will not again be within grape range of railroads until on our way home in October or November. Then, should there be any left, I will manifest for my own good and the edification of civilization a fruit capacity and fervor to be found only in savage camps.

Since our Lone Mountain experience we have not been thirsty. Our course hence is first south for eighty or ninety miles along the western flank of the White Pine Range, then east to the Snake Range near the boundary of the State, etc.

Our address will be Hamilton, Nevada, until the end of this month. Our movements being so uncertain, we prefer to have our mail forwarded to points where we chance to find ourselves. In southern Utah the greater portion of our course will be across deserts.

The roses are past bloom, but I'll send seeds from the first garden I find. Yesterday found on Mount Hamilton the *Pinus aristata* growing on limestone and presenting the most extravagant picturesqueness I have ever met in any climate or species. Glacial traces, too, of great interest. This is the famous White Pine mining region, now nearly dead. Twenty-eight thousand mining claims were located in the district, which is six miles by twelve. Now only fifteen are worked, and of these only one, the Eberhardt, gives much hope or money. Both Hamilton and Treasure City are silent now, but Nature goes on gloriously.

Cordially yours

JOHN MUIR

To Dr. John Strentzel

WARD, NEVADA, SATURDAY MORNING
September 28th, 1878

DEAR DOCTOR:

Your kind letter of the 8th ultimo reached me yesterday, having been forwarded from Hamilton. This is a little three-year-old mining town where we are making a few days' halt to transact some business and rest the weary animals. We arrived late, when it was too dark to set the tents, and we recklessly camped in a corral on a breezy hilltop. I have a great horror of sleeping upon any trodden ground near human settlements, not to say ammoniacal pens, but the Captain had his blankets spread alongside the wagon, and I dared the worst and lay down beside him. A wild equinoctial gale roared and tumbled down the mountain-side all through the night, sifting the dry fragrant snuff about our eyes and ears, notwithstanding all our care in tucking and rolling our ample blankets. The situation was not exactly distressing, but most absurdly and d——dly ludicrous. Our camp traps, basins, bowls, bags, went speeding wildly past in screeching rumbling discord with the earnest wind-tones. A heavy mill-frame was blown down, but we suffered no great damage, most of our runaway gear having been found in fence corners. But how terribly we stood in need of deodorizers! — not dealkalizers, as you suggest.

Next morning we rented a couple of rooms in town where we now are and washed, rubbed, dusted, and combed ourselves back again into countenance. Half an hour ago, after reading your letter a second time, I tumbled out my pine tails, tassels, and burrs, and was down on my knees on the floor making a selection for you according to your wishes and was casting about as to the chances of finding a suitable box, when the Captain, returning from the post-office, handed me your richly laden grape box, and now the grapes are out and the burrs are in. Now this was a coincidence worth noting, was it not? — better than most people's

special providences. The fruit was in perfect
condition, every individual spheroid of them
all fresh and bright and as tightly bent as
drums with their stored-up sun-juices. The big
bunch is hung up for the benefit of eyes, most
of the others have already vanished, causing,
as they fled, a series of the finest sensuous
nerve-waves imaginable.

The weather is now much cooler — the
nights almost bracingly cold — and all goes
well, not a thirst trace left. We were weather-
bound a week in a cañon of the Golden Gate
Range, not by storms, but by soft, balmy, hazy
Indian summer, in which the mountain aspens
ripened to flaming yellow, while the sky was
too opaque for observations upon the distant
peaks.

Since leaving Hamilton, have obtained more
glacial facts of great interest, very telling in the
history of the Great Basin. Also many charming additions to the thousand, thousand pictures of Nature's mountain beauty. I understand perfectly your criticism on the blind
pursuit of every scientific pebble, wasting a life
in microscopic examinations of every grain of
wheat in a field, but I am not so doing. The
history of this vast wonderland is scarce at all
known, and no amount of study in other fields
will develop it to the light. As to that special

thirst affair, I was in no way responsible. I was fully awake to the danger, but I was not in a position to prevent it.

Our work goes on hopefully towards a satisfactory termination. Will soon be in Utah. All the mountains yet to be climbed have been seen from other summits save two on the Wasatch, viz. Mount Nebo and a peak back of Beaver. Our next object will be Wheeler's Peak, forty miles east of here.

The fir I send you is remarkably like the Sierra *grandis*, but much smaller, seldom attaining a greater height than fifty feet. In going east from the Sierra it was first met on the Hot Creek Range, and afterwards on all the higher ranges thus far. It also occurs on the Wasatch and Oquirrh Mountains. Of the two pines, that with the larger cones is called "White Pine" by the settlers. It was first met on Cory's Peak west of Walker Lake, and afterwards on all the mountains thus far that reached an elevation of ten thousand feet or more. This, I have no doubt, is the species so rare on the Sierra, and which I found on the eastern slope opposite the head of Owens Valley. Two years ago I saw it on the Wasatch above Salt Lake. I mean to send specimens to Gray and Hooker, as they doubtless observed it on the Rocky Mountains. The other species is the *aristata* of the southern portion of the Sierra above the Kern and Kings Rivers. Is but little known, though exceedingly interesting. First met on the Hot Creek Range, and more abundantly on the White Pine Mountains — called Fox-Tail Pine by the miners, on account of its long bushy tassels. It is by far the most picturesque of all pines, and those of these basin ranges far surpass those of the Sierra in extravagant and unusual beauty of the picturesque kind. These three species and the Fremont or nut pine and junipers are the only coniferous trees I have thus far met in the State. Possibly the Yellow Pine (*ponderosa*) may be found on the Snake Range. I observed it last year on the Wasatch, together with one Abies. Of course that small portion of Nevada which extends into the Sierra about Lake Tahoe is not considered in this connection, for it is naturally a portion of California.

Cordially yours

JOHN MUIR

Upon his return from the mountains of Nevada Muir found that sickness had invaded the family of John Swett, with whom he had made his home for the last three years, and it became necessary for him to find new lodgings. In a letter addressed to Mrs. John Bidwell, under date of February 17, 1879, he writes: "I have settled for the winter at 920 Valencia Street [San Francisco], with my friend Mr. [Isaac] Upham, of Payot, Upham and Company, Booksellers; am comfortable, but not very fruitful thus far — reading more than writing." This remained his temporary abode until his marriage and removal to Martinez the following year. The famous wooden clock shared also this last removal and continued its service as a faithful timepiece for many years to come.

To Dr. and Mrs. John Strentzel

920 VALENCIA ST., SAN FRANCISCO
January 28th, 1879

DEAR FRIENDS:

The vast soul-stirring work of flitting is at length done and well done. Myself, wooden clock, and notebooks are once more planted for the winter out here on the outermost ragged edge of this howling metropolis of dwelling boxes.

And now, well what now? Nothing but work, book-making, brick-making, the transformation of raw bush sugar and mountain meal into magazine cookies and snaps. And though the spectacled critics who ken everything in wise ignorance say "well done, sir, well done," I always feel that there is some-

117

thing not quite honorable in thus dealing with God's wild gold — the sugar and meal, I mean.

Yesterday I began to try to cook a mess of bees, but have not yet succeeded in making the ink run sweet. The blessed brownies winna buzz in this temperature, and what can a body do about it? Maybe ignorance is the deil that is spoiling the — the — the broth — the nectar, and perhaps I ought to go out and gather some more Melissa and thyme and white sage for the pot.

The streets here are barren and beeless and ineffably muddy and mean-looking. How people can keep hold of the conceptions of New Jerusalem and immortality of souls with so much mud and gutter, is to me admirably strange. A Eucalyptus bush on every other corner, standing tied to a painted stick, and a geranium sprout in a pot on every tenth window sill may help heavenward a little, but how little amid so muckle down-dragging mud!

This much for despondency; per contra, the grass and grain is growing, and man will be fed, and the nations will be glad, etc., and the sun rises every day.

Helen [Swett] is well out of danger, and is very nearly her own sweet amiable engaging little self again, and I can see her at least once a week.

I'm living with Mr. Upham and am comfortable as possible. Summer will soon be again.

When you come to the city visit me, and see how bravely I endure; so touching a lesson of resignation to metropolitan evils and goods should not be lightly missed.

Hoping all goes well with you, I am,
Cordially your friend
JOHN MUIR

Frequently, in letters to friends, Muir complains that in town he is unable to compel the right mood for the production of readable articles. "As yet I have accomplished very nearly nothing," he writes some weeks after the above letter; he had only "reviewed a little book, and written a first sketch of our bee pastures!... How astoundingly empty and dry — box-like! — is our brain in a house built on one of those precious 'lots' one hears so much about!"

The fact is that Muir's personal letters, like his conversation, flowed smoothly and easily; but when he sat down to write an article, his critical faculty was called into play, and his thoughts, to employ his own simile, began to labor like a laden wagon in a bog. There was a consequent loss of that spontaneity which made him such a fascinating talker. "John polishes his articles until an ordinary man slips on them," remarked his friend and neighbor John Swett when he wished to underline his own sense of the difference between Muir's spoken and written words. Such was the brilliance of his conversation during the decades of his greatest power that the fame of it still lingers as a literary tradition in California. Organizations and individuals vied with each other to secure his attendance at public and private gatherings, convinced that the announcement "John Muir will be there" would assure the success of any meeting. It was with this thought in mind that the manager of a great Sunday-School convention, scheduled to meet in Yosemite in June, 1879, offered him a hundred dollars just to come and talk.

It seems a pity that in his earlier years no one thought of having his vivid recitals of observations and adventures recorded by a stenographer and then placed before him for revision. By direction of the late E. H. Harriman, Muir's boyhood memoirs were taken down from his conversation at Pelican Lodge to be subsequently revised for publication. Though he often entirely rewrote the conversational first draft, the possession of the raw material in typed form acted as a stimulus to literary production, and enabled him to bring to completion what otherwise might have been lost to the world.

But, however much he chafed and groaned under the necessity of meeting his contracts for articles, the remarkable series which he wrote during the late seventies for "Harper's Magazine" and "Scribner's Monthly" are conclusive demonstrations of his power. Among them was "The Humming-Bird of the California Waterfalls" which loaded his mail with letters from near and far, and evoked admiration from the foremost writers of the time. Though Muir was not without self-esteem, the flood of praise that descended upon him gave him more embarrassment than gratification, especially when his sisters desired to know the identity of this or that lady who had dedicated a poem to him.

Scarcely any one knew at this time that there was a lady not far from San Francisco who, though not writing poems, was playing rival to the boo pastures of his articles, and that when, during the spring of 1879, he disappeared occasionally from the Upham household on Valencia Street, he could have been found, and not alone, in the Strentzel orchards at Martinez. "Every one," writes John to Miss Strentzel in April — "every one, according to the eternal unfitness of civilized things, has been seeking me and calling on me while I was away. John Swett, on his second failure to find me, left word with Mr. Upham that he was coming to Martinez some time to see me during the summer vacation! The other day I chanced to find in my pocket that slippery, fuzzy mesh you wear round your neck." The feminine world probably will recognize in the last sentence a characteristically masculine description of a kind of head-covering fashionable in those days and known as a "fascinator."

The same letter contains evidence that the orchards did not let him forget them when he returned to San Francisco, for after reporting that he had finished "Snow Banners" and ʿɜ at work upon "Floods," he breaks off in the middle of a sentence to exclaim "Boo!!! aren't they lovely!!! The bushel of bloom, I mean. Just came this moment. Never was so blankly puzzled in making a guess before lifting the lid. An orchard in a band-box!!! Who wad ha thocht it? A swarm of bees and fifty humming-birds would have made the thing complete."

Early in the year Muir had carefully laid his plans for a new exploration trip, this time into the Puget Sound region. There doubtless was something in the circumstances and uncertainties of this new venture that brought to culmination his friendship with Miss Strentzel, for they became engaged on the eve of his departure, though for months no one outside of the family knew anything about it, so closely was the secret kept. Even to Mrs. Carr, who had ardently hoped for this outcome, he merely wrote: "I'm going home — going to my summer in the snow and ice and forests of the north coast. Will sail to-morrow at noon on the Dakota for Victoria and Olympia. Will then push inland and alongland. May visit Alaska."

He did, as it turned out, go to Alaska that summer, and the first literary fruitage of this trip took the form of eleven letters to the "San Francisco Evening Bulletin." Written on the spot, they preserve the freshness of his first impressions, and were read with breathless interest by an ever-enlarging circle of readers. Toward the close of his life these vivid sketches were utilized, together with his journals, in writing the first part of his "Travels in Alaska." It was at Fort Wrangell that he met the Reverend S. Hall Young, then stationed as a missionary among the Thlinkit Indians. Mr. Young later accompanied him on various canoe and land expeditions, particularly the one up Glacier Bay, that resulted in the discovery of a number of stupendous glaciers, the largest of which was afterwards to receive the name of Muir. In his book, "Alaska Days with John Muir," Mr. Young has given a most readable and vivid account of their experiences together, and the interested reader will wish to compare, among other things, the author's own account of his thrilling rescue from certain death on the precipices of Glenora Peak with Muir's modest description of the heroic part he played in the adventure.

It is Young also who relates how Muir, by his daring and original ways of inquiring into Nature's every mood, came to be regarded by the Indians as a mysterious being whose motives were beyond all conjecture. A notable instance was the occasion on which, one wild, stormy night, he left the shelter of Young's house and slid out into the inky darkness and wind-driven sheets of rain. At two o'clock in the morning a rain-soaked group of Indians hammered at the missionary's door, and begged him to pray. "We scare. All Stickeen scare," they said, for some wakeful ones had seen a red glow on top of a neighboring mountain and the mysterious, portentous phenomenon had immediately been communicated to the whole frightened tribe. "We want you play [pray] God; plenty play," they said.

The reader will not find it difficult to imag-

124

ine what had happened, for Muir was the unconscious cause of their alarm. He had made his way through the drenching blast to the top of a forested hill. There he had contrived to start "a fire, a big one, to see as well as to hear how the storm and trees were behaving." At midnight his fire, sheltered from the village by the brow of the hill, was shedding its glow upon the low-flying storm-clouds, striking terror to the hearts of the Indians, who thought they saw something that "waved in the air like the wings of a spirit." And while they were imploring the prayers of the missionary for their safety, Muir, according to his own account, was sitting under a bark shelter in front of his fire, with "nothing to do but look and listen and join the trees in their hymns and prayers."

Meanwhile Muir's "Bulletin" letters had greatly enlarged its circulation and were being copied all over the country, to the great delight of the editor, Sam Williams, who had long been a warm friend of Muir. The latter's descriptions reflected the boundless enthusiasm which these newfound wildernesses of Alaska aroused in him. In the Sierra Nevada his task was to reconstruct imaginatively, from vestiges of vanished glaciers, the picture of their prime during the ice period; but here he saw actually at work the stupendous landscape-making glaciers of Alaska, and in their action he found verified the conclusions of his "Studies in the Sierra." No wonder he tarried in the North months beyond the time he had set for his return. "Every summer," he wrote to Miss Strentzel from Fort Wrangell in October — "every summer my gains from God's wilds grow greater. This last seems the greatest of all. For the first few weeks I was so feverishly excited with the boundless exuberance of the woods and the wilderness, of great ice floods, and the manifest scriptures of the ice-sheet that modelled the lovely archipelagoes along the coast, that I could hardly settle down to the steady labor required in making any sort of Truth one's own. But I'm working now, and feel unable to leave the field. Had a most glorious time of it among the Stickeen glaciers, which in some shape or other will reach you."

Upon landing in Portland on his return in January, he was persuaded to give several public lectures and to make an observation trip up the Columbia River. At his lodgings in San Francisco there had gathered meanwhile an immense accumulation of letters, and among them one that bridged the memories of a dozen eventful years. It was from Katharine Merrill Graydon, one of the three little Samaritans who used to visit him after the accidental injury to one of his eyes in an Indianapolis wagon factory. "The three children you knew best," said the writer, "the ones who long ago in the dark room delighted to read to you and bring you flowers, are now men and women. Merrill is a young lawyer with all sorts of aspirations. Janet is at home, a young lady of leisure. Your 'little friend Katie' is teacher in a fashionable boarding-school, which I know is not much of a recommendation to a man who turns his eyes away from all flowers but the wild rose and the sweet-brier." The main occasion of the letter was to introduce Professor David Starr Jordan and Mr. Charles Gilbert, who were going to the Pacific Coast. "I send this," continued the writer, "with a little quaking of the heart. What if you should ask, 'Who is Kate Graydon?' Still I have faith that even ten or twelve years have not obliterated the pleasant little friendship formed one summer so long ago. The remembrance on my part was wonderfully quickened one morning nearly two years ago when Professor Jordan read to our class the sweetest, brightest, most musical article on the 'Water Ouzel' from 'Scribner's.' The writer, he said, was John Muir. The way my acquaintance of long ago developed into friendship, and the way I proudly said I knew you, would have made you laugh."

JOHN MUIR

This letter brought the following response:

To Miss Katharine Merrill Graydon

920 VALENCIA STREET, SAN FRANCISCO
February 5th, 1880

MY DEAR KATIE, MISS KATE GRAYDON,
Professor of Greek and English Literature,
etc.

MY DEAR, FRAIL, WEE, BASHFUL LASSIE AND
DEAR MADAM:

I was delighted with your bright charming
letter introducing your friends Professor [David
Starr] Jordan and Charles Gilbert. I have not
yet met either of the gentlemen. They are at
Santa Barbara, but expect to be here in April,
when I hope to see them and like them for your
sake, and Janet's, and their own worth.

Some time ago I learned that you were teaching Greek, and of all the strange things in this
changeful world, this seemed the strangest, and
the most difficult to get packed quietly down
into my awkward mind. Therefore I will have to
get you to excuse the confusion I fell into at the
beginning of my letter. I mean to come to you
in a year or two, or any time soon, to see you
all in your new developments. The sweet
blooming underbrush of boys and girls —
Moores, Merrills, Graydons, etc. — was very
refreshing and pleasant to me all my Indiana

128

days, and now that you have all grown up into trees, strong and thrifty, waving your out-reaching branches in God's Light, I am sure I shall love you all. Going to Indianapolis is one of the brightest of my hopes. It seems but yesterday since I left you all. And indeed, in very truth, all these years have been to me one unbroken day, one continuous walk in one grand garden.

I'm glad you like my wee dear ouzel. He is one of the most complete of God's small darlings. I found him in Alaska a month or two ago. I made a long canoe trip of seven hundred miles from Fort Wrangell northward, exploring the glaciers and icy fiords of the coast and inland channels with one white man and four Indians. And on the way back to Wrangell, while exploring one of the deep fiords with lofty walls like those of Yosemite Valley, and with its waters crowded with immense bergs discharged from the noble glaciers, I found a single specimen of his blessed tribe. We had camped on the shore of the fiord among huge icebergs that had been stranded at high tide, and next morning made haste to get away, fearing that we would be frozen in for the winter; and while pushing our canoe through the bergs, admiring and fearing the grand beauty of the icy wilderness, my blessed favorite came out from the shore to see me, flew once round the boat, gave one cheery note of welcome, while seeming to say, "You need not fear this ice and frost, for you see I am here," then flew back to the shore and alighted on the edge of a big white berg, not so far away but that I could see him doing his happy manners.

In this one summer in the white Northland I have seen perhaps ten times as many glaciers as there are in all Switzerland. But I cannot hope to tell you about them now, or hardly indeed at any time, for the best things and thoughts one gets from Nature we dare not tell. I will be so happy to see you again, not to renew my acquaintance, for that has not been for a moment interrupted, but to know you better in your new growth.

Ever your friend

JOHN MUIR

Years afterwards Dr. Jordan, as he notes in his autobiography, "The Days of a Man," took the opportunity to bestow the name Ouzel Basin on the old glacier channel "near which John Muir sketched his unrivaled biography of a water ouzel."

Any one who has heard the February merriment of Western meadowlarks in the Alhambra Valley must know that winter gets but a slight foothold there, for it tilts toward the sun, and is in full radiance of blossom and song during March and April. John Muir and Louie Wanda Strentzel chose the fourteenth of the latter flower month for their wedding day and were ready to share their secret with their friends. "Visited the immortals Brown and Swett," confesses John to his fiancée in one of his notes, and the announcement was followed immediately by shoals of congratulatory letters. The one from Mrs. John Swett, in whose home he had spent so many happy days, is not only fairly indicative of the common opinion, but draws some lines of Muir's character that make it worthy of a place here.

To Louie Wanda Strentzel

SAN FRANCISCO,
April 8, 1880

MY DEAR MISS STRENTZEL:

When Mr. Muir made his appearance the other night I thought he had a sheepish twinkle in his eye, but ascribed it to a guilty consciousness that he had been up to Martinez again and a fear of being rallied about it. Judge then of the sensation when he exploded his bombshell! At first laughing incredulity — it was April. We were on our guard against being taken in, but the mention of Dr. Dwinell's

name and a date settled it, and I have hunted
up a pen to write you a letter of congratulation.
For John and I are jubilant over the match. It
gratifies completely our sense of fitness, for you
both have a fair foundation of the essentials of
good health, good looks, good temper, etc.
Then you both have culture, and to crown all
you have "prospects" and he has talent and
distinction.

But I hope you are good at a hair-splitting
argument. You will need to be to hold your
own with him. Five times to-day has he van-
quished me. Not that I admitted it to him —
no, never! He not only excels in argument, but
always takes the highest ground — is always
on the right side. He told Colonel Boyce the
other night that his position was that of cham-
pion for a mean, brutal policy. It was with regard to Indian extermination, and that he
(Boyce) would be ashamed to carry it with one
Indian in personal conflict. I thought the
Colonel would be mad, but they walked off arm
in arm. Further, he is so truthful that he not
only will never embellish sketch or word-
picture by any imaginary addition, but even
retains every unsightly feature lest his picture
should not be true.

There, I have said all I can in his favor, and
as an offset I must tell you that I have been

trying all day to soften his hard heart of an old animosity and he won't yield an inch. It is sometimes impossible to please him. . . .

With hearty regard, I am

Yours very truly

MARY LOUISE SWETT

The occasion of the following letter was one from Miss Graydon in which she rallied him on her sudden discovery of how much sympathy she had wasted on him because she had imagined him without friends or companions except glaciers and icebergs, and without even a mother to wear out her anxious heart about him. "I heard," she wrote, "that your mother was still living and that you had not been near her for twelve years. And then, while I supposed you had not a lady friend in the world, I heard you were the center of an adoring circle of ladies in San Francisco. If you heard any one laugh about that time, it was I. See if I ever waste my sympathy on you again!"

To Miss Katharine Merrill Graydon

1419 TAYLOR ST., SAN FRANCISCO
April 12th, 1880

MY DEAR GIRL-WOMAN, KATIE AND MISS KATE:
Your letter of March 28th has reached me, telling how much loving sympathy I am to

133

have because I have a mother, and because of the story of my adoring circle of lady friends. Well, what is to become of me when I tell you that I am to marry one of those friends the day after to-morrow? What sympathy will be left the villain who has a mother and a wife also, and even a home and a circle, etc., and twice as muckle as a' that? But now, even now, Katie, don't, don't withdraw your sympathy. You know that I never did demand pity for the storm-beatings and rock-beds and the hunger and loneliness of all these years since you were a frail wee lass, for I have been very happy and strong through it all — the happiest man I ever saw; but, nevertheless, I want to hold on to and love all my friends, for they are the most precious of all my riches.

I hope to see you all this year or next, and no amount of marrying will diminish the enjoyment of meeting you again. And some of you will no doubt come to this side of the Continent, and then how happy I will be to welcome you to a warm little home in the Contra Costa hills near the bay.

I have been out of town for a week or two, and have not seen much of Professor Jordan and Mr. Gilbert. They are very busy about the fishes, crabs, clams, oysters, etc. Have called at his hotel two or three times, and have had some good Moores and Merrill talks, but nothing short of a good long excursion in the free wilderness would ever mix us as much as you seem to want.

Now, my brave teacher lassie, good luck to you. Heaven bless you, and believe me,

Ever truly your friend

JOHN MUIR

It was fitting, perhaps, that one who loved Nature in her wildest moods, should have his wedding day distinguished by a roaring rainstorm through which he drove Dr. I. E. Dwinell, the officiating clergyman, back to the Martinez station in a manner described by the latter as "like the rush of a torrent down the cañon." Both relatives and friends, to judge by their letters, were so completely surprised by the happy event that it proved "a nine days' wonder." The social stir occasioned by the wedding was, however, far from gratifying to Mr. Muir, who had to summon all his courage to prevent his besetting bashfulness from driving him to the seclusion of the nearest cañon.

But lest the reader imagine that Muir's home was henceforward to be on the beaten crossways of annoying crowds, let me hasten to add that the old Strentzel home, which the bride's parents vacated for their daughter, was a more than ordinarily secluded and quiet place. Cascades of ivy and roses fell over the corners of the wide verandas, and the slope upon which the house stood had an air of leaning upon its elbows and looking tranquilly down across hill-girt orchards to the blue waters of Carquinez Straits. There, a mile away, at the entrance of the valley, nestled the little town of Martinez, but scarcely a whisper of its activities might be heard above the contented hum of Alhambra bees. It was an ideal place for a honeymoon and there we leave the happy pair.

CHAPTER XIV

THE SECOND ALASKA TRIP AND THE SEARCH FOR THE JEANNETTE

1880–1882

I

AFTER his marriage Muir rented from his father-in-law a part of the Strentzel ranch, and then proceeded with great thoroughness to master the art of horticulture, for which he possessed natural and perhaps inherited aptitude. But when July came, the homing instinct for the wilderness again grew strong within him. He doubtless had an understanding with his wife that he was to continue during the next summer the unfinished explorations of 1879. The lure of "something lost behind the ranges" was in his case a glacier, as Mr. Young reports in his "Alaska Days with John Muir." The more immediate occasion of his departure was a letter from his friend Thomas Magee, of San Francisco, urging him to join him on a trip to southeastern Alaska. The two had traveled together before, and he acted at once upon the suggestion, leaving for the North on July 30th.

JOHN MUIR

To Mrs. Muir

Off Cape Flattery
Monday, August 2d, 1880
10 A.M.

MY DEAR WIFE:

All goes well. In a few hours we will be in Victoria. The voyage thus far has been singularly calm and uneventful. Leaving you is the only event that has marred the trip and it is marred sorely, but I shall make haste to you and reach you ere you have the time to grieve and weary. If you will only be calm and cheery all will be better for my short spell of ice-work.

The sea has been very smooth, nevertheless Mr. Magee has been very sick. Now he is better. As for me I have made no sign, though I have had some headache and heartache. We are now past the Flattery Rocks, where we were so roughly storm-tossed last winter, and Neah Bay, where we remained thirty-six hours. How placid it seems now — the water black and gray with reflections from the cloudy sky, fur seals popping their heads up here and there, ducks and gulls dotting the small waves, and Indian fishing-boats towards the shore, each with a small glaring red flag flying from the masthead.

Behind the group of white houses nestled in the deepest bend of the bay rise rounded, ice-swept hills, with mountains beyond them folding in and in, in beautiful braids, and all densely forested. We are so near the shore that with the mate's glasses I can readily make out some of the species of the trees. The forest is in the main scarce at all different from those of the Alaskan coast. Now the Cape Lighthouse is out of sight and we are fairly into the strait. Vancouver Island is on [the] left in fine clear view, with forests densely packed in every hollow and over every hill and mountain. How beautiful it is! How deep and shadowy its cañons, how eloquently it tells the story of its sculpture during the Age of Ice! How perfectly virgin it is! Ships loaded with Nanaimo coal and Puget Sound coal and lumber, a half-dozen of them, are about us, beating their way down the strait, and here and there a pilot boat to represent civilization, but not one scar on the virgin shore, nor the smoke of a hut or camp.

I have just been speaking with a man who has spent a good deal of time on the island. He says that so impenetrable is the underbrush, his party could seldom make more than two miles a day though assisted by eight Indians. Only the shores are known.

Now the wind is beginning to freshen and the small waves are tipped with white, milk-white, caps, almost the only ones we have seen since leaving San Francisco. The Captain and first officer have been very attentive to us, giving us the use of their rooms and books, etc., besides answering all our questions anent the sea and ships.

We shall reach Victoria about two or three o'clock. The California will not sail before tomorrow sometime, so that we shall have plenty [of] time to get the charts and odds and ends we need before leaving. Mr. Magee will undoubtedly go on to Wrangell, but will not be likely to stop over.

Ten minutes past two by your clock

We are just rounding the Esquimalt Lighthouse, and in a few minutes more will be tied up at the wharf. Quite a lively breeze is blowing from the island, and the strait is ruffled with small shining wavelets glowing in the distance like silver. Hereabouts many lofty moutonnéed rock-bosses rise above the forests, bare of trees, but brown looking from the mosses that cover them. Since entering the strait, the heavy swell up and down, up and down, has vanished and all the sick have got well and are out in full force, gazing at the harbor with the excitement one always feels after a voyage, whether the future offers much brightness or not.

140

The new Captain of the California is said to be good and careful, and the pilot and purser I know well, so that we will feel at home during the rest of our trip as we have thus far; and as for the main objects, all Nature is unchangeable, loves us all, and grants gracious welcome to every honest votary.

I hope you do not feel that I am away at all. Any real separation is not possible. I have been alone, as far as [concerns] the isolation that distance makes, so much of my lifetime that separation seems more natural than absolute contact, which seems too good and indulgent to be true.

Her Majesty's ironclad Triumph is lying close alongside. How huge she seems and impertinently strong and defiant, with a background of honest green woods! Jagged-toothed wolves and wildcats harmonize smoothly enough, but engines for the destruction of human beings are only devilish, though they carry preachers and prayers and open up views of sad, scant tears. Now we are making fast. "Make fast that line there, make fast," "let go there," "give way."

We will go on to Victoria this afternoon, taking our baggage with us, and stay there until setting out on the California. The ride of three miles through the woods and round the

glacial bosses is very fine. This you would enjoy. I shall look for the roses. Will mail this at
once, and write again before leaving this grand
old ice-ribbed island.

And now, my dear Louie, keep a good heart
and do the bits of work I requested you to do,
and the days in Alaska will go away fast enough
and I will be with you again as if I had been
gone but one day.

Ever your affectionate husband

JOHN MUIR

To Mrs. Muir

VICTORIA, B.C.
August 3, 1880, 3.45 P.M.

DEAR LOUIE:

The Vancouver roses are out of bloom hereabouts but I may possibly find some near
Nanaimo. I mailed you a letter yesterday
which you will probably receive with this.

Arriving at Esquimalt we hired a carriage
driven by a sad-eyed and sad-lipped negro to
take us with all our baggage to Victoria, some
three miles distant. The horses were also of
melancholic aspect, lean and clipper-built in
general, but the way they made the fire fly from
the glacial gravel would have made Saint Jose
and his jet beef-sides hide in the dust. By dint
of much blunt praise of his team he put them

142

to their wiry spring-steel metal and we passed
everything on the road with a whirr — cab,
cart, carriage, and carryall. We put up at the
Driard House and had a square, or cubical,
meal. Put on a metallic countenance to the
landlord on account of the money and experience we carried, nearly scared him out of
his dignity and made him give us good rooms.

At 6.45 P.M. the California arrived, and we
went aboard and had a chat with Hughes, the
purser. He at once inquired whether I had *any
one* with me, meaning you, as Vanderbilt had
given our news. Learned that the California
would not sail until this evening and made up
our minds to take a drive out in the highways
and byways adjacent to the town. While
strolling about the streets last evening I felt a
singular interest in the Thlinkit Indians I met
and something like a missionary spirit came
over me. Poor fellows, I wish I could serve
them.

There is good eating, but poor sleeping here.
My bed was but little like our own at home.
Met Major Morris, the Treasury agent, this
morning. He is going up with us. He is, you
remember, the writer of that book on Alaska
that I brought with me.

About nine o'clock we got a horse and buggy
at the livery stable and began our devious drive

by going back to the Dakota to call on First Officer Griffith and give him a box of weeds for his kind deeds. Then took any road that offered out into the green leafy country. How beautiful it is, every road banked high and embowered in dense, fresh, green, tall ferns six to eight feet high close to the wheels, then spiræa, two or three species, wild rose bushes, madroño, hazel, hawthorn, then a host of young Douglas spruces and silver firs with here and there a yew with its red berries and dark foliage, and a maple or two, then the tall firs and spruces forming the forest primeval. We came to a good many fields of grain, but all of them small as compared with the number of the houses. The oats and barley are just about ripe. We saw little orchards, too; a good many pears, little red-brown fellows, six hatfuls per tree, and the queerest little sprinkling of little red and yellow cherries just beginning to ripen. Many of the cottage homes about town are as lovely as a cottage may be, embowered in honeysuckle and green gardens and bits of lawn and orchard and grand oaks with lovely outlooks. The day has been delightful. How you would have enjoyed it — all three of you.

Our baggage is already aboard and the hour draws nigh. I must go. I shall write you again from Nanaimo.

THE SECOND ALASKA TRIP

Good-bye again, my love. Keep a strong heart and speedily will fly the hours that bring me back to thee. Love to mother and father. Farewell.

Ever your affectionate husband
JOHN MUIR

To Mrs. Muir

ON BOARD THE CALIFORNIA
10 A.M., August 4th, 1880

DEAR LOUIE:

We are still lying alongside the wharf at Victoria. It seems a leak was discovered in one of the watertanks that had to be mended, and the result was that we could not get off on the seven o'clock tide last night.

Victoria seems a dry, dignified, half-idle town, supported in great part by government fees. Every erect, or more than erect, back-leaning, man has an office, and carries himself with that peculiar aplomb that all the Hail Britannia people are so noted for. The wharf and harbor stir is very mild. The steamer Princess Louise lies alongside ours, getting ready for the trip to New Westminster on [the] Fraser River. The Hudson's Bay Company's steamer Otter, a queer old tubby craft, left for the North last night. A few sloops, plungers, and boats are crawling about the harbor or ly-

ing at anchor, doing or dreaming a business nobody knows. Yonder comes an Indian canoe
with its one unique sail calling up memories,
many, of my last winter's rambles among the
icebergs. The water is ruffled with a slight
breeze, scarce enough for small white-caps.
Though clearer than the waters of most har-
bors, it is not without the ordinary drift of old
bottles, straw, and defunct domestic animals.
How rotten the piles of the wharf are, and how
they smell, even in this cool climate!

They are taking hundreds of barrels of mo-
lasses aboard — for what purpose? To delight
the Alaska younglings with 'lasses bread and
smear their happy chubby cheeks, or to make
cookies and gingerbread? No, whiskey, Indian
whiskey! It will be bought by Indians, nine
tenths of it and more; they will give their hard-
earned money for it, and their hard-caught furs,
and take it far away along many a glacial
channel and inlet, and make it into crazing
poison. Onions, too, many a ton, are coming
aboard to boil and fry and raise a watery cry.

Alone on the wharf, I see a lone stranger
dressed in shabby black. He has a kind of un-
nerved, drooping look, his shoulders coming
together and his toes and his knees and the
two ends of his vertebral column, something
like a withering leaf in hot sunshine. Poor

fellow, he looks at our ship as if he wanted to go again to the mines to try his luck. And here come two Indian women and a little girl trotting after them. They seem as if they were coming aboard, but turn aside at the edge of the wharf and descend rickety stairs to their canoe, tied to a pile beneath the wharf. Now they reappear with change of toilet, and the little girl is carrying a bundle, something to eat or sell or sit on.

Yonder comes a typical John Bull, grand in size and style, carmine in countenance, abdominous and showing a fine tight curve from chin to knee, when seen in profile, yet benevolent withal and reliable, confidence-begetting. And here just landed opposite our ship is a pile of hundreds of bears' skins, black and brown, from Alaska, brought here by the Otter, a few deer skins too, and wildcat and wolverine. The Hudson's Bay Company men are about them, showing their ownership.

Ten minutes to twelve o'clock

"Let go that line there," etc., tells that we are about to move. Our steamer swings slowly round and heads for Nanaimo. How beautiful the shores are! How glacial, yet how leafy! The day becomes calmer, and brighter, and everybody seems happy. Our fellow passen-

147

gers are Major Morris and wife, whom I met last year, Judge Deady, a young Englishman, and [a] dreamy, silent old gray man like a minister.

8 P.M.

We are entering Nanaimo Harbor.

To Mrs. Muir

DEPARTURE BAY
A FEW MILES FROM NANAIMO
9 A.M., *August 5th*, 1880

DEAR LOUIE:

We are coaling here, and what a rumble they are making! The shores here are very imposing, a beveled bluff, topped with giant cedar, spruce, and fir and maple with varying green; here and there a small madroño too, which here is near its northern limit.

We went ashore last eve at Nanaimo for a stroll, Magee and I, and we happened to meet Mr. Morrison, a man that I knew at Fort Wrangell, who told me particulars of the sad Indian war in which Toyatte was killed. He was present and gave very graphic descriptions.

We sailed hither at daylight this morning, and will probably get away, the Captain tells me, about eleven o'clock, and then no halt

148

until we reach Wrangell, which is distant from here about sixty hours.

I hardly know, my lassie, what I've been writing, nothing, I fear, but very small odds and ends, and yet these may at least keep you from wearying for an hour, and the letters, poor though they be, shall yet tell my love, and that will redeem them. I mail this here, the other two were mailed in Victoria, my next from Wrangell.

Heaven bless you, my love, and mother and father. I trust that you are caring for yourself and us all by keeping cheery and strong, and avoiding the bad practice of the stair-dance. Once more, my love, farewell, I must close in haste. Farewell.

Ever your affectionate husband

JOHN MUIR

Missionary S. Hall Young was standing on the wharf at Fort Wrangell on the 8th of August, watching the California coming in, when to his great joy he spied John Muir standing on the deck and waving his greetings. Springing nimbly ashore, Muir at once fired at him the question, "When can you be ready?" In response to Young's expostulations over his haste, and his failure to bring his wife, he exclaimed: "Man, have you forgotten? Don't

149

you know we lost a glacier last fall? Do you think I could sleep soundly in my bed this winter with that hanging on my conscience? My wife could not come, so I have come alone and you've got to go with me to find the lost. Get your canoe and crew and let us be off."

To Mrs. Muir

SITKA ON BOARD THE CALIFORNIA
August 10th, 1880
10.30 P.M. *of your time*

MY OWN DEAR LOUIE:

I'm now about as far from you as I will be this year — only this wee sail to the North and then to thee, my lassie. And I'm not away at all, you know, for only they who do not love may ever be apart. There is no true separation for those whose hearts and souls are together. So much for love and philosophy. And now I must trace you my way since leaving Nanaimo.

We sailed smoothly through the thousand evergreen isles, and arrived at Fort Wrangell at 4.30 A.M. on the 8th. Left Wrangell at noon of the same day and arrived here on the 9th at 6 A.M. Spent the day in friendly greetings and saunterings. Found Mr. Vanderbilt and his wife and Johnnie and, not every way least, though last, little Annie, who is grown in stature and grace and beauty since last I kissed her.

To-day Mr. Vanderbilt kindly took myself and Mr. Magee and three other fellow passengers on an excursion on his steamer up Peril Strait, about fifty miles. (You can find it on one of the charts that I forgot to bring.) We returned to the California about half-past nine, completing my way thus far.

And now for my future plans. The California sails to-morrow afternoon some time for Fort Wrangell, and I mean to return on her and from there set out on my canoe trip. I do not expect to be detained at Wrangell, inasmuch as I saw Mr. [S. Hall] Young, who promised to have a canoe and crew ready. I mean to keep close along the mainland, exploring the deep inlets in turn, at least as far north as the Taku, then push across to Cross Sound and follow the northern shore, examining the glaciers that crowd into the deep inlet that puts back northward from near the south extremity of the Sound, where I was last year. Thence I mean to return eastward along the southern shore of the Sound to Chatham Strait, turn southward down the west shore of the Strait to Peril Strait, and follow this strait to Sitka, where I shall take the California. Possibly, however, I may, should I not be pushed for time, return to

Wrangell. Mr. Magee will, I think, go with me, though very unwilling to do so. . . .

August 11th, at noon

I have just returned from a visit to the Jamestown. The Commander, Beardslee, paid me a visit here last evening, and invited me aboard his ship. Had a pleasant chat, and an invitation to make the Jamestown my home while here.

I also found my friend Koshoto, the Chief of the Hoonas, the man who, I told you, had entertained Mr. Young and me so well last year on Cross Sound, and who made so good a speech. He is here trading, and seemed greatly pleased to learn that I was going to pay him another visit; said that meeting me was like meeting his own brother who was dead, his heart felt good, etc. . . .

I have been learning all about the death of the brave and good old Toyatte. I think that Dr. Corliss, one of the Wrangell missionaries, made a mistake in reference to the seizure of some whiskey, which caused the beginning of the trouble.

This is a bright, soft, balmy day. How you would enjoy it! You must come here some day when you are strong enough. . . . Everybody inquires first on seeing me, "Have you brought

your wife?" and then, "Have you a photo-
graph?" and then pass condemnation for coming alone! . . .

The mail is about to close, and I must write
to mother.

> Affectionately your husband
>
> JOHN MUIR

How eagerly I shall look for news when I
reach Fort Wrangell next month!

To Mrs. Muir

RESIDENCE OF MR. YOUNG, FORT WRANGELL
11.45 A.M., *August 14th*, 1880

DEAR LOUIE:

I am back in my old quarters, and how familiar it all seems! — the lovely water, the islands,
the Indians with their baskets and blankets
and berries, the jet ravens prying and flying
here and there, and the bland, dreamy, hushed
air drooping and brooding kindly over all. I
miss Toyatte so much. I have just been over
the battleground with Mr. Young, and have
seen the spot where he fell.

Instead of coming here direct from Sitka we
called at Klawak on Prince of Wales Island for
freight, — canned salmon, oil, furs, etc., — which
detained us a day. We arrived here last evening at half-past ten. Klawak is a fishing and

trading station located in a most charmingly
beautiful bay, and while lying there, the evening before last, we witnessed a glorious auroral
display which lasted more than three hours.
First we noticed long white lance-shaped
streamers shooting up from a dark cloud-like
mass near the horizon, then a well-defined arch,
the corona, almost black, with a luminous edge
appeared, and from it, radiating like spokes
from a hub, the streamers kept shooting with a
quick glancing motion, and remaining drawn
on the dark sky, distinct, and white, as fine
lines drawn on a blackboard. And when half
the horizon was adorned with these silky
fibrous lances of light reaching to and converg-
ing at the zenith, broad flapping folds and
waves of the same white auroral light came
surging on from the corona with astonishing
energy and quickness, the folds and waves
spending themselves near the zenith like
waves on a smooth sloping sand-beach. But
throughout the greater portion of their courses
the motion was more like that of sheet lightning, or waves made in broad folds of muslin
when rapidly shaken; then in a few minutes
those delicate billows of light rolled up among
the silken streamers, would vanish, leaving the
more lasting streamers with the stars shining
through them; then some of the seemingly

permanent streamers would vanish also, and appear again in vivid white, like rockets shooting with widening base, their glowing shafts reflected in the calm water of the bay among the stars.

It was all so rare and so beautiful and exciting to us that we gazed and shouted like children at a show, and in the middle of it all, after I was left alone on deck at about half-past eleven, the whole sky was suddenly illumined by the largest meteor I ever saw. I remained on deck until after midnight, watching. The corona became crimson and slightly flushed the bases of the streamers, then one by one the shining pillars of the glorious structure were taken down, the foundation arch became irregular and broke up, and all that was left was only a faint structureless glow along the northern horizon, like the beginning of the dawn of a clear frosty day. The only sounds were the occasional shouts of the Indians, and the impressive roar of a waterfall.

Mr. Young and I have just concluded a bargain with the Indians, Lot and his friend, to take us in his canoe for a month or six weeks, at the rate of sixty dollars per month. Our company will be those two Indians, and Mr. Young and myself, also an Indian boy that Mr. Young is to take to his parents at Chilkat, and possi-

bly Colonel Crittenden as far as Holkham
Bay. . . .

You will notice, dear, that I have changed the
plan I formerly sent you in this, that I go on to
the Chilkat for Mr. Young's sake, and farther;
now that Mr. Magee is out of the trip, I shall
not feel the necessity I previously felt of getting back to Sitka or Wrangell in time for the
next steamer, though it is barely possible that
I shall. Do not look for me, however, as it is
likely I shall have my hands full for two
months. To-morrow is Sunday, so we shall not
get away before Monday, the 16th. How hard
it is to wait so long for a letter from you! I
shall not get a word until I return. I am trying
to trust that you will be patient and happy,
and have that work done that we talked of.

Every one of my old acquaintances seems
cordially glad to see me. I have not yet seen
Shakes, the Chief, though I shall ere we leave.
He is now one of the principal church members,
while Kadachan has been getting drunk in the
old style, and is likely, Mr. Young tells me, to
be turned out of the church altogether. John,
our last year's interpreter, is up in the Cassiar
mines. Mrs. McFarlane, Miss Dunbar, and
the Youngs are all uncommonly anxious to
know you, and are greatly disappointed in not
seeing you here, or at least getting a peep at

your picture. "Why could she not have come up and stayed with us while you were about your ice business?" they ask in disappointed tone of voice.

Now, my dear wife, the California will soon be sailing southward, and I must again bid you good-bye. I must go, but you, my dear, will go with me all the way. How gladly when my work is done will I go back to thee! With love to mother and father, and hoping that God will bless and keep you all, I am ever in heart and soul the same, JOHN MUIR

6 P.M. I have just dashed off a short "Bulletin" letter.

The events that followed are graphically narrated in Part II of "Travels in Alaska." Eight days after his arrival at Fort Wrangell, Muir and Mr. Young got started with their party, which consisted of the two Stickeen Indians Lot Tyeen and Hunter Joe — and a half-breed named Smart Billy. There was also Mr. Young's dog Stickeen, whom Mr. Muir at first accepted rather grudgingly as a supercharge of the already crowded canoe, but who later won his admiration and became the subject of one of the noblest dog stories in English literature.

The course of the expedition led through Wrangell Narrows between Mitkof and Kupreanof Islands, up Frederick Sound past Cape Fanshaw and across Port Houghton, and then up Stephens Passage to the entrance of Holkham Bay, also called Sumdum. Fourteen and a half hours up the Endicott Arm of this bay, which Muir was the first white man to explore, he found the glacier he had suspected there — a stream of ice three quarters of a mile wide and eight or nine hundred feet deep, discharging bergs with sounds of thunder. He had scarcely finished a sketch of it when he observed another glacial cañon on the west side of the fiord and, directing his crew to pull around a glaciated promontory, they came into full view of a second glacier, still pouring its ice into a branch of the fiord. Muir gave the first of these glaciers the name Young in honor of his companion, who complains that some later chart-maker substituted the name Dawes, thus committing the larceny of stealing his glacier.

In retracing their course, after some days spent in exploring the head of the fiord, they struck a side-arm through which the water was rushing with great force. Threading the narrow entrance, they found themselves in what Muir described as a new Yosemite in the making. He called it Yosemite Bay, and has furnished a charming description of its flora, fauna, and physical characteristics in his "Travels in Alaska."

On August 21st, Young being detained by missionary duties, Muir set out alone with the Indians to explore what is now known as the Tracy Arm of Holkham Bay. The second day he found another kingly glacier hidden within the benmost bore of the fiord. "There is your lost friend," said the Indians, laughing, and as the thunder of its detaching bergs reached their cars, they added, "He says, Sagh-a-ya?" (How do you do?)

After leaving Taku Inlet, Muir laid his course north through Stephens Passage and around the end of Admiralty Island, where a camp was made only with difficulty. The next morning he crossed the Lynn Canal with his boat and crew and pitched camp, after a voyage of twenty miles, on the west end of Farewell Island, now Pyramid Island. Early the following day they turned Point Wimbledon, crept along the lofty north wall of Cross Sound, and entered Taylor Bay. During a part of this trip, the canoe was exposed to a storm and swells rolling in past Cape Spencer from the open ocean. It was an undertaking that called for courage, skill, and hardihood of no mean order.

At the head of Taylor Bay, Muir found a great glacier consisting of three branches whose combined fronts had an extent of about eight miles. Camp was made near one of these fronts in the evening of August 29th. Early the following morning, Muir became aware that "a wild storm was blowing and calling," and before any one was astir he was off — too eager to stop for breakfast—into the rain-laden gale, and out upon the glacier. It was one of the great, inspired days of his life, immortalized in the story of "Stickeen," the brave little dog [1] that had become his inseparable companion.

Muir's time was growing short, so he hastened on with his party the next day into Glacier Bay, where among other great glaciers he had discovered the previous autumn the one that now bears his name. Several days were spent there most happily, exploring and observing glacial action, and then the canoe was turned Sitka-ward by way of Icy, Chatham, and Peril Straits, arriving in time to enable him to catch there the monthly mail steamer

[1] Mr. Muir received so many letters inquiring about the dog's antecedents that he asked Mr. Young in 1897 to tell him what he knew of Stickeen's earlier history. Some readers may be interested in his reply, which was as follows: "Mrs. Young got him as a present from Mr. H——, that Irish sinner who lived in a cottage up the beach towards the Presbyterian Mission in Sitka."

to Portland. Thus ended the Alaska trip of 1880.

II

"After all, have you not found there is some happiness in this world outside of glaciers, and other glories of nature?" The friend who put this question to John Muir, in a letter full of pleasantries and congratulations, had just received from him a jubilant note announcing the arrival of a baby daughter on March 27th. His fondness of children now had scope for indulgence at home, and he became a most devoted husband and father.

But for the time being he was to be deprived of this new domestic joy. For when he received an invitation to accompany the United States Revenue steamer Corwin on an Arctic relief expedition in search of DeLong and the Jeannette, it was decided in family council that so unusual an opportunity to explore the northern parts of Alaska and Siberia must not be neglected. His preparations had to be made in great haste while the citizens of Oakland were giving a banquet in honor of Captain C. L. Hooper and the officers of the Corwin at the Galinda Hotel in Oakland on April 29th. Fortunately, the Captain was an old friend whom he had known in Alaska and to whom he could entrust the purchase of the necessary polar garments from the natives in Bering Straits.

The Corwin sailed from San Francisco on May 4, 1881, and the following series of letters was written to his wife during the cruise. They supplement at many points the more formal account of his experiences published in "The Cruise of the Corwin." One of the objectives of the expedition was Wrangell Land in the Arctic Ocean, north of the Siberian coast, because it had been the expressed intention of Commander DeLong to reach the North Pole by traveling along its eastern coast, leaving cairns at intervals of twenty-five miles. It was not known at this time that Wrangell Land did not extend toward the Pole, but was an island of comparatively small extent. It was found later, by the log of the Jeannette, that the vessel had drifted, within sight of the island, directly across the meridians between which it lies. While the Corwin was still searching for her and her crew, the Jeannette was crushed in the ice and sank on June 12, 1881, in the Arctic Ocean, one hundred and fifty miles north of the New Siberian Islands.

Meanwhile Captain Hooper succeeded in penetrating, with the Corwin, the ice barrier that surrounded Wrangell Land. So far as known, the first human beings that ever stood upon the shores of this mysterious island were in Captain Hooper's landing party, August 12, 1881, and John Muir was of the number. The earliest news of the event, and of the fact that DeLong had not succeeded in touching either Herald Island or Wrangell Land, reached the world at large in a letter from Muir published in the "San Francisco Evening Bulletin," September 29, 1881.

Since the greater part of the first two letters, written to his wife at sea and while approaching Unalaska, was quoted in the writer's introduction to "The Cruise of the Corwin," they are omitted here for the sake of brevity.

To Mrs. Muir

MONDAY, 4 P.M., *May* 16, [1881]

DEAR LOUIE:

Since writing this forenoon, we reached the mouth of the strait that separates Unalaska Island from the next to the eastward, against a strong headwind and through rough snow squalls, when the Captain told me that he thought he would not venture through the Strait to-day, because the swift floodtide setting through the Strait against the wind was surely raising a dangerously rough sea, but rather seek an anchorage somewhere in the lee of the bluffs, and wait the fall of the wind. As he approached the mouth of the Strait, however, he changed his mind and determined to try it.

When the vessel began to pitch heavily and the hatches and skylights were closed, I knew that we were in the Strait, and made haste to get on my overcoat and get up into the pilot-house to enjoy the view of the waves. The view proved to be far wilder and more exciting than I expected. Indeed, I never before saw water in so hearty a storm of hissing, blinding foam. It was all one leaping, clashing, roaring mass of white, mingling with the air by means of the long hissing streamers dragged from the wave-tops, and the biting scud. Our little vessel, swept onward by the flood pouring into Bering's Sea and by her machinery, was being buffeted by the head-gale and the huge, white, over-combing waves that made her reel and tremble, though she stood it bravely and obeyed the helm as if in calm water. After proceeding about five or six miles into the heart of this grand uproar, it seemed to grow yet wilder and began to bid defiance to any farther headway against it. At length, when we had nearly lost our boats and [were] in danger of having our decks swept, we turned and fled for refuge before the gale. The giant waves, exulting in their

164

strength, seemed to be chasing us and threatening to swallow us at a gulp, but we finally made our escape, and were perhaps in no great danger farther than the risk of losing our boats and having the decks swept.

After going back about ten miles, we discovered a good anchorage in fifteen fathoms of water in the lee of a great bluff of lava about two thousand feet high, and here we ride in comfort while the blast drives past overhead. If we do not get off to-morrow, I will go ashore and see what I can learn.

Have learned already since the snow ceased falling that all the region hereabouts has been glaciated just like that thousand miles to the eastward. All the sculpture shows this clearly.

How pleasant it seems to be able to walk once more without holding on and to have your plate lie still on the table!

It is clearing up. The mountains are seen in groups rising back of one another, all pure white. The sailors are catching codfish. There are two waterfalls opposite our harbor.

Good-night to all. Oh, if I could touch my baby and thee!

This has been a very grand day — snow, waves, wind, mountains!

[JOHN MUIR]

JOHN MUIR

To Mrs. Muir

UNALASKA HARBOR
TUESDAY, *May* 17, 1881

DEAR LOUIE:

The gale having abated early this morning,
we left our anchorage on the south side of the
island and steamed round into the Strait to try
it again after our last evening's defeat, and this
time we were successful, after a hard contest
with the tide, which flows here at a speed of ten
miles an hour.

The clouds lifted and the sun shone out
early this morning, revealing a host of mountains nobly sculptured and grouped and robed
in spotless white. Turn which way you would,
the mountains were seen towering into the
dark sky, some of them with streamers of
mealy snow wavering in the wind, a truly
glorious sight. The most interesting feature to
me was the fine, clear, telling, glacial advertise-
ment displayed everywhere in the trends of the
numerous inlets and bays and valleys and
ridges, in the peculiar shell-shaped névé am-
phitheaters and in the rounded valley bottoms
and forms of the peaks and the cliff fronts
facing the sea. No clearer glacial inscriptions
are to be found in any mountain range, though
I had been led to believe that these islands were
all volcanic upheavals, scarce at all changed

166

since their emergence from the waves, but on the contrary I have already discovered that the amount of glacial degradation has been so great as to cut the peninsula into islands. I have already been repaid for the pains of the journey.

My health is improving every day in this bracing cold, and you will hardly recognize me when I return. The summer will soon pass, and we hope to be back to our homes by October or November. . . . This is a beautiful harbor, white mountains shutting it in all around — white nearly to the water's edge. . . .

I will write again ere we leave, and then you will not hear again, probably, until near the middle of June, when we expect to meet the St. Paul belonging to the Alaska Commercial Company at St. Michael. Then I will write and you may receive my letter a month or two later.

Good-bye until to-morrow.

[JOHN MUIR]

To Mrs. Muir

UNALASKA
WEDNESDAY, *May 18th*, 1881

DEAR LOUIE:

The Storm-King of the North is again up and doing, rolling white, combing waves through the jagged straits between this marvel-

ous chain of islands, circling them about with
beaten, updashing foam, and piling yet more
and more snow on the clustering cloud-wrapped
peaks. But we are safe and snug in this land-
locked haven enjoying the distant storm-roar
of wave and wind. I have just been on deck;
it is snowing still and the deep bass of the gale
is sounding on through the mountains. How
weird and wild and fascinating all this hearty
work of the storm is to me. I feel a strange
love of it all, as I gaze shivering up the dim
white slopes as through a veil darkly, becoming
fainter and fainter as the flakes thicken and at
length hide all the land.

Last evening I went ashore with the Captain, and saw the chief men of the place and the
one white woman, and a good many of the
Aleuts. We were kindly and cordially entertained by the agent of the Alaska Commercial
Company, Mr. Greenbaum, and while seated
in his "elegant" parlor could hardly realize
that we were in so remote and cold and silent
a wilderness.

As we were seated at our ease discussing
Alaskan and Polar affairs, a knock came to the
door, and a tall, hoary, majestic old man slowly
entered, whom I at once took for the Russian
priest, but to whom I was introduced as Dr.
Holman. He shook hands with me very

heartily and said, "Mr. Muir, I am glad to see you. I had the pleasure of knowing you in San Francisco." Then I recognized him as the dignified old gentleman that I first met three or four years ago at the home of the Smiths at San Rafael, and we had a pleasant evening together. He has been in the employ of the Alaska Commercial Company here for a year, caring for the health of the Company's Aleuts. His own health has been suffering the meanwhile, and to-day I sent him half a dozen bottles of the Doctor's wine to revive him. This notable liberality under the circumstances was caused, first, by his having advised me years ago to take good care of my steps on the mountains; second, to get married; third, for his pictures, drawn for me, of the bliss of having children; fourth, for the sake of our mutual friends; fifth, for his good looks and bad health; and half-dozenth, because fifteen or twenty years ago on a dark night, while seeking one of his patients in the Contra Costa hills, he called at the house of Doctor Strentzel for directions and was invited in and got a glass of good wine. A half-dozen bottles for a half-dozen reasons! "That's consistent, isn't it?" I mean to give a bottle to a friend of the Captain who is stationed at St. Michael, and save one bottle for our first contact with the polar ice-pack, and one with which to celebrate the hour of our return to home, friends, wives, bairns.

We had fresh-baked stuffed codfish for breakfast, of which I ate heartily, stuffing and all, though the latter was gray and soft and much burdened with minced onions, and then I held out my plate for a spoonful of opaque, oleaginous gravy! This last paragraph is for grandmother as a manifestation of heroic, all-enduring, all-engulfing health.

We have not yet commenced to coal, so that we will not get off for the North before Sunday. There is a schooner here that will sail for Shoalwater Bay, Oregon, in a few days, and by it I will send four or five letters. The three or four more that I intend writing ere we leave this port I will give to the agent of the Company here to be forwarded by the next opportunity in case the first batch should be lost. Then others will be sent from St. Michael by the Company's steamer, and still others from the Seal Islands and from points where we fall in with any vessel homeward bound.

Good-night to all. I am multiplying letters in case some be lost. A thousand kisses to my child. This is the fifth letter from Unalaska. Will write two more to be sent by other vessels.

[JOHN MUIR]

THE SECOND ALASKA TRIP

To Mrs. Muir

SUNDAY AFTERNOON, *May* 22, 1881

DEAR LOUIE:

We left Unalaska this morning at four o'clock and are now in Bering Sea on our way to St. George and St. Paul Islands.... Next Tuesday or Wednesday we expect to come in sight of the ice, but hope to find open water, along the west shore, that will enable us to get through the Strait to Cape Serdze or thereabouts. In a month or so we expect to be at St. Michael, where we will have a chance to send more letters and still later by whalers.

You will, therefore, have no very long period of darkness, though on my side I fear I shall have to wait a long time for a single word, and it is only by trusting in you to be cheerful and busy for the sake of your health and for the sake of our little love and all of us that I can have any peace and rest throughout this trip, however long or short. Now you must be sure to sleep early to make up for waking during the night, and occupy all the day with light work and cheerful thoughts, and never brood and dream of trouble, and I will come back with the knowledge that I need and a fresh supply of the wilderness in my health. I am already quite well and eat with savage appetite whatsoever is brought within reach.

JOHN MUIR

This morning I devoured half of a salmon trout eighteen inches long, a slice of ham, half a plateful of potatoes, two biscuits, and four or five slices of bread, with coffee and something else that I have forgotten, but which was certainly buried in me and lost. For lunch, two platefuls of soup, a heap of fat compound onion hash, two pieces of toast, and three or four slices of bread, with potatoes, and a big sweet cake, and now at three o'clock I am very hungry — a hunger that no amount of wave-tossing will abate. Furthermore, I look forward to fat seals fried and boiled, and to walrus steaks and stews, and doughnuts fried in train oil, and to all kinds of bears and fishy fowls with eager longing. There! Is that enough, grandmother? All my table whims are rapidly passing into the sere and yellow leaf and falling off.

I promise to comfort and sustain you beyond your highest aspirations when I return and fall three times a day on your table like a wolf on the fold. You know those slippery yellow custards — well, I eat those also!

You must not forget Sam Williams.[1] And now, my love, good-night. I hope you are feeling strong-hearted. I wish I could write anything, sense or nonsense, to cheer you up

[1] Editor of the *San Francisco Evening Bulletin*.

and brighten the outlook into the North. I
will try to say one more line or two when we
reach the Islands to-morrow.

Love to all. Kiss Annie for me.

[JOHN MUIR]

To Mrs. Muir

PLOVER BAY, SIBERIA
June 16th, 1881

MY BELOVED WIFE:

We leave this harbor to-morrow morning at
six o'clock, for St. Michael, and the northward.
The Corwin is in perfect condition, and since
the season promises to be a favorable one, we
hope to find the Jeannette and get home this
fall. I have not yet seen the American shore,
but hope to see it very thoroughly, as everything seems to work towards my objects. That
the Asiatic and American continents were one
a very short geological time ago is already clear
to me, though I shall probably obtain much
more available proof than I now have. This is
a grand fact. While the crystal glaciers were
creating Yosemite Valley, a thousand were
uniting here to make Bering Strait and Bering
Sea. The south side of the Aleutian chain of
islands was the boundary of the continent and
the ocean.

Since the Tom Pope came into the harbor,

I have written five "Bulletin" letters, which are for you mostly, and therefore I need the less to write any detailed narrative of the cruise. She will sail at the same hour as we do, and her Captain, Mr. Millard, who has been many times in the Arctic both here and on the Greenland side, has promised to make you a visit, and will be able to give you much information.

If I could only get a line, one word, from you to know that you were all well, I would be content to await the end of the voyage with patience and fortitude. But, my dear, it's terrible at times to have to endure for so long a dark silence. We will not be likely to get a word before September. No doubt you have already received the six or seven letters that I sent from Unalaska and St. Paul, also the two or three "Bulletin" letters from Unalaska. Write [W.C.] Bartlett or the office for a dozen copies of each, and save them for me.

We are drifting in the harbor among cakes of ice about the size of the orchard, but they can do us no harm. The great mountains forming the walls are covered yet with snow, except on a few bare spots near their bases, and there is not a single tree. Scarce a hint of any spring or summer have I seen since leaving San Francisco and the orchard. I hope you will

174

see Mr. Millard. You must keep Annie Wanda downstairs or she may fall; and now, my wife and child, daughter and mother, I must bid good-bye. Heaven bless you all! Send copies of my "Bulletin" letters to my mother, and put this letter with my papers and notebooks. You will get many other letters now that the whalers are returning.

My heart aches, not to go home ere I have done my work, but just to know that you are well.

Your affectionate husband

JOHN MUIR

To Mrs. Muir

· ST. MICHAEL, ALASKA

June 21, 1881

Sunshine, dear Louie, sunshine all the day, ripe and mellow sunshine, like that which feeds the fruits and vines! It came to us just [three] days ago when we were approaching this little old-fashioned trading post at the mouth of the Yukon River. . . .

On the day of our arrival from Plover Bay, a little steamer came into the harbor from the Upper Yukon, towing three large boats loaded with traders, Indians, and furs — all the furs they had gathered during the winter. We went across to the storeroom of the Company to see them. A queer lot they were, whites and Indians, as they unloaded their furs. It was worth while to look at the furs too — big bundles of bear skins brown and black, wolf, fox, beaver, marten, ermine, moose, wolverine, wildcat — many of them with claws spread and hair on end as if still alive and fighting for their lives. Some of the Indian chiefs, the wildest animals of all, and the more notable of the traders, not at all wild save in dress, but rather gentle and refined in manners, like village parsons. They held us in long interesting talks and gave us some valuable information concerning the broad wilds of the Yukon.

Yesterday I took a long walk of twelve or fourteen miles over the tundra to a volcanic cone and back, leaving the ship about twelve in the forenoon and getting back at half-past eight. I found a great number of flowers in full bloom, and birds of many species building their nests, and a capital view of the surrounding country from the rim of an old crater, altogether making a delightful day, though a very wearisome one on account of the difficult walking.

The ground back of St. Michael stretches away in broad brown levels of boggy tundra promising fine walking, but proving about as tedious and exhausting as possible. The spongy covering [is] roughened with tussocks of grass and sedge and creeping heathworts and willows, among which the foot staggers about and sinks and squints, seeking rest and finding none, until far down between the rocking tussocks. This covering is composed of a plush of mosses, chiefly sphagnum, about eight inches or a foot deep, resting on ice that never melts, while about half of the surface of the moss is covered with white, yellow, red, and gray lichens, and the other half is planted more or less with grasses, sedges, heathworts, and creeping willows, and a flowering plant here and there such as primula and purple-spiked *Pedicularis*. Out in this grand solitude — solitary as far as man is concerned — we met a great many of the Arctic grouse, ptarmigan, cackling and screaming at our approach like old laying hens; also plovers, snipes, curlews, sandpipers, loons in ponds, and ducks and geese, and finches and wrens about the crater and rocks at its base. . . .

And now good-bye again, and love to all, wife, darling baby Anna, grandmother, and grandfather.

[JOHN MUIR]

JOHN MUIR

To Mrs. Muir

BETWEEN PLOVER BAY AND
ST. LAWRENCE ISLAND,
July 2d, 1881

MY BELOVED WIFE:

After leaving St. Michael, on the twenty-second of June . . . we went again into the Arctic Ocean to Tapkan, twelve miles northwest of Cape Serdze, to seek the search party that we left on the edge of the ice-pack opposite Koliuchin Island, and were so fortunate as to find them there, having gone as far as the condition of the ice seemed to them safe, and after they had reached the fountain-head of all the stories we had heard concerning the lost whaler Vigilance and determined them to be in the main true. At Cape Wankarem they found three Chukchis who said that last year when the ice was just beginning to grow, and when the sun did not rise, they were out seal-hunting three or four miles from shore when they saw a broken ship in the drift ice, which they boarded and found some dead men in the cabin and a good many articles of one sort and another which they took home and which they showed to our party. This evidence reveals the fate of at least one of the ships we are seeking.

Our party, when they saw us, came out to the edge of the ice. which extended about three miles from shore, and after a good deal of difficulty reached the steamer. The north wind was blowing hard, sending huge black swells and combing waves against the jagged, grinding edge of the pack with terrible uproar, making it impossible for us to reach them with a boat. We succeeded, however, in throwing a line to them, which they made fast to a skin boat that they had pushed over the ice from the shore, and, getting into it, they were dragged over the stormy edge of ice waves and water waves and soon got safely aboard, leaving the tent, provisions, dogs, and sleds at the Indian village, to be picked up some other time.

Then we sailed southward again to take our interpreter Chukchi Joe to his home, which we reached two hours ago. Now we are steering for St. Michael again, intending to land for a few hours on the north side of St. Lawrence Island on the way. At St. Michael we shall write our letters, which will be carried to San Francisco by the Alaska Commercial Company's steamer St. Paul, take on more provisions, and then sail north again along the American shore, spending some time in Kotzebue Sound, perhaps exploring some of the rivers that flow into it, and then push on around Point Barrow and out into the ocean northward as we can, our movements being always determined by the position and movements of the ice-pack.

Before making a final effort in August or September to reach Wrangell Land in search of traces of the Jeannette, we will return yet once more to St. Michael for coal and provisions which we have stored there in case we should be compelled to pass a winter north of Bering Strait. The season, however, is so favorable that we have sanguine hopes of finding an open way to Wrangell Land and returning to our homes in October. The Jeannette has not been seen, nor any of her crew, on the Asiatic coast as far west as Cape Yaken, and I have no hopes of the vessel ever escaping from the ice; but her crew, in case they saved their provisions, may yet be alive, though it is strange that they did not come over the ice in the spring. Possibly they may have reached the American coast. If so, they will be found this summer. Our vessel is in perfect condition, and our Captain is very cautious and will not take any considerable chances of being caught in the North pack.

How long it seems since I left home, and yet according to the almanac it will not be two months until the day after to-morrow! I have seen so much and gone so far, and the nightless days are so strangely joined, it seems more

180

than a year. And yet how short a time is the busy month at home among the fruit and the work! My wee lass will be big and bright now, and by the time I can get her again in my arms she will be afraid of my beard. I have a great quantity of ivory dolls and toys — ducks, bears, seals, walruses, etc. — for her to play with, and some soft white furs to make a little robe for her carriage. But it is a sore, hard thing to be out of sight of her so long, and of thee, Lassie, but still sorer and harder not to hear. Perhaps not one word until I reach San Francisco! You, however, will hear often. . . .

This is a lovely, cool, clear, bright day, and the mountains along the coast of Asia stand in glorious array, telling the grand old story of their birth beneath the sculpturing ice of the glacial period. But the snow still lingers here and there down to the water's edge, and a little beyond the mouth of Bering Strait the vast, mysterious ice-field of the North stretches away beneath a dark, stormy sky for thousands of miles. I landed on East Cape yesterday and found unmistakable evidence of the passage over it of a rigid ice-sheet from the North, a fact which is exceedingly telling here. . . .

My health is so good now that I never notice it. I climbed a mountain at East Cape yesterday, about three thousand feet high, a mile through snow knee-deep, and never felt fatigue, my cheeks tingling in the north wind. .... I have a great quantity of material in my note-books already, lots of sketches [of] glaciers, mountains, Indians, Indian towns, etc. So you may be sure I have been busy, and if I could only hear a word now and then from that home in the California hills I would be the happiest and patientest man in all Hyperborea.

I am alone in the cabin; the engine is grinding away, making the lamp that is never lighted now rattle, and the joints creak everywhere, and the good Corwin is gliding swiftly over smooth blue water about half way to St. Lawrence Island. And now I must to bed! But before I go I reach my arms towards you, and pray God to keep you all. Good-night.

[JOHN MUIR]

To Mrs. Muir

ST. MICHAEL, *July 4th*, 1881

DEAR LOUIE:

We arrived here this afternoon at three o'clock and intend to stay about three days, taking in coal and provisions, and then to push off to the North. We intend to spend nearly a month along the American shore, perhaps as far north as Point Barrow, before we attempt to go out into the Arctic Ocean among the ice, for it is in August and September that the ice is most open. Then, if, as we hope from the favorableness of the season, we succeed in reaching Wrangell Land to search for traces of the Jeannette, or should find any sure tidings of her, we will be back in sunny, iceless California about the end of October, in grape-time. Otherwise we will probably return to St. Michael and take on a fresh supply of coal and nine months' provisions, and go north again prepared to winter in case we should get caught in the north of Bering Strait.

A few miles to the north of Plover Bay some thirteen or fourteen canoe-loads of natives came out to trade; more than a hundred of them were aboard at once, making a very lively picture. When we proceeded on our way, they allowed us to tow them for a mile or two in order to take advantage of the northerly current in going back to their village. They were dragged along, five or six canoes on each side, making the Corwin look like a mother field-mouse with a big family hanging to her teats, one of the first country sights that filled me with astonishment when a boy.

In coming here I had very fine views of St. Lawrence Island from the north side, showing the trend of the ice-sheet very plainly, much to my delight. The middle of the island is crowded with volcanic cones, mostly post-glacial, and therefore regular in form and but little wasted, and I counted upwards of fifty from one point of view. Just in front of this volcanic portion on the coast there is a dead Esquimo village where we landed and found that every soul of the population had died two years ago of starvation. More than two hundred skeletons were seen lying about like rubbish, in one hut thirty, most of them in bed. Mr. E. W. Nelson, a zealous collector for the Smithsonian Institution, gathered about one hundred skulls as specimens, throwing them together in heaps to take on board, just as when a boy in Wisconsin I used to gather pumpkins in the fall after the corn was shocked. The boxfuls on deck looked just about as unlike a cargo of cherries as possible, but I will not oppress you with grim details.

Some of the men brought off guns, axes, spears, etc., from the abandoned huts, and I found a little box of child's playthings which might please Anna Wanda, but which, I suppose, you will not let into the house. Well, I have lots of others that I bought, and when last here I engaged an Indian to make her a little fur suit, which I hope is ready so that I can send it down by the St. Paul. I hope it may fit her. I wish she were old enough to read the stories that I should like to write her.

Love to all. Good-night.

Ever yours

JOHN MUIR

To Mrs. Muir

ST. MICHAEL, *July 9th*, 1881

MY DEAR WIFE:

We did not get away last evening, as we expected, on account of the change in plans — as to taking all our winter stores on board, instead of leaving them until another visit in September. It is barely possible we might get caught off Point Barrow or on Wrangell [Land] by movements in the ice-pack that never can be anticipated. Therefore we will be more comfortable with abundance of bread about us. In the matter of coal, there is a mine on the north coast where some can be obtained in case of need, and also plenty of driftwood.

Our cruise, notwithstanding we have already made two trips into a portion of the Arctic usually blocked most of the summer, we consider is just really beginning. For we have not yet made any attempt to get to the packed region about Herald Island and Wrangell Land. Perhaps not once in twenty years would it be possible to get a ship alongside the shores of Wrangell Land, although its southern point is about nine degrees south of points attained on the eastern side of the continent. To find the ocean ice thirty or forty feet thick away from its mysterious shores seems to be about as hopeless as to find a mountain glacier out of its cañon. Still, this has been so remarkably open and mild a winter, and so many north gales have been blowing this spring, [gales] calcu-lated to break up the huge packs and grind the cakes and blocks against one another, that we have sanguine hopes of accomplishing all that we are expected to do and get home by the end of October. If I can see as much of the Amer-ican coast as I have of the Asiatic, I will be satisfied, and should the weather be as favor-able I certainly shall. . . .

We may, possibly, be home ere you receive any more [letters]. If not, think of me, dear, as happily at work with no other pain than the pain of separation from you and my wee lass. I have many times been weighing chances as to whether you have sent letters by the Mary-and-Helen, now called the "Rodgers," which was to sail about the middle of June. She is a slow sailer, and has to go far out of her course by Petropavlovskii, the capital of Kamchatka, for dogs, and will not be through the Strait before the end of the season nearly. Yet a letter by her is my only hope for hearing from you this season.

How warm and bland the weather is here, 60° in the shade, and how fine a crop of grass and flowers is growing up along the shores and back on the spongy tundra! The Captain says I can have a few hours on shore this afternoon. I mean to go across the bay three miles to a part of the tundra I have not yet seen. I shall at least find a lot of new flowers and see some of the birds. Once more, good-bye. I send Anna's parka by the St. Paul. Give my love to Sam Williams. You must not forget him.

[JOHN MUIR]

A month and three days after the date of the preceding letter the Corwin succeeded in making a landing on Wrangell Land. From some unpublished notes of Muir under the heading "Our New Arctic Territory" we excerpt the following account of the event:

Next morning [August 12th] the fog lifted, and we were delighted to see that though there was now about eight miles of ice separating us from the shore, it was less closely packed, and the Corwin made her way through it without great difficulty until within two miles of the shore, where the craggy berg-blocks were found to be extremely hard and wedged closely together. But a patch of open water near the beach, now plainly in sight, encouraged a continuance of the struggle, and with a full head of steam on, the barrier was forced. By 10 o'clock A.M. our little ship was riding at anchor less than a cable's length from the beach, opposite the mouth of a river.

This landing point proved to be in latitude 71° 4', longitude 177° 40' 30" W., near the East Cape. After taking formal possession of the country, one party examined the level beach about the mouth of the river, and the left bank for a mile or two, and a hillside that slopes gently down to the river, while another party of officers, after building a cairn, depositing records in it, and setting the flag on a conspicuous point of the bluff facing the ocean, proceeded northwestward along the brow of the short bluff to a marked headland, a distance of three or four miles, searching attentively for traces of the Jeannette expedition and of any native inhabitants that might chance to be in the country. Then all were hurriedly recalled and a way was forced to open water through ten miles of drift ice which began to close upon us.

To Mrs. Muir

POINT BARROW, *August 16th*, 1881

MY BELOVED WIFE:

Heaven only knows my joy this night in hearing that you were well. Old as the letter is and great as the number of days and nights that have passed since your love was written, it yet seems as if I had once more been upstairs and held you and Wanda in my arms. Ah, you little know the long icy days, so strangely nightless, that I have longed and longed for one word from you. The dangers, great as they were, while groping and grinding among the vast immeasurable ice-fields about that mysterious Wrangell Land would have seemed as nothing before I knew you. But most of the special dangers are past, and I have grand news for you, my love, for we have succeeded in landing on that strange ice-girt country and our work is nearly all done and I am coming home by the middle of October. No thought of wintering now and attempting to cross the frozen ocean from Siberia. We will take no more risks. All is well with our stanch little ship. She is scarce at all injured by the pounding and grinding she has undergone, and sailing home seems nothing more than crossing San Francisco Bay. We have added a large territory [Wrangell Land] to the domain of the United States and amassed a grand lot of knowledge of one sort and another.

Now we sail from here to-morrow for Cape Lisburne, or, if stormy, to Plover Bay, to coal and repair our rudder, which is a little weak. Thence we will go again around the margin of the main polar pack about Wrangell Land, but not into it, and possibly discover a clear way to land upon it again and obtain more of its geography; then leave the Arctic about the 10th of September, call at St. Michael, at Unalaska, and then straight home.

I shall not write at length now, as this is to go down by the Legal Tender, which sails in a few days and expects to reach San Francisco by the 20th of September, but we may reach home nearly as soon as she. I have to dash off a letter for the "Bulletin" to-night, though I ought to go to bed. Not a word of it is yet written.

We came poking and feeling our way along this icy shore a few hours ago through the fog, little thinking that a letter from you was just ahead. Then the fog lifted, and we saw four whalers at anchor and a strange vessel. When the Captain of the Belvidere shouted, "Letters for you, Captain, by the Legal Tender," which was the strange vessel, our hearts leaped, and a boat was speedily sent alongside. I got the letter package and handed them round, and yours, love, was the very last in the package, and I dreaded there was none. The Rodgers had not yet been heard from. One of the whale ships was caught here and crushed in the ice and sank in twenty minutes a month ago.

Good-bye, love. I shall soon be home. Love to all. My wee lass-love — she seems already

in my arms. Not in dreams this time! From
father and husband and lover.

JOHN MUIR

Muir's collection of plants, gathered in the
Arctic lands touched by the Corwin, was naturally of uncommon interest to botanists.
Asa Gray returned from a European trip in
November, and in response to an inquiry from
Muir at once wrote him to send on his Arctic
plants for determination. Those from Herald
Island and Wrangell Land, represented by a
duplicate set in the Gray Herbarium at Harvard, are still the only collections known to
science from those regions. In determining
the plants, Gray found among them a new
species of erigeron, and in reporting it to the
American Academy of Arts and Sciences
named it *Erigeron Muirii* in honor of its dis-
coverer. Muir found it in July at Cape
Thompson on the Arctic shore of Alaska.[1]

This cruise in the Arctic Ocean, as it turned
out, was to be the last of his big expeditions
for some time. Domestic cares and joys, and
the development of the fruit ranch, absorbed
his attention more and more. The old freedom

---

[1] A complete list of his various collections and of his glacial
observations will be found in the appendix to *The Cruise of
the Corwin* (1917).

was gone, but the following paragraph, from a letter written to Mrs. John Bidwell, of Rancho Chico, on January 2, 1882, suggests that he had found a satisfying substitute for the independence of earlier years:

I have been anxious to run up to Chico in the old free way to tell you about the majestic icy facts that I found last summer in the Lord's Arctic palaces, but, as you can readily guess, it is not now so easy a matter to wing hither and thither like a bird, for here is a wife and a baby and a home, together with the old press of field studies and literary work, which I by no means intend to lose sight of even in the bright bewitching smiles of my wee bonnie lassie. Speaking of brightness, I have been busy, for a week or two just past, letting more light into the house by means of dormer windows, and in making two more open brick fireplaces. Dormer-windows, open wood-fires, and perfectly happy babies make any home glow with warm sunny brightness and bring out the best that there is in us.

CHAPTER XV

THERE was an interval of ten years during which Mr. Muir devoted himself with great energy and success to the development of the Alhambra fruit ranch. According to a fictitious story, still encountered in some quarters, he was penniless at the time of his marriage. On the contrary, he had several thousand dollars at interest and, according to a fragment of uncompleted memoirs, was receiving from one hundred to two hundred and fifty dollars for each of his magazine articles. "After my first article," he wrote, "I was greatly surprised to find that everything else I offered was accepted and paid for. That I could earn money simply with written words seemed very strange."

In the same memoirs Muir generalizes as follows on the decade between 1881 and 1891:

About a year before starting on the Arctic expedition I was married to Louie Strentzel, and for ten years I was engaged in fruit-raising in the Alhambra Valley, near Martinez, clearing land, planting vineyards and orchards, and selling the fruit, until I had more money than I thought I would ever need for my family or for all expenses of travel and study, however far or however long continued. But this farm work never seriously interrupted my studies. Every spring when the snow on the mountains had melted, until the approach of winter, my explorations were pushed farther and farther. Only in the early autumn, when the table grapes were gathered, and in winter and early spring, when the vineyards and orchards were pruned and cultivated, was my personal supervision given to the work. After these ten years I sold part of the farm and leased the balance, so as to devote the rest of my life, as care-free as possible, to travel and study. Thus, in 1891, I was again free from the farm and all bread-winning cares.

In the extant correspondence of the early eighties one gets only indirect and fugitive hints of Muir's activities. Worthy of notice is the fact that during July, 1884, he took his wife to the Yosemite Valley, and their joint letters to the grandparents and the little daughter, left at home, afford amusing glimpses of a husband who has never played courier to a wife and of a wife who mistakes trout for catfish and suspects a bear behind every bush. It should be added that in Mrs. Muir's letters there is a note of concern for her husband's health, which had begun to suffer under the exacting cares of the ranch. "I am anxious about John," she writes. "The journey was hard for him, and he looks thin and pale and tired. He must not leave the mountains until he is well and strong again."

The arrival, in 1886, of a second daughter, believed to have been of frail health during her infant years, brought an increase of parental cares and anchored the family to the ranch more closely than ever. Mrs. Muir was naturally disinclined to travel, and both of them were full of misgivings regarding anything that might imperil the safety of the children. Under the circumstances Muir became more and more absorbed in the management of the ranch and care for his own.

Meanwhile time was working changes in the Wisconsin family circle from which John had gone out in 1867. Nearly eighteen years had gone by since he had seen his father and mother, brothers and sisters. His brother-in-law David Galloway died suddenly in September, 1884, his father and mother were growing infirm, the wife of his brother David was smitten with an incurable malady, and death was thinning the ranks of the friends of his youth. In view of these circumstances he began to feel more and more strongly the desire to revisit the scenes and friends of his boyhood. "I mean to see you all some time this happy new year

[1885]," he wrote to his brother David at the close of December. "Seeing you after so long a journey in earth's wildest wildernesses will make [the experience] indeed new to me. I could not come now without leaving the ranch to go to wreck, a score of workmen without a head, and no head to be found, though I have looked long for a foreman. Next spring after the grapes are pruned and sulphured, etc., and the cherry crop sold, I mean to pay off all but a half-dozen or so and leave things to take their course for a month or two. Can't you send me some good steady fellow to learn this fruit business and take some of the personal supervision off my shoulders? Such a person could be sure of a job as long as he liked."

It seems worth while to record, in this connection, an incident of dramatic and pathetic interest which occurred during the summer of 1885, just before Muir made his first return trip to his old Wisconsin home. Helen Hunt Jackson had come to San Francisco in June after months of illness, caused, as she thought, by defective sanitation in a Los Angeles boarding-house. Having recently been appointed Special Commissioner to inquire into the conditions surrounding the Mission Indians of California, she gave herself with devotion and ability to the righting of their wrongs. Among her particular friends was Mrs. Carr, at whose suburban Pasadena home, "Carmelita," she had written a part of her Indian story "Ramona." It was quite natural, therefore, that she should apply to John Muir for help in planning a convalescent's itinerary in the mountains. "I know with the certainty of instinct," she wrote, "that nothing except three months out of doors night and day will get this poison out of my veins. The doctors say that in six weeks I may be strong enough to be laid on a bed in a wagon and drawn about."

It is easy to imagine the surprise and amusement of Muir when he read her statement of the conditions and equipment required for her comfort. She wished to be among trees where it was moist and cool, being unable to endure heat. She wanted to keep moving, but the altitudinal range must not exceed four thousand feet, and, above all, she must not get beyond easy reach of express and post-offices. Her outfit was to consist of eight horses, an ambulance, two camp-wagons for tents, and a phaeton buggy. The attendants were to comprise four servants, a maid, and a doctor.

"Now do you know any good itinerary," she inquired, "for such a cumbrous caravan as this? How you would scorn such lumbering methods! I am too ill to wish any other. I shall do this as a gamester throws his last card!" In conclusion she stated that she had always cherished the hope of seeing him some time. "I believe," she adds, "I know every word you have written. I never wished myself a man but once. That was when I read how it seemed to be rocked in the top of a pine tree in a gale!"

Muir's reply to this request, according to the draft of a letter found among his papers, was as follows:

To Helen Hunt Jackson

MARTINEZ, *June 16th*, 1885

MY DEAR MRS. JACKSON:

Your letter of June 8th has shown me how sick you are, but also that your good angel is guiding you to the mountains, and therefore I feel sure that you will soon be well again.

When I came to California from the swamps of Florida, full of malarial poison, I crawled up the mountains over the snow into the blessed woods about Yosemite Valley, and the exquisite pleasure of convalescence and exuberant rebound to perfect health that came to me at once seem still as fresh and vivid after all these years as if enjoyed but yesterday.

The conditions you lay down for your itinerary seem to me desperately forbidding. No path accessible to your compound congregation can be traced across the range, maintaining anything like an elevation of four thousand feet, to say nothing of coolness and moisture, while along the range the topography is still less compliant to your plans. When I was tracing the Sequoia belt from the Calaveras to the Kern River I was compelled to make a descent of nine thousand feet in one continuous swoop in crossing the Kings River Valley, while the ups and downs from ridge to ridge throughout the whole course averaged nearly five thousand feet.

No considerable portion of the middle and southern Sierra is cool and moist at four thousand feet during late summer, for there you are only on the open margin of the main forest zone, which is sifted during the day by the dry warm winds that blow across the San Joaquin plains and foothills, though the night winds from the summit of the range make the nights delightfully cool and refreshing.

The northern Sierra is considerably cooler and moister at the same heights. From the end of the Oregon Railroad beyond Redding you might work up by a gentle grade of fifty miles or so to Strawberry Valley where the elevation is four thousand feet. There is abundance of everything, civilized as well as wild, and from thence circle away all summer around Mount Shasta where the circumference is about one hundred miles, and only a small portion of your way would lie much above or below the required elevation, and only the north side, in Shasta Valley, would you find rather dry and warm, perhaps, while you would reach an express station at every round or a good messenger could find you in a day from the station at any point in your orbit. And think how glorious a center you would have! — so glorious and inspiring that I would gladly revolve there, weary, afoot, and alone for all eternity.

The Kings River yosemite would be a delightful summer den for you, abounding in the best the mountains have to give. Its elevation is about five thousand feet, length nine miles, and it is reached by way of Visalia and Hyde's Mills among the Sequoias of the Kaweah, but not quite accessible to your wheels and pans, I fear. Have you considered the redwood region of the Coast Range about Mendocino? There you would find coolness, moist air, and spicy woods at a moderate elevation.

If an elevation of six thousand feet were considered admissible, I would advise your going on direct to Truckee by rail, rather than to Dutch Flat, where the climate may be found too dry and hot. From Truckee by easy stages to Tahoe City and thence around the Lake and over the Lake all summer. This, as you must know, is a delightful region — cool and moist and leafy, with abundance of food and express stations, etc.

What an outfit you are to have — terrible as an army with banners! I scarce dare think of it. What will my poor Douglas squirrels say at the sight? They used to frisk across my feet, but I had only two feet, which seemed too many for the topography in some places, while you have a hundred, besides wooden spokes and spooks. Under ordinary circumstances they would probably frighten the maid and stare the doctor out of countenance, but every tail will be turned in haste and hidden at the bottom of the deepest knot-holes. And what shuffling and haste there will be in the chaparral when the bears are getting away! Even the winds might hold their breath, I fancy, "pause and die," and the great pines groan aghast at the oncoming of so many shining cans and carriages and strange colors.

But go to the mountains where and how you will, you soon will be free from the effects of this confusion, and God's sky will bend down about you as if made for you alone, and the pines will spread their healing arms above you

and bless you and make you well again, and so
delight the heart of

JOHN MUIR

"If nothing else comes of my camping air-
castle," she wrote from 1600 Taylor Street,
San Francisco, two days after receiving Muir's
answer, "I have at least one pleasure from it —
your kind and delightful letter. I have read it
so many times I half know it. I wish Mrs. Carr
were here that I might triumph over her. She
wrote me that I might as well ask one of the
angels of heaven as John Muir, 'so entirely out
of his line' was the thing I proposed to do. I
knew better, however, and I was right. You
are the only man in California who could tell
me just what I needed to know about ranges
of climate, dryness, heat, etc., also roads."

But the author of "Ramona" was never to
have an opportunity to play her last card, for
she was beyond even the healing of the mountains if she could have reached them. Indeed,
one detects a presentiment of her doom in the
closing lines of her letter to the man who had
fired her imagination with his contagious faith
in the restorative powers of nature. "If you
could see me," she writes, "you would only
wonder that I have courage to even dream of
such an expedition. I am not at all sure it is

not of the madness which the gods are said to send on those whom they wish to destroy. They tell me Martinez is only twenty miles away: do you never come into town? The regret I should weakly feel at having you see the 'remains' (ghastly but inimitable word) of me would, I think, be small in comparison with the pleasure I should feel in seeing you. I am much too weak to see strangers — but it is long since you were a stranger." Whether the state of his own health had permitted him to call on "H. H.," as she was known among her friends, before he started East, in August, to see his parents, is not clear. Certain it is that by a singular coincidence he was ringing her doorbell almost at the moment when the brave spirit of this noble friend of the Indians was taking flight. "Mrs. Jackson may have gone away somewhere," he remarked in writing to his wife the next day: "could get no response to my ringing — blinds down."

The immediate occasion of his decision to go East is best told in some further pages from unpublished memoirs under the title of "Mysterious Things." Though Muir's boyhood was passed in communities where spooks, and ghosts, and clairvoyance were firmly believed in, he was as a man singularly free from faith in superstitions of this kind. But there were several occasions when he acted upon sudden and mysterious impulses for which he knew no explanation, and which he contents himself simply to record. One of these relates to the final illness and death of his father and is told as follows:

In the year 1885, when father was living with his youngest daughter in Kansas City, another daughter, who was there on a visit, wrote me that father was not feeling as well as usual on account of not being able to take sufficient exercise. Eight or ten years before this, when he was about seventy years of age, he fell on an icy pavement and broke his leg at the hip joint, a difficult break to heal at any time, but in old age particularly so. The bone never knitted, and he had to go on crutches the balance of his life.

One morning, a month or two after receiving this word from my sister, I suddenly laid down my pen and said to my wife: "I am going East, because somehow I feel this morning that if I don't go now I won't see father again." At this time I had not seen him for eighteen years. Accordingly I went on East, but, instead of going direct to Kansas City, I first went to Portage, where one of my brothers and my mother were living.

As soon as I arrived in Portage, I asked mother whether she thought she was able to take the journey to Kansas City to see father, for I felt pretty sure that if she didn't go now she wouldn't see him again alive. I said the same to my brother David. "Come on, David: if you don't go to see father now,

I think you will never see him again." He seemed greatly surprised and said: "What has put that in your head? Although he is compelled to go around on crutches, he is, so far as I have heard, in ordinary health." I told him that I had no definite news, but somehow felt that we should all make haste to cheer and comfort him and bid him a last good-bye. For this purpose I had come to gather our scattered family together. Mother, whose health had long been very frail, said she felt it would be impossible for her to stand the journey. David spoke of his business, but I bought him a railway ticket and compelled him to go.

On the way out to Kansas City I stopped at Lincoln, Nebraska, where my other brother, Daniel, a practicing physician, was living. I said, "Dan, come on to Kansas City and see father." "Why?" he asked. "Because if you don't see him now, you never will see him again. I think father will leave us in a few days." "What makes you think so?" said he; "I have not heard anything in particular." I said, "Well, I just kind of feel it. I have no reason." "I cannot very well leave my patients, and I don't see any necessity for the journey." I said, "Surely you can turn over your patients to some brother physician. You will not probably have to be away more than four or five days, or a week, until after the funeral." He said, "You seem to talk as though you knew everything about it." I said, "I don't know anything about it, but I have that feeling — that presentiment, if you like — nothing more." I then bought him a ticket and said, "Now let's go: we have no time to lose." Then I sent the same word to two sisters living in Kearney and

Crete, Nebraska, who arrived about as soon as we did.

Thus seven of the eight in our family assembled around father for the first time in more than twenty years. Father showed no sign of any particular illness, but simply was confined to his bed and spent his time reading the Bible. We had three or four precious days with him before the last farewell. He died just after we had had time to renew our acquaintance with him and make him a cheering, comforting visit. And after the last sad rites were over, we all scattered again to our widely separated homes.

The reader who recalls, from the opening chapters of this work, the paternal severity which embittered for John Muir the memory of the youthful years he spent on the farm, will be interested in a few additional details of this meeting of father and son after eighteen years. In spite of the causes which had estranged them so long ago, John had never withheld his admiration for the nobler traits of his father's character, and he apparently cherished the hope that some day he might be able to sit down quietly with him and talk it all out. It seemed futile to do this so long as the old man was actively engaged in evangelistic work, which shut out from calm consideration anything that seemed to him to have been or to be an embarrassment of his calling. Now that he was laid low, John deemed that the proper time had arrived, but for this purpose he had come too late.

"Father is very feeble and helpless," he wrote to his wife from the aged man's bedside. "He does not know me, and I am very sorry. He looks at me and takes my hand and says, 'Is this my dear John?' and then sinks away on the pillow, exhausted, without being able to understand the answer. This morning when I went to see him and was talking broad Scotch to him, hoping to stir some of the old memories of Scotland before we came here, he said, 'I don't know much aboot it noo,' and then added, 'You're a Scotchman, aren't you?' When I would repeat that I was his son John that went to California long ago and came back to see him, he would start and raise his head a little and gaze fixedly at me and say, 'Oh, yes, my dear wanderer,' and then lose all memory again. ... I'm sorry I could not have been here two or three months earlier, though I suppose all may be as well, as it is."

A few months earlier, when Daniel Muir was still in full possession of his faculties, he had particularly mentioned to his daughter Joanna some of the cruel things he had said and done to his "poor wandering son John." This wanderer, crossing the mountains and the plains in response to a mysterious summons, had gathered the scattered members of the former Fountain Lake home to his dying father's bedside, and, as the following letter shows, was keeping solitary vigil there, when the hour of dissolution came.

To Mrs. Muir

803 WABASH AVENUE
KANSAS CITY, MISSOURI
October 6th, 1885

DEAR LOUIE:

You will know ere this that the end has come and father is at rest. He passed away in a full summer day evening peace, and with that peace beautifully expressed, and remaining on his countenance as he lies now, pure and clean like snow, on the bed that has borne him so long.

Last evening David and I made everybody go to bed and arranged with each other to keep watch through the night, promising the girls to give warning in time should the end draw near while they slept. David retired in an adjoining room at ten o'clock, while I watched alone, he to be called to take my place at two or three in the morning, should no marked change take place before that time.

About eleven o'clock his breathing became calm and slow, and his arms, which had been

208

moved in a restless way at times, at length were folded on his breast. About twelve o'clock his breathing was still calmer, and slower, and his brow and lips were slightly cold and his eyes grew dim. At twelve-fifteen I called David and we decided to call up the girls, Mary, Anna, and Joanna, but they were so worn out with watching that we delayed a few minutes longer, and it was not until about one minute before the last breath that all were gathered together to kiss our weary affectionate father a last good-bye, as he passed away into the better land of light.

Few lives that I know were more restless and eventful than his — few more toilsome and full of enthusiastic endeavor onward towards light and truth and eternal love through the midst of the devils of terrestrial strife and darkness and faithless misunderstanding that well-nigh overpowered him at times and made bitter burdens for us all to bear.

But his last years as he lay broken in body and silent were full of calm divine light, and he oftentimes spoke to Joanna of the cruel mistakes he had made in his relations towards his children, and spoke particularly of me, wondering how I had borne my burdens so well and patiently, and warned Joanna to be watchful to govern her children by love alone. . . .

Seven of the eight children will surely be present [at the funeral]. We have also sent telegrams to mother and Sarah, though I fear neither will be able to endure the fatigues of the journey. . . . In case they should try to be present, David or I would meet them at Chicago. Then the entire family would be gathered once more, and how gladly we would bring that about! for in all our devious ways and wanderings we have loved one another.

In any case, we soon will be scattered again, and again gathered together. In a few days the snow will be falling on father's grave and one by one we will join him in his last rest, all our separating wanderings done forever.

Love to all, Wanda, Grandma, and Grandpa.

Ever yours, Louie

JOHN MUIR

To Mrs. Muir

PORTAGE CITY, WISCONSIN
September 10th, 1885

DEAR LOUIE:

I have just returned from a visit to the old people and old places about our first home in America, ten or twelve miles to the north of this place, and am glad to hear from you at last. Your two letters dated August 23d and 28th and the Doctor's of September 1st have

just been received, one of them having been
forwarded from the Yellowstone, making
altogether four letters from home besides
Wanda's neat little notes which read and look
equally well whichever side is uppermost. Now
I feel better, for I had begun to despair of hearing from you at all, and the weeks since leaving
home, having been crowded with novel scenes
and events, seemed about as long as years.

As for the old freedom I used to enjoy in the
wilderness, that, like youth and its enthusiasms,
is evidently a thing of the past, though I feel
that I could still do some good scientific work
if the necessary leisure could be secured. Your
letters and the Doctor's cheer and reassure me,
as I felt that I was staying away too long and
leaving my burdens for others to carry who had
enough of their own, and though you encourage
me to prolong my stay and reap all the benefit
I can in the way of health and pleasure and
knowledge, I cannot shut my eyes to the fact
that the main vintage will soon be on and require my presence, to say nothing of your uncertain state of health. Therefore I mean to
begin the return journey next Saturday morning by way of Chicago and Kansas City. . . .

Still another of your letters has just arrived,
dated August 31st, by which I learn that
Wanda is quite well and grandma getting

stronger, while you are not well as you should be. I have tried to get you conscious of the necessity of the utmost care of your health — especially at present — and again remind you of it.

The Yellowstone period was, as you say, far too short, and it required bitter resolution to leave all. The trip, however, as a whole has been far from fruitless in any direction. I have gained telling glimpses of the Continent from the car windows, and have seen most of the old friends and neighbors of boyhood times, who without exception were almost oppressively kind, while a two weeks' visit with mother and the family is a great satisfaction to us all, however much we might wish it extended. . . .

I saw nearly all of the old neighbors, the young folk, of course, grown out of memory and unrecognizable; but most of the old I found but little changed by the eighteen years since last I saw them, and the warmth of my welcome was in most instances excruciating. William Duncan, the old Scotch stone-mason who loaned me books when I was little and always declared that "Johnnie Moor will mak a name for himsel some day," I found hale and hearty, eighty-one years of age, and not a gray hair in his curly, bushy locks — erect, firm of step, voice firm with a clear calm ring to it, memory as good as ever apparently, and his interest in all the current news of the world as fresh and as far-reaching. I stopped overnight with [him] and talked till midnight.

We were four days in making the round and had to make desperate efforts to get away. We climbed the Observatory that used to be the great cloud-capped mountain of our child's imagination, but it dwindled now to a mere hill two hundred and fifty feet high, half the height of that vineyard hill opposite the house. The porphyry outcrop on the summit is very hard, and I was greatly interested in finding it grooved and polished by the ice-sheet. I began to get an appetite and feel quite well. Tell Wanda I'll write her a letter soon. Everybody out in the country seemed disappointed, not seeing you also. Love to all.

Ever yours   JOHN MUIR

Early in 1887 a letter from Janet Moores, one of the children who had visited Muir in his dark-room in Indianapolis many years ago, brought him news that she had arrived in Oakland. She was the daughter of his friend Mrs. Julia Merrill Moores, and a sister of Merrill Moores, who spent a season with John in Yosemite and in 1915 was elected a member of Congress from Indiana.

JOHN MUIR

To Miss Janet Douglass Moores

MARTINEZ, CALIFORNIA
February 23, 1887

MY DEAR FRIEND JANET:

Have you really turned into a woman, and have you really come to California, the land of the sun, and Yosemite and a' that, through the whirl of all these years! Seas between us braid hae roared, my lassie, sin' the auld lang syne, and many a storm has roared over broad mountains and plains since last we parted. Yet, however, we are but little changed in all that signifies, saved from many dangers that we know, and from many more that we never shall know — kept alive and well by a thousand, thousand miracles!

Twenty years! How long and how short a time that seems to-day! How many times the seas have ebbed and flowed with their white breaking waves around the edges of the continents and islands in this score of years, how many times the sky has been light and dark, and the ground between us been shining with rain, and sun, and snow: and how many times the flowers have bloomed, but for a' that and a' that you seem just the same to me, and time and space and events hide you less than the thinnest veil. Marvelous indeed is the permanence of the impressions of those sunrise

214

days, more enduring than granite mountains.
Through all the landscapes I have looked into,
with all their wealth of forests, rivers, lakes,
and glaciers, and happy living faces, your
face, Janet, is still seen as clear and keenly
outlined as on the day I went away on my long
walk.

Aye, the auld lang syne is indeed young.
Time seems of no avail to make us old except
in mere outer aspects. To-day you appear the
same little fairy girl, following me in my walks
with short steps as best you can, stopping now
and then to gather buttercups, and anemones,
and erigenias, sometimes taking my hand in
climbing over a fallen tree, threading your way
through tall grasses and ferns, and pushing
through very small spaces in thickets of underbrush. Surely you must remember those holiday walks, and also your coming into my
dark-room with light when I was blind! And
what light has filled me since that time, I am
sure you will be glad to know — the richest
sun-gold flooding these California valleys, the
spiritual alpenglow steeping the high peaks,
silver light on the sea, the white glancing sun-
spangles on rivers and lakes, light on the
myriad stars of the snow, light sifting through
the angles of sun-beaten icebergs, light in
glacier caves, irised spray wafting from white

215

waterfalls, and the light of calm starry nights beheld from mountain-tops dipping deep into the clear air. Aye, my lassie, it is a blessed thing to go free in the light of this beautiful world, to see God playing upon everything, as a man would play on an instrument, His fingers upon the lightning and torrent, on every wave of sea and sky, and every living thing, making all together sing and shine in sweet accord, the one love-harmony of the Universe. But what need to write so far and wide, now you are so near, and when I shall so soon see you face to face?

I only meant to tell you that you were not forgotten. You think I may not know you at first sight, nor will you be likely to recognize me. Every experience is recorded on our faces in characters of some sort, I suppose, and if at all telling, my face should be quite picturesque and marked enough to be readily known by anybody looking for me: but when I look in the glass, I see but little more than the marks of rough weather and fasting. Most people would see only a lot of hair, and two eyes, or one and a half, in the middle of it, like a hillside with small open spots, mostly overgrown with shaggy chaparral, as this portrait will show [drawing]. Wanda, peeping past my elbow, asks, "Is that you, Papa?" and then goes on to

A SELF-PORTRAIT
Drawing in letter of February 23, 1887
to Miss Janet Douglass Moores

say that it is just like me, only the hair is not curly enough; also that the little ice and island sketches are just lovely, and that I must draw a lot just like them for her. I think that you will surely like her. She remarked the other day that she was well worth seeing now, having got a new gown or something that pleased her. She is six years old.

The ranch and the pasture hills hereabouts are not very interesting at this time of year. In bloom-time, now approaching, the orchards look gay and Dolly Vardenish, and the home-garden does the best it can with rose bushes and so on, all good in a food and shelter way, but about as far from the forests and gardens of God's wilderness as bran-dolls are from children. I should like to show you my wild lily and Cassiope and Bryanthus gardens, and homes not made with hands, with their daisy carpets and woods and streams and other fine furniture, and singers, not in cages; but legs and ankles are immensely important on such visits. Unfortunately most girls are like flowers that have to stand and take what comes, or at best ride on iron rails around and away from what is worth seeing; then they are still something like flowers — flowers in pots carried by express.

I advised you not to come last Friday be-

cause the weather was broken, and the tele-
phone was broken, and the roads were muddy,
but the weather will soon shine again, and then
you and Mary can come, with more comfort
and safety. Remember me to Mary, and
believe me,

Ever truly your friend

JOHN MUIR

Muir's literary unproductiveness during the
eighties began to excite comment among his
friends if one may judge by several surviving
letters in which they inquire whether he has
forsaken literature. His wife, also, was eager
to have him continue to write, and it was, perhaps, due to this gentle pressure from several
quarters that he accepted in 1887 a proposal
from the J. Dewing Company to edit and contribute to an elaborately illustrated work entitled "Picturesque California." As usual with
such works, it was issued in parts, sold by sub-
scription, and while it bears the publication
date of 1888, it was not finished until a year or
two later.

As some of the following letters show, Muir
found it a hard grind to supply a steady stream
of copy to the publishers and to supervise his
corps of workmen on the ranch at the same
time. "I am all nerve-shaken and lean as a

crow — loaded with care, work, and worry,"
he wrote to his brother David after a serious
illness of his daughter Helen in August, 1887.
"The care and worry will soon wear away, I
hope, but the work seems rather to increase.
There certainly is more than enough of it to
keep me out of mischief forever. Besides the
ranch I have undertaken a big literary job, an
illustrated work on California and Alaska. I
have already written and sent in the two first
numbers and the illustrations, I think, are
nearly ready."

The prosecution of this task involved various
trips, and on some of them he was accompanied
by his friend William Keith, the artist. Perhaps the longest was the one on which they
started together early in July, 1888, traveling
north as far as Vancouver and making many
halts and side excursions, both going and coming. Muir was by no means a well man when
he left home, but in a train letter to his wife he
expressed confidence that he would "be well
at Shasta beneath a pine tree." The excursion
took him to Mount Hood, Mount Rainier,
Snoqualmie and Spokane Falls, and Victoria,
up the Columbia, and to many places of minor
interest in the Puget Sound region. In spite of
his persistent indisposition he made the ascent
of Mount Rainier. "Did not mean to climb

it," he wrote to his wife, "but got excited and soon was on top."

It did not escape the keen eyes of his devoted wife that the work of the ranch was in no small measure responsible for the failure of his health. "A ranch that needs and takes the sacrifice of a noble life," she wrote to her husband on this trip, "ought to be flung away beyond all reach and power for harm. . . . The Alaska book and the Yosemite book, dear John, must be written, and you need to be your own self, well and strong, to make them worthy of you. There is nothing that has a right to be considered beside this except the welfare of our children."

Muir's health, however, improved during the following winter and summer, notwithstanding the fact that the completion of "Picturesque California" kept him under tension all the time. By taking refuge from the tasks of the ranch at a hotel in San Francisco, during periods of intensive application, he learned to escape at least the strain of conflicting responsibilities. But even so he had to admit at times that he was "hard at work on the vineyards and orchards while the publishers of 'Picturesque California' are screaming for copy." In letters written to his wife, during periods of seclusion in San Francisco, Muir was accustomed to quote choice passages for comment and approval. The fact is of interest because it reveals that he had in her a stimulating and appreciative helper.

To Mrs. Muir

GRAND HOTEL, SAN FRANCISCO, CAL.
July 4th, 1889

DEAR LOUIE:

I'm pegging away and have invented a few good lines since coming here, but it is a hard subject and goes slow. However, I'll get it done somehow and sometime. It was cold here last evening and I had to put on everything in my satchel at once. . . .

Last evening an innocent-looking "Examiner" reporter sent up his card, and I, really innocent, told the boy to let him come up. He began to speak of the Muir Glacier, but quickly changed the subject to horned toads, snakes, and Gila monsters. I asked him what made him change the subject so badly and what there was about the Muir Glacier to suggest such reprobate reptiles. He said snakes were his specialty and wanted to know if I had seen many, etc. I talked carelessly for a few minutes, and judge of my surprise in seeing this villainous article. "John Muir says they kill hogs and eat rabbits, but don't eat hogs because too big, etc." What poetry! It's so perfectly ridiculous, I have at least had a good laugh out of it. "The toughness of the skin makes a difference," etc. — should think it would!

The air has been sulphurous all day and noisy as a battle-field. Heard some band music, but kept my room and saw not the procession.

Hope your finger is not going to be seriously sore and that the babies are well. I feel nervous about them after reading about those geological snakes of John Muir. . . .

My room is better than the last, and I might at length feel at home with my Puget Sound scenery had I not seen and had nerves shaken with those Gila monsters. I hope I'll survive, though the "Examiner" makes me say, "If the poison gets into them it takes no time at all to kill them" (the hogs), and my skin is not as thick. Remember me to Grandma, Grandpa, and the babies, and tell them not the sad story of the snakes of Fresno.

Ever yours

JOHN MUIR

To Mrs. Muir

GRAND HOTEL, SAN FRANCISCO, CAL.
July 5th, 1889

DEAR LOUIE:

Here are more snakes that I found in the

"Call" this morning! The curly, crooked things have fairly gained the papers and bid fair to crawl through them all, leaving a track never, I fear, to be obliterated. The "Chronicle's" turn will come next, I fancy, and others will follow. I suppose I ought to write a good post-glacial snake history for the "Bulletin," for just see how much better this lady's snakes are than mine in the "Examiner!" "The biggest snake that ever waved a warning rattle" — almost poetry compared with "John Muir says they don't eat sheep." "Wriggling and rattling aborigines!" I'm ashamed of my ramshackle "Examiner" prose. The Indians "tree the game" and "hang up his snakeship" "beautifully cured" in "sweet fields arrayed in living green," "and very beautiful they are," etc., etc., etc. Oh, dear, how scrawny and lean and mean my snake composition seems! Worse in its brutal simplicity than Johnnie's composition about "A Owl." Well, it must be borne.

I'm pegging away. Saw Upham to-day. Dr. Vincent is at the Palace. Haven't called on him; too busy. Love to all. Don't tell anybody about my poor snakes. Kiss the babies.

J. M.

JOHN MUIR

To Mrs. Muir

Oh, dear Louie, here are more of "them snakes" — "whirled and whizzed like a wheel," "big as my thigh, and head like my fist," all of them, you see, better and bigger than John Muir's.

And when, oh, when, is that fatal interview to end? How many more idiotic articles are to grow out of it? "Muir's Strange Story," "Elephants' bones are sticking in the Yukon River, says geologist John Muir"! "Bering Straits may be bridged because Bering Sea is shallow!" Oh! Oh! if the "Examiner" would only examine its logic!!! Anyhow, I shall take fine cautious care that the critter will not examine me again.

Oh, dear Louie, here's more, and were these letters not accompanied by the documentary evidence, you might almost think that these reptiles were bred and born in alcohol! "The Parson and the Snakes!" Think of that for Sunday reading! What is to become of this nation and the "Examiner"?

It's Johnson, too. Who would have thought it? And think of Longfellow's daughter being signed to such an article!

Well, I'm pegging away, but very slowly. Have got to the thirtieth page. Enough in four days for five minutes' reading. And yet I work hard, but the confounded subject has got so many arms and branches, and I am so cruelly severe on myself as to quality and honesty of work, that I can't go fast. I just get tired in the head and lose all power of criticism until I rest awhile.

It's very noisy here, but I don't notice it. I sleep well, and eat well, and my queer throat feeling has nearly vanished. The weather is very cool. Have to put my overcoat on the bed to reinforce the moderate cover. . . . Goodnight. Love to babies and all.

J. M.

To Mrs. Muir

GRAND HOTEL, SAN FRANCISCO, CAL.
July 11, 1889

DEAR LOUIE:

I was very glad to get your letter to-day, for somehow I was getting anxious about you all as if, instead of a week, I had been gone a year and had nothing but lonesome silence all the time.

You must see, surely, that I am getting literary, for I have just finished writing for the day and it is half-past twelve. Last evening I went to bed at this time and got up at six and have written twenty pages to-day, and feel

proud that now I begin to see the end of this
article that has so long been a black, growling
cloud in my sky. Some of the twenty pages
were pretty good, too, I think. I'll copy a
little bit for you to judge. Of course, you say,
"go to bed." Well, never mind a little writing
more or less, for I'm literary now, and the
fountains flow. Speaking of climate here,
I say:

The Sound region has a fine, fresh, clean climate,
well washed, both winter and summer with copious
rains, and swept with winds and clouds from the
mountains and the sea. Every hidden nook in the
depths of the woods is searched and refreshed, leaving no stagnant air. Beaver-meadows, lake-basins,
and low, willowy bogs are kept wholesome and
sweet, etc.

Again:

The outer sea margin is sublimely drenched and
dashed with ocean brine, the spicy scud sweeping
far inland in times of storm over the bending woods,
the giant trees waving and chanting in hearty accord, as if surely enjoying it all.

Here's another bit: [Quotes what is now the
concluding paragraph of Chapter XVII in
"Steep Trails," beginning "The most charming days here are days of perfect calm," etc.].

Well, I may be dull to-morrow, and then
too, I have to pay a visit to that charming,

entertaining, interesting [dentist] "critter" of files and picks, called Cutlar. So much, I suppose, for cold wind in my jaw. Good-night.
Love to all,

J. M.

To Mrs. Muir

GRAND HOTEL, SAN FRANCISCO
July 12, 1889

DEAR LOUIE:

Twelve and a half o'clock again, so that this letter should be dated the 13th. Was at the dentist's an hour and a half.... Still, have done pretty well, seventeen pages now, eighty-six altogether. Dewing is telegraphing like mad from New York for Muir's manuscript. He will get it ere long. Most of the day's work was prosy, except the last page just now written. Here it is. Speaking of masts sent from Puget Sound, I write:

Thus these trees, stripped of their leaves and branches, are raised again, transplanted and set firmly erect, given roots of iron, bare cross-poles for limbs, and a new foliage of flapping canvas, and then sent to sea, where they go merrily bowing and waving, meeting the same winds that rocked them when they stood at home in the woods. After standing in one place all their lives, they now, like sightseeing tourists, go round the world, meeting many a relative from the old home forest, some, like them-

227

selves, arrayed in broad canvas foliage, others planted close to shore, head downward in the mud, holding wharf platforms aloft to receive the wares of all nations.

Imaginative enough, but I don't know what I'll think of it in the sober morning. I see by the papers that [John] Swett is out of school, for which I am at once glad, sorry, and indignant, if not more.

Love to all. Good-night.

J. M.

To Mrs. Muir

GRAND HOTEL, SAN FRANCISCO
July 14, 1889

DEAR LOUIE:

It is late, but I will write very fast a part of to-day's composition. Here is a bit you will like:

The upper Snoqualmie Fall is about seventy-five feet high, with bouncing rapids at head and foot, set in a romantic dell thatched with dripping mosses and ferns and embowered in dense evergreens and blooming bushes. The road to it leads through ᴉajestic woods with ferns ten feet long beneath the crees, and across a gravelly plain disforested by fire many years ago, where orange lilies abound and bright shiny mats of kinnikinick sprinkled with scarlet berries. From a place called "Hunt's," at the end of the wagon road, a trail leads through fresh dripping woods never dry — Merten, Menzies, and Douglas spruces and maple and Thuja. The ground is covered with the best moss-work of the moist cool woods of the north, made up chiefly of the various species of hypnum, with *Marchantia jungermannia,* etc., in broad sheets and bosses where never a dust particle floated, and where all the flowers, fresh with mist and spray, are wetter than water-lilies.

In the pool at the foot of the fall there is good trout-fishing, and when I was there I saw some bright beauties taken. Never did angler stand in a spot more romantic, but strange it seemed that anyone could give attention to hooking in a place so surpassingly lovely to look at — the enthusiastic rush and song of the fall; the venerable trees overhead leaning forward over the brink like listeners eager to catch every word of their white refreshing waters; the delicate maidenhairs and asploniums, with fronds outspread, gathering the rainbow spray, and the myriads of hooded mosses, every cup fresh and shining.

Here's another kind — starting for Mount Rainier:

The guide was well mounted, Keith had bones to ride, and so had small queer Joe, the camp boy, and I. The rest of the party traveled afoot. The distance to the mountain from Yelm in a straight line is about fifty miles. But by the Mule-and-Yellow-Jacket trail, that we had to follow, it is one hundred miles. For, notwithstanding a part of the trail runs in the air where the wasps work hardest, it is far from being an air-line as commonly understood.

JOHN MUIR

At the Soda Springs near Rainier:

Springs here and there bubble up from the margin of a level marsh, both hot and cold, and likely to tell in some way on all kinds of ailments. At least so we were assured by our kind buxom hostess, who advised us to drink without ceasing from all in turn because "every one of 'em had medicine in it and [was] therefore sure to do good!" All our party were sick, perhaps from indulging too freely in "canned goods" of uncertain age. But whatever the poison might have been, these waters failed to wash it away though we applied them freely and faithfully internally and externally, and almost eternally as one of the party said.

Next morning all who had come through the ordeal of yellow-jackets, ancient meats, and medicinal waters with sufficient strength, resumed the journey to Paradise Valley and Camp of the Clouds, and, strange to say, only two of the party were left behind in bed too sick to walk or ride. Fortunately at this distressing crisis, by the free application of remedies ordinary and extraordinary, such as brandy, paregoric, pain-killer, and Doctor somebody-or-other's Golden Vegetable Wonder, they were both wonderfully relieved and joined us at the Cloud Camp next day, etc., etc., etc.

The dentist is still hovering like an angel or something over me. The writing will be finished to-morrow if all goes well. But punctuation and revision will take some time, and as there is now enough to fill two numbers, I suppose it will have to be cut down a little.

Guess I'll get home Thursday, but will try for Wednesday. Hoping all are well, I go to slumber.

With loving wishes for all

[JOHN MUIR]

To James Davie Butler

MARTINEZ, *September* 1, 1889

MY DEAR OLD FRIEND PROFESSOR BUTLER:

You are not forgotten, but I am stupidly busy, too much so to be able to make good use of odd hours in writing. All the year I have from fifteen to forty men to look after on the ranch, besides the selling of the fruit, and the editing of "Picturesque California," and the writing of half of the work or more. This fall I have to contribute some articles to the "Century Magazine," so you will easily see that I am laden.

It is delightful to see you in your letters with your family and books and glorious surroundings. Every region of the world that has been recently glaciated is pure and wholesome and abounds in fine scenery, and such a region is your northern lake country. How gladly I would cross the mountains to join you all for a summer if I could get away! But much of my old freedom is now lost, though I run away right or wrong at times. Last summer I spent

231

a few months in Washington Territory studying the grand forests of Puget Sound. I then
climbed to the summit of Mount Rainier, about
fifteen thousand feet high, over many miles of
wildly shattered and crevassed glaciers. Some
twenty glaciers flow down the flanks of this
grand icy cone, most of them reaching the
forests ere they melt and give place to roaring
turbid torrents. This summer I made yet another visit to my old Yosemite home, and out
over the mountains at the head of the Tuolumne River. I was accompanied by one of the
editors of the "Century," and had a delightful
time. When we were passing the head of the
Vernal Falls I told our thin, subtle, spiritual
story to the editor.

In a year or two I hope to find a capable
foreman to look after this ranch work, with its
hundreds of tons of grapes, pears, cherries, etc.,
and find time for book-writing and old-time
wanderings in the wilderness. I hope also to
see you ere we part at the end of the day.

You want my manner of life. Well, in short,
I get up about six o'clock and attend to the
farm work, go to bed about nine and read until
midnight. When I have a literary task I leave
home, shut myself up in a room in a San Francisco hotel, go out only for meals, and peg away
awkwardly and laboriously until the wee sma'

hours or thereabouts, working long and hard and accomplishing little. During meals at home my little girls make me tell stories, many of them very long, continued from day to day for a month or two. . . .

Will you be likely to come again to our side of the continent? How I should enjoy your visit! To think of little Henry an alderman! I am glad that you are all well and all together. Greek and ozone holds you in health. . . .

With love to Mrs. Butler and Henry, James, the girls, and thee, old friend, I am ever

Your friend

JOHN MUIR

The event of greatest ultimate significance in the year 1889 was the meeting of Muir with Robert Underwood Johnson, the "Century" editor mentioned in the preceding letter. Muir had been a contributor to the magazine ever since 1878, when it still bore the name of "Scribner's Monthly," and therefore he was one of the men with whom Mr. Johnson made contact upon his arrival in San Francisco. Muir knew personally many of the early California pioneers and so was in a position to give valuable advice in organizing for the "Century" a series of articles under the general title of "Gold-Hunters." This accomplished, it was arranged that Muir was to take Mr. Johnson into the Yosemite Valley and the High Sierra. Beside a camp-fire in the Tuolumne Meadows, Mr. Johnson suggested to Muir that he initiate a project for the establishment of the Yosemite National Park.[1] In order to further the movement it was agreed that he contribute a series of articles to the "Century," setting forth the beauties of the region. Armed with these articles and the public sentiment created by them, Johnson proposed to go before the House Committee on Public Lands to urge the establishment of a national park along the boundaries to be outlined by Muir.

Our country has cause for endless congratulation that the plan was carried out with ability and success. In August and September, 1890, appeared Muir's articles "The Treasures of Yosemite" and "Features of the Proposed Yosemite National Park," both of which aroused strong public support for the project. A bill introduced in Congress by General William Vandever embodied the limits of the park as proposed by Mr. Muir, and on October 1, 1890, the Yosemite National Park became an accomplished fact. The following letters

[1] For a very readable account of this eventful incident see Robert Underwood Johnson's *Remembered Yesterdays* (1923).

relate to the beginning and consummation of this far-sighted beneficial project.

To Mrs. Muir

DEAR LOUIE:

We arrived here about one o'clock after a fine glorious ride through the forests; not much dust, not very hot. The entire trip very delightful and restful and exhilarating. Johnson was charming all the way. I looked out as we passed Martinez about eleven o'clock, and it seemed strange I should ever go past that renowned town. I thought of you all as sleeping and safe. Whatever more of travel I am to do must be done soon, as it grows ever harder to leave my nest and young.

The foothills and all the woods of the Valley are flowery far beyond what I could have looked for, and the sugar pines seemed nobler than ever. Indeed, all seems so new I fancy I could take up the study of these mountain glories with fresh enthusiasm as if I were getting into a sort of second youth, or dotage, or something of that sort. Governor W—— was in our party, big, burly, and somewhat childishly jolly; also some other jolly fellows and fellowesses.

Saw Hill and his fine studio. He has one large Yosemite — very fine, but did not like it so well as the one you saw. He has another Yosemite about the size of the Glacier that I fancy you would all like. It is sold for five hundred dollars, but he would paint another if you wished.

Everybody is good to us. Frank Pixley is here and Ben Truman that wrote about Tropical California. I find old Galen Clark also. He looks well, and is earning a living by carrying passengers about the Valley. Leidig's and Black's old hotels are torn down, so that only Bernards' and the new Stoneman House are left. This last is quite grand; still it has a silly look amid surroundings so massive and sublime. McAuley and the immortal twins still flounder and flourish in the ethereal sky of Glacier Point.

I mean to hire Indians, horses, or something and make a trip to the Lake Tenaya region or Big [Tuolumne] Meadows and Tuolumne Cañon. But how much we will be able to accomplish will depend upon the snow, the legs, and the resolution of the Century. Give my love to everybody at the two houses and kiss and keep the precious babies for me as for thee.

Will probably be home in about a week.

Ever thine   J. M.

WINNING A COMPETENCE

To Robert Underwood Johnson

MARTINEZ, *March* 4, 1890

DEAR MR. JOHNSON:

... The love of Nature among Californians is desperately moderate; consuming enthusiasm almost wholly unknown. Long ago I gave up the floor of Yosemite as a garden, and looked only to the rough taluses and inaccessible or hidden benches and recesses of the walls. All the flowers are wall-flowers now, not only in Yosemite, but to a great extent throughout the length and breadth of the Sierra. Still, the Sierra flora is not yet beyond redemption, and much may be done by the movement you are making.

As to the management, it should, I think, be taken wholly out of the Governor's hands. The office changes too often and must always be more or less mixed with politics in its bearing upon appointments for the Valley. A commission consisting of the President of the University, the President of the State Board of Agriculture, and the President of the Mechanics Institute would, I think, be a vast improvement on the present commission. Perhaps one of the commissioners should be an army officer. Such changes would not be likely, as far as I can see, to provoke any formidable opposition on the part of Californians in

237

general. Taking back the Valley on the part
of the Government would probably be a
troublesome job. . . . Everybody to whom I
have spoken on the subject sees the necessity
of a change, however, in the management, and
would favor such a commission as I have suggested. For my part, I should rather see the
Valley in the hands of the Federal Government. But how glorious a storm of growls and
howls would rend our sunny skies, bursting
forth from every paper in the state, at the out-
rage of the "Century" Editor snatching with
unholy hands, etc., the diadem from California's brow! Then where, oh, where would
be the "supineness" of which you speak?
These Californians now sleeping in apathy,
caring only for what "pays," would then blaze
up as did the Devil when touched by Ithuriel's
spear. A man may not appreciate his wife,
but let her daddie try to take her back!

. . . As to the extension of the grant, the
more we can get into it the better. It should
at least comprehend all the basins of the
streams that pour into the Valley. No great
opposition would be encountered in gaining
this much, as few interests of an antagonistic
character are involved. On the Upper Merced
waters there are no mines or settlements of any
sort, though some few land claims have been

established. These could be easily extinguished by purchase. All the basins draining into Yosemite are really a part of the Valley, as their streams are a part of the Merced. Cut off from its branches, Yosemite is only a stump. However gnarly and picturesque, no tree that is beheaded looks well. But like ants creeping in the furrows of the bark, few of all the visitors to the Valley see more than the stump, and but little of that. To preserve the Valley and leave all its related rocks, waters, forests to fire and sheep and lumbermen is like keeping the grand hall of entrance of a palace for royalty, while all the other apartments from cellar to dome are given up to the common or uncommon use of industry — butcher-shops, vegetable-stalls, liquor-saloons, lumber-yards, etc.

But even the one main hall has a hog-pen in the middle of the floor, and the whole concern seems hopeless as far as destruction and desecration can go. Some of that stink, I'm afraid, has got into the pores of the rocks even. Perhaps it was the oncoming shadow of this desecration that caused the great flood and earthquake — "Nature sighing through all her works giving sign of woe that all was lost." Still something may be done after all. I have indicated the boundary line on the map in dotted line as proposed above. A yet greater extension I have marked on the same map, extending north and south between Lat. 38° and 37° 30′ and from the axis of the range westward about thirty-six or forty miles. This would include three groves of Big Trees, the Tuolumne Cañon, Tuolumne Meadows, and Hetch Hetchy Valley. So large an extension would, of course, meet more opposition. Its boundary lines would not be nearly so natural, while to the westward many claims would be encountered; a few also about Mounts Dana and Warren, where mines have been opened.

Come on out here and take another look at the Cañon. The earthquake taluses are all smooth now and the chaparral is buried, while the river still tosses its crystal arches aloft and the ouzel sings. We would be sure to see some fine avalanches. Come on. I'll go if you will, leaving ranch, reservations, Congress bills, "Century" articles, and all other terrestrial cares and particles. In the meantime I am

Cordially yours

JOHN MUIR

To Robert Underwood Johnson

MARTINEZ, *April 19th*, 1890

MY DEAR MR. JOHNSON:

I hope you have not been put to trouble by the delay of that manuscript. I have been interrupted a thousand times, while writing, by coughs, grippe, business, etc. I suppose you will have to divide the article. I shall write a sketch of the Tuolumne Cañon and Kings River yosemite, also the charming yosemite of the Middle Fork of Kings River, all of which may, I think, be got into one article of ten thousand words or twenty. If you want more than is contained in the manuscript sent you on the peaks and glaciers to the east of Yosemite, let me know and I will try to give what is wanted with the Tuolumne Cañon.

The Yosemite "Century" leaven is working finely, even thus far, throughout California. I enclose a few clippings. The "Bulletin" printed the whole of Mack's "Times" letter on our honest Governor. [Charles Howard] Shinn says that the "Overland" is going out into the battle henceforth in full armor. The "Evening Post" editorial, which I received last night and have just read, is a good one and I will try to have it reprinted. . . .

Mr. Olmsted's paper was, I thought, a little soft in some places, but all the more telling, I suppose, in some directions. Kate, like fate, has been going for the Governor, and I fancy he must be dead or at least paralyzed ere this.

How fares the Bill Vandever? I hope you gained all the basin. If you have, then a thou-

sand trees and flowers will rise up and call you
blessed, besides the other mountain people and
the usual "unborn generations," etc.

In the meantime for what you have already
done I send you a reasonable number of Yosemite thanks, and remain

Very truly your friend

JOHN MUIR

To Mr. and Mrs. John Bidwell

MARTINEZ, CALIFORNIA
April 19th, 1890

DEAR MRS. BIDWELL AND GENERAL:

I've been thinking of you every day since
dear Parry [1] died. It seems as if all the good
flower people, at once great and good, have
died now that Parry has gone — Torrey, Gray,
Kellogg, and Parry. Plenty more botanists
left, but none we have like these. Men more
amiable apart from their intellectual power I
never knew, so perfectly clean and pure they
were — pure as lilies, yet tough and unyielding
in mental fibre as live-oaks. Oh, dear, it makes
me feel lonesome, though many lovely souls
remain. Never shall I forget the charming

[1] Charles C. Parry, 1823–90. Explored and collected on
the Mexican boundary, in the Rocky Mountains, and in
California. The other botanists mentioned are John Torrey,
1796–1873; Asa Gray, 1810–88; and Albert Kellogg, who
died in 1887.

242

evenings I spent with Torrey in Yosemite, and with Gray, after the day's rambles were over and they told stories of their lives, Torrey fondly telling all about Gray, Gray about Torrey, all in one summer; and then, too, they told me about Parry for the first time. And then how fine and how fruitful that trip to Shasta with you! Happy days, not to come again! Then more than a week with Parry around Lake Tahoe in a boat; had him all to myself — precious memories. It seems easy to die when such souls go before. And blessed it is to feel that they have indeed gone before to meet us in turn when our own day is done.

The Scotch have a proverb, "The evenin' brings a' hame." And so, however separated, far or near, the evening of life brings all together at the last. Lovely souls embalmed in a thousand flowers, embalmed in the hearts of their friends, never for a moment does death seem to have had anything to do with them. They seem near, and are near, and as if in bodily sight I wave my hand to them in loving recognition.

Ever yours

JOHN MUIR

JOHN MUIR

To Robert Underwood Johnson

Martinez, *May 8th*, 1890

My dear Mr. Johnson:

. . . As I have urged over and over again, the Yosemite Reservation ought to include all the Yosemite fountains. They all lie in a compact mass of mountains that are glorious scenery, easily accessible from the grand Yosemite center, and are not valuable for any other use than the use of beauty. No other interests would suffer by this extension of the boundary. Only the summit peaks along the axis of the range are possibly gold-bearing, and not a single valuable mine has yet been discovered in them. Most of the basin is a mass of solid granite that will never be available for agriculture, while its forests ought to be preserved. The Big Tuolumne Meadows should also be included, since it forms the central camping-ground for the High Sierra adjacent to the Valley. The Tuolumne Cañon is so closely related to the Yosemite region it should also be included, but whether it is or not will not matter much, since it lies in rugged rocky security, as one of Nature's own reservations.

As to the lower boundary, it should, I think, be extended so far as to include the Big Tree groves below the Valley, thus bringing under Government protection a section of the forest containing specimens of all the principal trees of the Sierra, and which, if left unprotected, will vanish like snow in summer. Some private claims will have to be bought, but the cost will not be great.

Yours truly

JOHN MUIR

While traveling about with Keith in the Northwest during July, 1888, gathering materials for "Picturesque California," Muir was one day watching at Victoria the departure of steamers for northern ports. Instantly he heard the call of the "red gods" of Alaska and began to long for the old adventurous days in the northern wildernesses. "Though it is now ten years since my last visit here," he wrote to his wife in the evening, "Alaska comes back into near view, and if a steamer were to start now it would be hard indeed to keep myself from going aboard. I must spend one year more there at the least. The work I am now doing seems much less interesting and important. . . . Only by going alone in silence, without baggage, can one truly get into the heart of the wilderness. All other travel is mere dust and hotels and baggage and chatter."

The longed-for opportunity came two years later. During the winter of 1890 he had suffered an attack of the grippe which brought on a severe bronchial cough. He tried to wear it out at his desk, but it grew steadily worse. He then, as he used to relate with a twinkle in his eye, decided upon the novel experiment of trying to wear it out by going to Alaska and exploring the upper tributaries of the Muir Glacier. In the following letter we get a glimpse of him after two weeks of active exploration around Glacier Bay.

To Mrs. Muir

GLACIER BAY
CAMP NEAR EASTERN END OF ICE WALL
July 7th, [1890]

DEAR LOUIE:

The steamer Queen is in sight pushing up Muir Inlet through a grand crowd of bergs on which a clear sun is shining. I hope to get a letter from you to hear how you and the little ones and older ones are.

I have had a good instructive and exciting time since last I wrote you by the Elder a week ago. The weather has been fine and I have climbed two mountains that gave grand general views of the immense mountain fountains of the glacier and also of the noble St. Elias Range along the coast mountains, La Pérouse, Crillon, Lituya, and Fairweather. Have got

246

some telling facts on the forest question that has so puzzled me these many years, etc., etc. Have also been making preliminary observations on the motion of the glacier. Loomis and I get on well, and the Reid [1] and Cushing party camped beside us are fine company and energetic workers. They are making a map of the Muir Glacier and Inlet, and intend to make careful and elaborate measurements of its rate of motion, size, etc. They are well supplied with instruments and will no doubt do good work.

I have yet to make a trip round Glacier Bay, to the edge of the forest and over the glacier as far as I can. Probably Reid and Cushing and their companions will go with me. If this weather holds, I shall not encounter serious trouble. Anyhow, I shall do the best I can. I mean to sew the bear skin into a bag, also a blanket and a canvas sheet for the outside. Then, like one of Wanda's caterpillars, I can lie warm on the ice when night overtakes me, or storms rather, for here there is now no night. My cough has gone and my appetite has come, and I feel much better than when I left home. Love to each and all.

If I have time before the steamer leaves I will write to my dear Wanda and Helen. The

---

[1] Professor Harry Fielding Reid.

crowd of visitors are gazing at the grand blue crystal wall, tinged with sunshine.

Ever thine

J. M.

The crowning experience of this Alaska trip was the sled-trip which he made across the upper reaches of the Muir Glacier between the 11th and the 21st of July. Setting out from his little cabin on the terminal moraine, Muir pushed back on the east side of the glacier toward Howling Valley, fifteen miles to the northward, examined and sketched some of the lesser tributaries, then turned to the westward and crossed the glacier near the confluence of the main tributaries, and thence made his way down the west side to the front. No one was willing to share this adventure with him so he faced it, as usual, alone.

Chapter XVIII of "Travels in Alaska" gives, in journal form, an account of Muir's experiences and observations on this trip. To this may be added his description of two incidents as related in fragments of unpublished memoirs:

In the course of this trip I encountered few adventures worth mention apart from the common dangers encountered in crossing crevasses. Large timber wolves were common around Howling

Valley, feeding apparently on the wild goats of the adjacent mountains.

One evening before sundown I camped on the glacier about a mile above the head of the valley, and, sitting on my sled enjoying the wild scenery, I scanned the grassy mountain on the west side above the timber-line through my field glasses, expecting to see a good many wild goats in pastures so fine and wild. I discovered only two or three at the foot of a precipitous bluff, and as they appeared perfectly motionless, and were not lying down, I thought they must be held there by attacking wolves. Next morning, looking again, I found the goats still standing there in front of the cliff, and while eating my breakfast, preparatory to continuing my journey, I heard the dismal long-drawn-out howl of a wolf, soon answered by another and another at greater distances and at short intervals coming nearer and nearer, indicating that they had discovered me and were coming down the mountain to observe me more closely, or perhaps to attack me, for I was told by my Indians while exploring in 1879 and 1880 that these wolves attack either in summer or winter, whether particularly hungry or not; and that no Indian hunter ever ventured far into the woods alone, declaring that wolves were much more dangerous than bears. The nearest wolf had evidently got down to the margin of the glacier, and although I had not yet been able to catch sight of any of them, I made haste to a large square boulder on the ice and sheltered myself from attack from behind, in the same manner as the hunted goats. I had no firearms, but thought I could make a good fight with my Alpine ice axe. This, however, was only a threatened attack, and I went on my journey, though keeping a careful watch to see whether I was followed.

At noon, reaching the confluence of the eastmost of the great tributaries and observing that the ice to the westward was closely crevassed, I concluded to spend the rest of the day in ascending what is now called Snow Dome, a mountain about three thousand feet high, to scan the whole width of the glacier and choose the route that promised the fewest difficulties. The day was clear and I took the bearings of what seemed to be the best route and recorded them in my notebook so that in case I should be stopped by a blinding snowstorm, or impassable labyrinth of crevasses, I might be able to retrace my way by compass.

In descending the mountain to my sled camp on the ice I tried to shorten the way by sliding down a smooth steep fluting groove nicely lined with snow; but in looking carefully I discovered a bluish spot a few hundred feet below the head, which I feared indicated ice beneath the immediate surface of the snow; but inasmuch as there were no heavy boulders at the foot of the slope, but only a talus of small pieces an inch or two in diameter, derived from disintegrating metamorphic slates, lying at as steep an angle as they could rest, I felt confident that even if I should lose control of myself and be shot swiftly into them, there would be no risk of broken bones. I decided to encounter the adventure. Down I glided in a smooth comfortable swish until I struck the blue spot. There I suddenly lost control of myself and went rolling and bouncing like a boulder until stopped by plashing into the loose gravelly delta.

WINNING A COMPETENCE

As soon as I found my legs and senses I was startled by a wild, piercing, exulting, demoniac yell, as if a pursuing assassin long on my trail were screaming: "I've got you at last." I first imagined that the wretch might be an Indian, but could not believe that Indians, who are afraid of glaciers, could be tempted to venture so far into the icy solitude. The mystery was quickly solved when a raven descended like a thunderbolt from the sky and alighted on a jag of a rock within twenty or thirty feet of me. While soaring invisible in the sky, I presume that he had been watching me all day, and at the same time keeping an outlook for wild goats, which were sometimes driven over the cliffs by the wolves. Anyhow, no sooner had I fallen, though not a wing had been seen in all the clear mountain sky, than I had been seen by these black hunters who now were eagerly looking me over and seemed sure of a meal. The explanation was complete, and as they eyed me with a hungry longing stare I simply called to them: "Not yet!"

CHAPTER XVI

THE sudden death of Dr. Strentzel on the last
of October, 1890, brought in its train a change
of residence for the Muir family. At the time
of his marriage, Muir had first rented and later
purchased from his father-in-law the upper
part of the Alhambra ranch. Dr. Strentzel
thereupon left the old home to his daughter,
and removed to the lower half of the ranch,
where he and his wife built and occupied a
large new frame house on a sightly hill-top.
Since Mrs. Strentzel, after her husband's death,
needed the care of her daughter, the Muirs
left the upper ranch home, in which they had
lived for ten years, and moved to the more
spacious, but on the whole less comfortable,
house which thereafter became known as the
Muir residence.

At the beginning of his father-in-law's illness,
Muir was on the point of starting on a trip up
the Kings River Cañon in order to secure additional material for a "Century" article. The
project, naturally, had to be abandoned. "It

252

is now so snowy and late," he wrote to Mr. Johnson in November, "I fear I shall not be able to get into the cañons this season. I think, however, that I can write the article from my old notes. I made three trips through the Kings River Cañon, and one through the wild Middle Fork Cañon with its charming Yosemite." The deeper purpose of this article was to serve as a starter for another national park. It means that two weeks after the successful issue of the campaign for the creation of the Yosemite National Park, Muir, ably assisted by Mr. R. U. Johnson, began to advocate the enlargement of the Sequoia National Park so as to embrace the Kings River region and the Kaweah and Tule Sequoia groves. John W. Noble was then Secretary of the Interior (1889–93), and it is fair to say that, measured by the magnitude of benefits conferred upon the country, no more useful incumbent has ever filled that office. He at once declared himself ready to withdraw the region from entry if Muir would delimit upon Land Office maps the territory that should go into a park.

"I am going to San Francisco this morning," Muir wrote to Johnson on May 13, 1891, "and will get the best map I can and will draw the boundaries of the proposed new park. . . . This map I shall send you to-morrow." During the same month he made another trip up the cañon of the Kings River, particularly the South Fork, and afterwards wrote for the "Century"[1] an unusually telling description of it under the title of "A Rival of the Yosemite." "This region," he said in concluding the article, "contains no mines of consequence; it is too high and too rocky for agriculture, and even the lumber industry need suffer no unreasonable restriction. Let our law-givers then make haste, before it is too late, to save this surpassingly glorious region for the recreation and well-being of humanity, and the world will rise up and call them blessed."

Advance sheets of the article, placed in the hands of Secretary Noble, moved him to bring Muir's proposal to the immediate attention of Congress with the recommendation of "favorable consideration and action." But over thirty years have passed since then, and Muir's dream of good still awaits realization at the hands of our law-givers. The Roosevelt-Sequoia National Park bill, now before Congress, is substantially Muir's original proposal, and fittingly recognizes the invaluable service which Theodore Roosevelt rendered to the cause of forests and parks, partly in coöperation with Muir, as shown in a succeeding chap-

[1] November, 1891.

ter. This bill should be speedily passed, over the paltering objections of adventurers who place their private farthing schemes above the immeasurable public benefit of a national playground that not only rivals the already overcrowded Yosemite in beauty and spaciousness, but is, in the words of Muir, "a veritable song of God."

Muir had now reached the stage in his career when he had not only the desire, but also the power, to translate his nature enthusiasms into social service. Increasing numbers of progressive citizens, both East and West, were looking to him for leadership when corrupt or incompetent custodians of the public domain needed to be brought to the bar of public opinion. And there was much of this work to be done by a man who was not afraid to stand up under fire. Muir's courageous and outspoken criticism of the mismanagement of Yosemite Valley by the State Commissioners aroused demands in Washington for an investigation of the abuses and a recession of the Valley to the Federal Government as part of the Yosemite National Park.

Since there was likelihood of a stiff battle over this and other matters, Muir's friends, particularly Mr. R. U. Johnson, urged him to get behind him a supporting organization on the Pacific Coast through which men of kindred aims could present a united front. This led to the formal organization of the Sierra Club on the 4th of June, 1892. It declared its purpose to be a double one: first, "to explore, enjoy, and render accessible the mountain regions of the Pacific Coast," and "to publish authentic information concerning them"; and, second, "to enlist the support and coöperation of the people and government in preserving the forests and other natural features of the Sierra Nevada Mountains." The Club, in short, was formed with two sets of aims, and it gathered into its membership on the one hand persons who were primarily lovers of mountains and mountaineering, and on the other hand those whose first interest was to conserve the forests and other natural features for future generations. In no single individual were both these interests better represented than in the person of Muir, who became the first president of the Club, and held the office continuously until his death twenty-two years later. Among the men who deserve to be remembered in connection with the organization and early conservation activities of the Club were Warren Olney, Sr., and Professors Joseph LeConte, J. H. Senger, William Dallam Armes, and Cornelius Beach Bradley.

One of the first important services of the

Club was its successful opposition to the so-called "Caminetti Bill," a loosely drawn measure introduced into Congress in 1892 with the object of altering the boundaries of the Yosemite National Park in such a way as to eliminate about three hundred alleged mining claims, and other large areas desired by stockmen and lumbermen. The bill underwent various modifications, and finally, in 1894, it was proposed to authorize the Secretary of the Interior to make the alterations. Muir's public interviews and the organized resistance of the Club, fortunately, repelled this contemplated raid upon the new park; for watchful guardians of the public domain regarded it as of ill omen that Secretary Hoke Smith, who had succeeded John W. Noble in 1893, reported that he had no objection to interpose to the bill's passage.

It should be recorded to the lasting honor of President Harrison and the Honorable John W. Noble that they established the first forest reserves under an Act of Congress [1] passed March 3, 1891. It was the first real recognition of the practical value of forests in conserving

[1] The authorization of the President to make forest reservations is contained in a clause inserted in the Sundry Civil Bill of that year. The credit of it belongs to Edward A. Bowers ,whose name deserves to be held in remembrance for other noble services to the cause of forest conservation.

water-flow at the sources of rivers. The Boone and Crockett Club on April 8, 1891, made it the occasion of a special vote of thanks addressed to the President and Secretary Noble on the ground that "this society recognizes in these actions the most important steps taken in recent years for the preservation of our forests." Though not so recognized at the time, it was a happy augury for the future that the resolution was inspired, signed, and transmitted by Theodore Roosevelt.

Among the few surviving Muir letters of the early nineties is the following one to his Indianapolis friend Mrs. Graydon, who had expressed a hope that, if he returned to her home city during the current year, she might be able to arrange for a social evening with the poet James Whitcomb Riley.

To Mrs. Mary Merrill Graydon

MARTINEZ, *February* 28, 1893

MY DEAR MRS. GRAYDON:

I am glad to hear from you once more. You say you thought on account of long silence we might be dead, but the worst that could be fairly said is "not dead but sleeping" — hardly even this, for, however silent, sound friendship never sleeps, no matter how seldom paper letters fly between.

My heart aches about Janet — one of the sad, sad, sore cases that no human wisdom can explain. We can only look on the other side through tears and grief and pain and see that pleasure surpasses the pain, good the evil, and that, after all, Divine love is the sublime boss of the universe.

The children greatly enjoy the [James Whitcomb] Riley book you so kindly sent. I saw Mr. Riley for a moment at the close of one of his lectures in San Francisco, but I had to awkwardly introduce myself, and he evidently couldn't think who I was. Professor [David Starr] Jordan, who happened to be standing near, though I had not seen him, surprised me by saying, "Mr. Riley, this man is the author of the Muir Glacier." I invited Mr. Riley to make us a visit at the ranch, but his engagements, I suppose, prevented even had he cared to accept, and so I failed to see him save in his lecture.

I remember my visit to your home with pure pleasure, and shall not forget the kindness you bestowed, as shown in so many ways. As to coming again this year, I thank you for the invitation, but the way is not open so far as I can see just now.

I think with Mr. Jackson that Henry Riley [1]

[1] One of his fellow workmen in the wagon factory in

shows forth one of the good sides of human nature in so vividly remembering the little I did for him so long ago. I send by mail with this letter one of the volumes of "Picturesque California" for him in your care, as I do not know his address. Merrill Moores knows him, and he can give him notice to call for the book. It contains one of my articles on Washington, and you are at liberty to open and read it if you wish.

Katie [Graydon] I have not seen since she went to Oakland, though only two hours away. But I know she is busy and happy through letters and friends. I mean to try to pass a night at McChesney's, and see her and find out all about her works and ways. The children and all of us remember her stay with us as a great blessing.

Remember me to the Hendricks family, good and wholesome as sunshine, to the venerable Mr. Jackson, and all the grand Merrill family, your girls in particular, with every one of whom I fell in love, and believe me, noisy or silent,

Ever your friend

JOHN MUIR

Indianapolis, 1866–67. "Your name is a household word with us," wrote Mr. Riley in acknowledging Muir's gift. "The world has traveled on at a great rate in the twenty-five years since you and I made wheels together, and you, I am proud to say, have traveled with it."

TREES AND TRAVEL

Muir had long cherished the intention of returning to Scotland in order to compare his boyhood memories of the dingles and dells of his native land with what he described, before the California period of his life, as "all the other less important parts of our world." In the spring of 1893 he proceeded to carry out the plan. The well-remembered charms of the old landscapes were still there, but he was to find that his standards of comparison had been changed by the Sierra Nevada. On the way East he paid a visit to his mother in Wisconsin, lingered some days at the Chicago World's Fair, and then made his first acquaintance with the social and literary life of New York and Boston. The following letters give some hint of the rich harvest of lasting friendships which he reaped during his eastern sojourn.

To Mrs. Muir

3420 Michigan Ave., Chicago
May 29, 1893, 9 a.m.

Dear Louie:

I leave for New York this evening at five o'clock and arrive there to-morrow evening at seven, when I expect to find a letter from you in care of Johnson at the "Century" Editorial Rooms. The Sellers' beautiful home has been made heartily my own, and they have left

nothing undone they could think of that would
in any way add to my enjoyment. Under their
guidance I have been at the [World's] Fair
every day, and have seen the best of it, though
months would be required to see it all.

You know I called it a "cosmopolitan rat's [1]
nest," containing much rubbish and commonplace stuff as well as things novel and precious.
Well, now that I have seen it, it seems just
such a rat's nest still, and what, do you think,
was the first thing I saw when I entered the
nearest of the huge buildings? A high rat's
nest in a glass case about eight feet square,
with stuffed wood rats looking out from the
mass of sticks and leaves, etc., natural as life!
So you see, as usual, I am "always right."

I most enjoyed the art galleries. There are
about eighteen acres of paintings by every
nation under the sun, and I *wandered* and *gazed*
until I was ready to fall down with utter exhaustion. The Art Gallery of the California
building is quite small and of little significance,
not more than a dozen or two of paintings all
told: four by Keith, not his best, and four by
Hill, not his best, and a few others of no special
character by others, except a good small one

[1] Refers to the wood rat or pack rat (*Neotoma*) which
builds large mound-like nests and "packs" into them all
kinds of amusing odds and ends.

by Yelland. But the National Galleries are perfectly overwhelming in grandeur and bulk and variety, and years would be required to make even the most meager curiosity of a criticism.

The outside view of the buildings is grand and also beautiful. For the best architects have done their best in building them, while Frederick Law Olmsted laid out the grounds. Last night the buildings and terraces and fountains along the canals were illuminated by tens of thousands of electric lights arranged along miles of lines of gables, domes, and cornices, with glorious effect. It was all fairyland on a colossal scale and would have made the Queen of Sheba and poor Solomon in all their glory feel sick with helpless envy. I wished a hundred times that you and the children and Grandma could have seen it all, and only the feeling that Helen would have been made sick with excitement prevented me from sending for you.

I hope Helen is well and then all will be well. I have worked at my article at odd times now and then, but it still remains to be finished at the " Century " rooms. Tell the children I'll write them from New York to-morrow or next day. Love to all. Good-bye.

Ever yours

JOHN MUIR

JOHN MUIR

To Mrs. Muir

THE THORNDIKE
BOSTON, MASS., *June* 12, 1893

DEAR LOUIE:

I have been so crowded and overladen with enjoyments lately that I have lost trace of time and have so much to tell you I scarce know where and how to begin. When I reached New York I called on Johnson, and told him I meant to shut myself up in a room and finish my articles and then go with Keith to Europe. But he paid no attention to either my hurry or Keith's, and quietly ordered me around and took possession of me.

NEW YORK, *June* 13

DEAR LOUIE:

I was suddenly interrupted by a whole lot of new people, visits, dinners, champagne, etc., and have just got back to New York by a night boat by way of Fall River. So I begin again. Perhaps this is the 13th, Tuesday, for I lose all track of time.

First I was introduced to all the " Century " people, with their friends also as they came in. Dined with Johnson first. Mrs. J. is a bright, keen, accomplished woman. . . .

Saw Burroughs the second day. He had been at a Walt Whitman Club the night before, and had made a speech, eaten a big dinner, and had a headache. So he seemed tired, and gave no sign of his fine qualities. I chatted an hour with him and tried to make him go to Europe with me. The "Century" men offered him five hundred dollars for some articles on our trip as an inducement, but he answered to-day by letter that he could not go, he must be free when he went, that he would above all things like to go with me, etc., but circumstances would not allow it. The "circumstances" barring the way are his wife. I can hardly say I have seen him at all.

Dined another day with [Richard Watson] Gilder. He is charming every way, and has a charming home and family. . . . I also dined in grand style at Mr. Pinchot's, whose son is studying forestry. The home is at Gramercy Park, New York. Here and at many other places I had to tell the story of the minister's dog. Everybody seems to think it wonderful for the views it gives of the terrible crevasses of the glaciers as well as for the recognition of danger and the fear and joy of the dog. I must have told it at least twelve times at the request of Johnson or others who had previously heard it. I told Johnson I meant to write it out for "St. Nicholas," but he says it is too good for "St. Nick," and he wants it for the "Century" as a separate article. When I am telling it at the dinner-tables, it is curious to see how eagerly the liveried servants listen from behind screens, half-closed doors, etc.

Almost every day in town here I have been called out to lunch and dinner at the clubs and soon have a crowd of notables about me. I had no idea I was so well known, considering how little I have written. The trip up the Hudson was delightful. Went as far as West Point, to Castle Crags, the residence of the [Henry Fairfield] Osborns. Charming drives in the green flowery woods, and, strange to say, all the views are familiar, for the landscapes are all freshly glacial. Not a line in any of the scenery that is not a glacial line. The same is true of all the region hereabouts. I found glacial scoring on the rocks of Central Park even.

Last Wednesday evening Johnson and I started for Boston, and we got back this morning, making the trip both ways in the night to economize time. After looking at the famous buildings, parks, monuments, etc., we took the train for Concord, wandered through the famous Emerson village, dined with Emerson's son, visited the Concord Bridge, where the first blood of the Revolution was shed, and where "the shot was fired heard round the world." Went through lovely, ferny, flowery woods and meadows to the hill cemetery and laid flowers

on Thoreau's and Emerson's graves. I think it
is the most beautiful graveyard I ever saw. It
is on a hill perhaps one hundred and fifty feet
high in the woods of pine, oak, beech, maple,
etc., and all the ground is flowery. Thoreau
lies with his father, mother, and brother not
far from Emerson and Hawthorne. Emerson
lies between two white pine trees, one at his
head, the other at [his] feet, and instead of a
mere tombstone or monument there is a mass
of white quartz rugged and angular, wholly un-
cut, just as it was blasted from the ledge. I
don't know where it was obtained. There is not
a single letter or word on this grand natural
monument. It seems to have been dropped
there by a glacier, and the soil he sleeps in is
glacial drift almost wholly unchanged since
first this country saw the light at the close of
the glacial period. There are many other graves
here, though it is not one of the old cemeteries.
Not one of them is raised above ground. Sweet
kindly Mother Earth has taken them back to
her bosom whence they came. I did not imagine I would be so moved at sight of the resting-
places of these grand men as I found I was, and
I could not help thinking how glad I would be
to feel sure that I would also rest here. But I
suppose it cannot be, for Mother will be in
Portage. . . .

After leaving Thoreau and Emerson, we walked through the woods to Walden Pond. It is a beautiful lake about half a mile long, fairly embosomed like a bright dark eye in wooded hills of smooth moraine gravel and sand, and with a rich leafy undergrowth of huckleberry, willow, and young oak bushes, etc., and grass and flowers in rich variety. No wonder Thoreau lived here two years. I could have enjoyed living here two hundred years or two thousand. It is only about one and a half or two miles from Concord, a mere saunter, and how people should regard Thoreau as a hermit on account of his little delightful stay here I cannot guess.

We visited also Emerson's home and were shown through the house. It is just as he left it, his study, books, chair, bed, etc., and all the paintings and engravings gathered in his foreign travels. Also saw Thoreau's village residence and Hawthorne's old manse and other home near Emerson's. At six o'clock we got back from Walden to young Emerson's father-in-law's place in Concord and dined with the family and Edward Waldo Emerson. The latter is very like his father — rather tall, slender, and with his father's sweet perennial smile. Nothing could be more cordial and loving than his reception of me. When we called at the house, one of the interesting old colonial

ones, he was not in, and we were received by
his father-in-law, a college mate of Thoreau,
who knew Thoreau all his life. The old man
was sitting on the porch when we called. Johnson introduced himself, and asked if this was
Judge Keyes, etc. The old gentleman kept his
seat and seemed, I thought, a little cold and
careless in his manner. But when Johnson said,
"This is Mr. Muir," he jumped up and said
excitedly, "John Muir! Is this John Muir?"
and seized me as if I were a long-lost son. He
declared he had known me always, and that
my name was a household word. Then he took
us into the house, gave us refreshments, cider,
etc., introduced us to his wife, a charming old-
fashioned lady, who also took me for a son.
Then we were guided about the town and
shown all the famous homes and places. But
I must hurry on or I will be making a book of it.

We went back to Boston that night on a late
train, though they wanted to keep us, and next
day went to Professor Sargent's grand place,
where we had a perfectly wonderful time for
several days. This is the finest mansion and
grounds I ever saw. The house is about two
hundred feet long with immense verandas
trimmed with huge flowers and vines, standing
in the midst of fifty acres of lawns, groves, wild
woods of pine, hemlock, maple, beech, hickory,

etc., and all kinds of underbrush and wild flowers and cultivated flowers — acres of rhododendrons twelve feet high in full bloom, and a pond covered with lilies, etc., all the ground waving, hill and dale, and clad in the full summer dress of the region, trimmed with exquisite taste.

The servants are in livery, and everything is fine about the house and in it, but Mr. and Mrs. Sargent are the most cordial and unaffected people imaginable, and in a few minutes I was at my ease and at home, sauntering where I liked, doing what I liked, and making the house my own. Here we had grand dinners, formal and informal, and here I told my dog story, I don't know how often, and described glaciers and their works. Here, the last day, I dined with Dana, of the New York "Sun," and Styles, of the "Forest and Stream," Parsons, the Superintendent of Central Park, and Matthews, Mayor of Boston. Yesterday the Mayor came with carriages and drove us through the public parks and the most interesting streets of Boston, and he and Mr. and Mrs. Sargent drove to the station and saw us off. While making Sargent's our headquarters, Mr. Johnson took me to Cambridge, where we saw the classic old shades of learning, found Royce, who guided us, saw Porter, and the historian Parkman, etc., etc. We called at Eliot's house, but he was away.

We also went to the seaside at Manchester, forty miles or so from Boston, to visit Mrs. [James T.] Fields, a charming old lady, and how good a time! Sarah Orne Jewett was there, and all was delightful. Here, of course, Johnson made me tell that dog story as if that were the main result of glacial action and all my studies, but I got in a good deal of ice-work better than this, and never had better listeners.

Judge Howland, whom I met in Yosemite with a party who had a special car, came in since I began this letter to invite me to a dinner to-morrow evening with a lot of his friends. I must get that article done and set the day of sailing for Europe, or I won't get away at all. This makes three dinners ahead already. I fear the tail of my article will be of another color from the body. Johnson has been most devoted to me ever since I arrived, and I can't make him stop. I think I told you the "Century" wants to publish my book. They also want me to write articles from Europe.

Must stop. Love to all. How glad I was to get Wanda's long good letter this morning, dated June 2! All letters in Johnson's care will find me wherever I go, here or in Europe.

[JOHN MUIR]

JOHN MUIR

To Mrs. Muir

DUNBAR, SCOTLAND
July 6, 1893

DEAR LOUIE:

I left Liverpool Monday morning, reached
Edinburgh early the same day, went to a hotel,
and then went to the old book-publisher David
Douglas, to whom Johnson had given me a
letter. He is a very solemn-looking, dignified
old Scotchman of the old school, an intimate
friend and crony of John Brown, who wrote
"Rab and His Friends," knew Hugh Miller,
Walter Scott, and indeed all the literary men,
and was the publisher of Dean Ramsay's
"Reminiscences of Scottish Life and Character," etc. He had heard of me through my
writings, and, after he knew who I was, burst
forth into the warmest cordiality and became a
perfect gushing fountain of fun, humor, and
stories of the old Scotch writers. Tuesday
morning he took me in hand, and led me over
Edinburgh, took me to all the famous places
celebrated in Scott's novels, went around the
Calton Hill and the Castle, into the old
churches so full of associations, to Queen
Mary's Palace Museum, and I don't know how
many other places.

In the evening I dined with him, and had a
glorious time. He showed me his literary treas-

ures and curiosities, told endless anecdotes of
John Brown, Walter Scott, Hugh Miller, etc.,
while I, of course, told my icy tales until very
late — or early — the most wonderful night
as far as humanity is concerned I ever had in
the world. Yesterday forenoon he took me out
for another walk and filled me with more wonders. His kindness and warmth of heart, once
his confidence is gained, are boundless. From
feeling lonely and a stranger in my own native
land, he brought me back into quick and living
contact with it, and now I am a Scotchman
and at home again.

In the afternoon I took the train for Dunbar
and in an hour was in my own old town. There
was no carriage from the Lorne Hotel that
used to be our home, so I took the one from the
St. George, which I remember well as Cossar's
Inn that I passed every day on my way to
school. But I'm going to the Lorne, if for
nothing else [than] to take a look at that
dormer window I climbed in my nightgown,
to see what kind of an adventure it really
was.

I sauntered down the street and went into a
store on which I saw the sign Melville, and soon
found that the proprietor was an old playmate
of mine, and he was, of course, delighted to see
me. He had been reading my articles, and said

he had taken great pride in tracing my progress through the far-off wildernesses. Then I went to William Comb, mother's old friend, who was greatly surprised, no doubt, to see that I had changed in forty years. "And this is Johnnie Muir! Bless me, when I saw ye last ye were naething but a small mischievous lad." He is very deaf, unfortunately, and was very busy. I am to see him again to-day.

Next I went in search of Mrs. Lunam, my cousin, and found her and her daughter in a very pretty home half a mile from town. They were very cordial, and are determined to get me away from the hotel. I spent the evening there talking family affairs, auld lang syne, glaciers, wild gardens, adventures, etc., till after eleven, then returned to the hotel.

Here are a few flowers that I picked on the Castle hill on my walk with Douglas, for Helen and Wanda. I pray Heaven in the midst of my pleasure that you are all well. Edinburgh is, apart from its glorious historical associations, far the most beautiful town I ever saw. I cannot conceive how it could be more beautiful. In the very heart of it rises the great Castle hill, glacier-sculptured and wild like a bit of Alaska in the midst of the most beautiful architecture to be found in the world. I wish you could see it, and you will when the babies grow up. . . .

Good-bye.

J. M.

To Helen Muir

DUNBAR, SCOTLAND
July 12, 1893

HELLO, MIDGE, MY SWEET HELEN:

Are you all right? I'm in Scotland now, where I used to live when I was a little boy, and I saw the places where I used to play and the house I used to live in. I remember it pretty well, and the school where the teacher used to whip me so much, though I tried to be good all the time and learn my lessons. The round tower on the hill in the picture at the beginning of the letter is one of the places I used to play at on Saturdays when there was no school.

Here is a little sprig of heather a man gave me yesterday and another for Wanda. The heather is just beginning to come into bloom. I have not seen any of it growing yet, and I don't know where the man found it. But I'm going pretty soon up the mountains, and then I'll find lots of it, and won't it be lovely, miles and miles of it, covering whole mountains and making them look purple. I think I must camp out in the heather.

I'm going to come home just as soon as I get back from Switzerland, about the time the grapes are ripe, I expect. I wish I could see you, my little love.

Your papa

JOHN MUIR

To Mrs. Muir

DUNBAR, SCOTLAND
July 12, 1893

DEAR LOUIE:

I have been here nearly a week and have seen most of my old haunts and playgrounds, and more than I expected of my boy playmates. Of course it is all very interesting, and I have enjoyed it more than I anticipated. Dunbar is an interesting place to anybody, beautifully located on a plateau above the sea and with a background of beautiful hills and dales, green fields in the very highest state of cultivation, and many belts and blocks of woods so arranged as to appear natural. I have had a good many rides and walks into the country among the fine farms and towns and old castles, and had long talks with people who listen with wonder to the stories of California and far Alaska.

I suppose, of course, you have received my Edinburgh letter telling the fine time with

David Douglas. I mean to leave here next
Monday for the Highlands, and then go to
Norway and Switzerland.

I am stopping with my cousin, who, with
her daughter, lives in a handsome cottage just
outside of town. They are very cordial and
take me to all the best places and people, and
pet me in grand style, but I must on and away
or my vacation time will be past ere I leave
Scotland.

At Haddington I visited Jeanie Welch
Carlyle's grave in the old abbey. Here are two
daisies, or gowans, that grew beside it.

I was on a visit yesterday to a farmer's family three miles from town — friends of the Lunams. This was a fine specimen of the gentle-
man-farmers' places and people in this, the
best part of Scotland. How fine the grounds
are, and the buildings and the people! . . .

I begin to think I shall not see Keith again
until I get back, except by accident, for I have
no time to hunt him up; but anyhow I am not
so lonesome as I was and with David Douglas's
assistance will make out to find my way to fair
advantage.

The weather here reminds me of Alaska, cool
and rather damp. Nothing can surpass the
exquisite fineness and wealth of the farm crops,
while the modulation of the ground stretching

away from the rocky, foamy coast to the green Lammermoor Hills is charming. Among other famous places I visited the old castle of the Bride of Lammermoor and the field of the battle of Dunbar. Besides, I find fine glacial studies everywhere.

I fondly hope you are all well while I am cut off from news.

Ever yours

JOHN MUIR

To Wanda Muir

DUNBAR, SCOTLAND
July 13, 1893

DEAR WANDA:

It is about ten o'clock in the forenoon here, but no doubt you are still asleep, for it is about midnight at Martinez, and sometimes when it is to-day here it is yesterday in California on account of being on opposite sides of the round world. But one's thoughts travel fast, and I seem to be in California whenever I think of you and Helen. I suppose you are busy with your lessons and peaches, peaches especially. You are now a big girl, almost a woman, and you must mind your lessons and get in a good store of the best words of the best people while your memory is retentive, and then you will go through the world rich.

278

Ask mother to give you lessons to commit to memory every day. Mostly the sayings of Christ in the gospels and selections from the poets. Find the hymn of praise in Paradise Lost "These are thy glorious works, Parent of Good, Almighty," and learn it well.

Last evening, after writing to Helen, I took a walk with Maggie Lunam along the shore on the rocks where I played when a boy. The waves made a grand show breaking in sheets and sheaves of foam, and grand songs, the same old songs they sang to me in my childhood, and I seemed a boy again and all the long eventful years in America were forgotten while I was filled with that glorious ocean psalm.

Tell Maggie I'm going to-day to see Miss Jaffry, the minister's daughter who went to school with us. And tell mamma that the girl Agnes Purns, that could outrun me, married a minister and is now a widow living near Prestonpans. I may see her. Good-bye, dear. Give my love to grandma and everybody.

Your loving father
JOHN MUIR

JOHN MUIR

To Mrs. Muir

STATION HOTEL, OBAN, N.B.
July 22, 1893

DEAR LOUIE:

I stayed about ten days at Dunbar, thinking I should not slight my old home and cousins. I found an extra cousin in Dunbar, Jane Mather, that I had not before heard of, and she is one to be proud of, as are the Lunams. I also found a few of the old schoolmates, now gray old men, older-looking, I think, and grayer than I, though I have led so hard a life. I went with Maggie Lunam to the old schoolhouse where I was so industriously thrashed half a century ago. The present teacher, Mr. Dick, got the school two years after I left, and has held it ever since. He had been reading the "Century," and was greatly interested. I dined with him and at table one of the guests said, "Mr. Dick, don't you wish you had the immortal glory of having whipped John Muir?"

I made many short trips into the country, along the shores, about the old castle, etc. Then I went back to Edinburgh, and then to Dumfries, Burns's country for some years, where I found another cousin, Susan Gilroy, with whom I had a good time. Then I went through Glasgow to Stirling, where I had a charming walk about the castle and saw the famous battle-field, Bruce's and Wallace's monuments, and glacial action.

This morning I left Stirling and went to Callander, thence to Inversnaid by coach and boat, by the Trossachs and Loch Katrine, thence through Loch Lomond and the mountains to a railroad and on to this charming Oban. I have just arrived this day on Lochs Katrine and Lomond, and the drives through the passes and over the mountains made famous by Scott in the "Lady of the Lake" will be long remembered — "Ower the muir amang the heather."

The heather is just coming into bloom and it is glorious. Wish I could camp in it a month. All the scenery is interesting, but nothing like Alaska or California in grandeur. To-morrow I'm going back to Edinburgh and next morning intend to start for Norway, where I will write.

Possibly I may not be able to catch the boat, but guess I will. Thence I'll return to Edinburgh and then go to Switzerland. Love to all. Dear Wanda and Helen, here is some bell heather for you.

Ever yours

J. M.

To Mrs. Muir

EUSTON HOTEL, LONDON
September 1, 1893

DEAR LOUIE:

Yesterday afternoon I went to the home of Sir Joseph Hooker at Sunningdale with him and his family.... Now I am done with London and shall take the morning express to Edinburgh to-morrow, go thence to the Highlands and see the heather in full bloom, visit some friends, and go back to Dunbar for a day....

I have been at so many places and have seen so much that is new, the time seems immensely long since I left you. Sir Joseph and his lady were very cordial. They have a charming country residence, far wilder and more retired than ours, though within twenty-five miles of London. We had a long delightful talk last evening on science and scientific men, and this forenoon and afternoon long walks and talks through the grounds and over the adjacent hills. Altogether this has been far the most interesting day I have had since leaving home. I never knew before that Sir Joseph had accompanied Ross in his famous Antarctic expedition as naturalist. He showed me a large number of sketches he made of the great ice-cap, etc., and gave me many facts concerning that little known end of the world entirely new to me. Long talks, too, about Huxley, Tyndall, Darwin, Sir Charles Lyell, Asa Gray, etc. My, what a time we had! I never before knew either that he had received the Copley Medal, the highest scientific honor in the world.

I hope to hear from you again before sailing, as I shall order my mail forwarded from London the last thing. I feel that my trip is now all but done, though I have a good many people to see and small things to do, ere I leave. The hills in full heather bloom, however, is not a small thing.

Much love   JOHN MUIR

To Helen Muir

KILLARNEY, IRELAND
September 7, 1893

MY OWN DEAR HELEN:

After papa left London he went to the top of Scotland to a place called Thurso, where a queer Scotch geologist [Robert Dick] once lived; hundreds of miles thereabouts were covered with heather in full bloom. Then I went to Inverness and down the canal to Oban again. Then to Glasgow and then to Ireland to see the beautiful bogs and lakes and Macgillicuddy's Reeks. Now I must make haste tomorrow back towards Scotland and get ready to sail to New York on the big ship Campania, which leaves Liverpool on the sixteenth day of this month, and then I'll soon see darling Helen again. Papa is tired traveling so much, and wishes he was home again, though he has seen many beautiful and wonderful places, and learned a good deal about glaciers and mountains and things. It is very late, and I must go to bed. Kiss everybody for me, my sweet darling, and soon I'll be home.

[JOHN MUIR]

To James and Hardy Hay

CUNARD ROYAL MAIL STEAMSHIP CAMPANIA
September 16, 1893

James and Hardy Hay
and all the glorious company
about them, young and old.

DEAR COUSINS:

I am now fairly aff and awa' from the old home to the new, from friends to friends, and soon the braid sea will again roar between us; but be assured, however far I go in sunny California or icy Alaska, I shall never cease to love and admire you, and I hope that now and then you will think of your lonely kinsman, whether in my bright home in the Golden State or plodding after God's glorious glaciers in the storm-beaten mountains of the North.

TREES AND TRAVEL

Among all the memories that I carry away with me this eventful summer none stand out in so divine a light as the friends I have found among my own kith and kin: Hays, Mathers, Lunams, Gilroys. In particular I have enjoyed and admired the days spent with the Lunams and you Hays. Happy, Godful homes; again and again while with you I repeated to myself those lines of Burns: "From scenes like these old Scotia's grandeur springs, that makes her loved at home, revered abroad."

Don't forget me and if in this changing world you or yours need anything in it that I can give, be sure to call on

Your loving and admiring cousin
JOHN MUIR

From George W. Cable

DRYADS' GREEN
NORTHAMPTON, MASSACHUSETTS
December 18, 1893

MY DEAR MR. MUIR:

I am only now really settled down at home for a stay of a few weeks. I wanted to have sent to you long ago the book I mail now and which you kindly consented to accept from me — Lanier's poems. There are in Lanier such wonderful odors of pine, and hay, and salt sands and cedar, and corn, and such whisperings of

285

Eolian strains and every outdoor sound — I think you would have had great joy in one another's personal acquaintance.

And this makes me think how much I have in yours. Your face and voice, your true, rich words, are close to my senses now as I write, and I cry hungrily for more. The snow is on us everywhere now, and as I look across the white, crusted waste I see such mellowness of yellow sunlight and long blue and purple shadows that I want some adequate manly partnership to help me reap the rapture of such beauty. In one place a stretch of yellow grass standing above the snow or blown clear of it glows golden in the slant light. The heavens are blue as my love's eyes and the elms are black lace against their infinite distance.

Last night I walked across the frozen white under a moonlight and starlight that made the way seem through the wastes of a stellar universe and not along the surface of one poor planet.

Write and tell me, I pray you, what those big brothers of yours, the mountains, have been saying to you of late. It will compensate in part, but only in part, for the absence of your spoken words.

Yours truly

G. W. CABLE

TREES AND TRAVEL

To Robert Underwood Johnson

MARTINEZ, *April* 3, 1894

MY DEAR MR. JOHNSON:

The book, begotten Heaven knows when, is finished and out of me, therefore hurrah, etc., and thanks to you, very friend, for benevolent prodding. Six of the sixteen chapters are new, and the others are nearly so, for I have worked hard on every one of them, leaning them against each other, adding lots of new stuff, and killing adjectives and adverbs of redundant growth — the *verys, intenses, gloriouses, ands,* and *buts,* by the score. I feel sure the little alpine thing will not disappoint you. Anyhow I've done the best I could. Read the opening chapter when you have time. In it I have ventured to drop into the poetry that I like, but have taken good care to place it between bluffs and buttresses of bald, glacial, geological facts.

Mrs. Muir keeps asking me whether it is possible to get Johnson to come out here this summer. She seems to regard you as a Polish brother. Why, I'll be hanged if I know. I always thought you too cosmically good to be of any clannish nation. By the way, during these last months of abnormal cerebral activity I have written another article for the "Century" which I'll send you soon.

JOHN MUIR

The book mentioned in the preceding letter was his "Mountains of California," which appeared in the autumn of 1894 from the press of the Century Company. "I take pleasure in sending you with this a copy of my first book," he wrote to his old friend Mrs. Carr. "You will say that I should have written it long ago; but I begrudged the time of my young mountain-climbing days." To a Scotch cousin, Margaret Hay Lunam, he characterized it as one in which he had tried to describe and explain what a traveler would see for himself if he were to come to California and go over the mountain-ranges and through the forests as he had done.

The warmth of appreciation with which the book was received by the most thoughtful men and women of his time did much to stimulate him to further literary effort. His friend Charles S. Sargent, director of the Arnold Arboretum, then at work upon his great work "The Silva of North America," wrote as follows: "I am reading your Sierra book and I want to tell you that I have never read descriptions of trees that so picture them to the mind as yours do. No fellow who was at once a poet, naturalist, and keen observer has to my knowledge ever written about trees before, and I believe you are the man who ought to have written a silva of North America. Your book

is one of the great productions of its kind and
I congratulate you on it."

Equally enthusiastic was the great English
botanist J. D. Hooker. "I have just finished
the last page of your delightful volume," he
wrote from his home at Sunningdale, " and can
therefore thank you with a full heart. I do not
know when I have read anything that I have
enjoyed more. It has brought California back
to my memory with redoubled interest, and
with more than redoubled knowledge. Above
all it has recalled half-forgotten scientific facts,
geology, geography, and vegetation that I
used to see when in California and which I have
often tried to formulate in vain. Most especially this refers to glacial features and to the
conifers; and recalling them has recalled the
scenes and surroundings in which I first heard
them."

The acclaim of the book by reviewers was so
enthusiastic that the first edition was soon exhausted. It was his intention to bring out at
once another volume devoted to the Yosemite
Valley in particular. With this task he busied
himself in 1895, revisiting during the summer
his old haunts at the headwaters of the Tuolumne and passing once more alone through
the cañon to Hetch-Hetchy Valley. As in the
old days he carried no blanket and a minimum

of provisions, so that he had only a handful of crackers and a pinch of tea left when he reached Hetch-Hetchy. "The bears were very numerous," he wrote to his wife on August 17th, "this being berry time in the cañon. But they gave no trouble, as I knew they wouldn't. Only in tangled underbrush I had to shout a good deal to avoid coming suddenly on them."

Having no food when he reached Hetch-Hetchy, he set out to cover the twenty miles from there to Crocker's on foot, but had gone only a few miles when he met on the trail two strangers and two well-laden pack-animals. The leader, T. P. Lukens, asked his name, and then told him that he had come expressly to meet John Muir in the hope that he might go back with him into Hetch-Hetchy. "On the banks of the beautiful river beneath a Kellogg oak" the bonds of a new mountain friendship were sealed while beautiful days rolled by unnoticed. "I am fairly settled at home again," he wrote to his aged mother on his return, "and the six weeks of mountaineering of this summer in my old haunts are over, and now live only in memory and notebooks like all the other weeks in the Sierra. But how much I enjoyed this excursion, or indeed any excursion in the wilderness, I am not able to tell. I must have been born a mountaineer and the climbs and 'scootchers' of boyhood days about the old Dunbar Castle and on the roof of our house made fair beginnings. I suppose old age will put an end to scrambling in rocks and ice, but I can still climb as well as ever. I am trying to write another book, but that is harder than mountaineering."

During the spring of the following year, Mr. Johnson saw some article on Muir which moved him to ask whether he had ever been offered a professorship at Harvard, and whether Professor Louis Agassiz had declared him to be "the only living man who understood glacial action in the formation of scenery."

To Robert Underwood Johnson

MARTINEZ, *May* 3, 1895

MY DEAR MR. JOHNSON:

To both your questions the answer is, No. I hate this personal rubbish, and I have always sheltered myself as best I could in the thickest shade I could find, celebrating only the glory of God as I saw it in nature.

The foundations for the insignificant stories you mention are, as far as I know, about as follows. More than twenty years ago Professor Runkle was in Yosemite, and I took him into the adjacent wilderness and, of course, night and day preached to him the gospel of glaciers. When he went away he urged me to go with him, saying that the Institute of Technology in Boston was the right place for me, that I could have the choice of several professorships there, and every facility for fitting myself for the duties required, etc., etc.

Then came Emerson and more preaching. He said, Don't tarry too long in the woods. Listen for the word of your guardian angel. You are needed by the young men in our colleges. Solitude is a sublime mistress, but an intolerable wife. When Heaven gives the sign, leave the mountains, come to my house and live with me until you are tired of me and then I will show you to better people.

Then came Gray and more fine rambles and sermons. He said, When you get ready, come to *Harvard*. You have good and able and enthusiastic friends there and we will gladly push you ahead, etc., etc. So much for *Ha-a-a-rvard.* But you must surely know that I never for a moment thought of leaving God's big show for a mere profship, call who may.

The Agassiz sayings you refer to are more nearly true than the college ones. Yosemite was my home when Agassiz was in San Francisco, and I never saw him. When he was there I wrote him a long icy letter, telling what glorious things I had to show him and urging him to come to the mountains. The reply to this letter was written by Mrs. Agassiz, in which she told me that, when Agassiz read my letter, he said excitedly, "Here is the first man I have ever found who has any adequate conception of glacial action." Also that he told her to say in reply to my invitation that if he should accept it now he could not spend more than six weeks with me at most. That he would rather go home now, but next year he would come and spend all summer with me. But, as you know, he went home to die.

Shortly afterward I came down out of my haunts to Oakland and there met Joseph LeConte, whom I had led to the Lyell Glacier a few months before Agassiz's arrival. He (LeConte) told me that, in the course of a conversation with Agassiz on the geology of the Sierra, he told him that a young man by the name of Muir studying up there perhaps knew more about the glaciation of the Sierra than any one else. To which Agassiz replied warmly, and bringing his fist down on the table, "He knows *all* about it." Now there! You've got it all, and what a mess of mere J. M. you've made me write. Don't you go and publish it. Burn it.

Ever cordially yours

JOHN MUIR

What of the summer day now dawning? Remember you have a turn at the helm. How are you going to steer? How fares Tesla and the auroral lightning? Shall we go to icy Alaska or to the peaks and streets and taluses of the Sierra? That was a good strong word you said for the vanishing forests.

To Robert Underwood Johnson

MARTINEZ, *September* 12, 1895

MY DEAR MR. JOHNSON:

I have just got home from a six weeks' ramble in the Yosemite and Yosemite National Park. For three years the soldiers have kept the sheepmen and sheep out of the park, and I looked sharply at the ground to learn the value of the military influence on the small and great flora. On the sloping portions of the forest floor, where the soil was loose and friable, the vegetation has not yet recovered from the dibbling and destructive action of the sheep feet and teeth. But where a tough sod on meadows was spread, the grasses and blue gentians and erigerons are again blooming in all their wild glory.

The sheepmen are more than matched by the few troopers in this magnificent park, and the wilderness rejoices in fresh verdure and bloom. Only the Yosemite itself in the middle of the grand park is downtrodden, frowsy, and like an abandoned backwoods pasture. No part of the Merced and Tuolumne wilderness is so dusty, downtrodden, abandoned, and pathetic as the Yosemite. It looks ten times worse now than when you saw it seven years ago. Most of the level meadow floor of the Valley is fenced with barbed and unbarbed wire and about three hundred head of horses are turned loose every night to feed and trample the flora out of existence. I told the hotel and horsemen that they were doing all they could to prevent lovers of wild beauties from visiting the Valley, and that soon all *tourist travel* would cease. This year only twelve hundred regular tourists visited the Valley, while two thousand campers came in and remained a week or two. . . .

I have little hope for Yosemite. As long as the management is in the hands of eight politicians appointed by the ever-changing Governor of California, there is but little hope. I never saw the Yosemite so frowsy, scrawny, and downtrodden as last August, and the horsemen began to inquire, "Has the Yosemite begun to play out?". . .

Ever yours

JOHN MUIR

At the June Commencement in 1896, Harvard bestowed upon Muir an honorary M. A. degree.[1] The offer of the honor came just as he was deciding, moved by a strange presentiment of her impending death, to pay another visit to his mother. Among Muir's papers, evidently intended for his autobiography, I find the following description of the incident under the heading of "Mysterious Things":

As in the case of father's death, while seated at work in my library in California in the spring of 1896, I was suddenly possessed with the idea that I ought to go back to Portage, Wisconsin, to see my mother once more, as she was not likely to live long, though I had not heard that she was failing. I had not sent word that I was coming. Two of her daughters were living with her at the time, and, when one of them happened to see me walking up to the house through the garden, she came running out, saying, "John, God must have sent you, because mother is very sick." I was with her about a week before she died, and managed to get my brother Daniel, the doctor, to come down from Nebraska to be with her. He insisted that he knew my mother's case very well, and didn't think that there was the slightest necessity for his coming. I told him I thought he would never see her again if he didn't come, and he would always regret neglecting

[1] President Eliot's salutation, spoken in Latin, was as follows: "Johannem Muir, locorum incognitorum exploratorem insignem; fluminum qui sunt in Alaska serratisque montibus conglaciatorum studiosum; diligentem silvarum et rerum agrestium ferarumque indagatorem, artium magistrum."

this last duty to mother, and finally succeeded in getting him to come. But brother David and my two eldest sisters, who had since father's death moved to California, were not present.

The following letter gives a brief summary of his Eastern experiences up to the time when he joined the Forestry Commission in Chicago. It should be added that Muir went along unofficially at the invitation of C. S. Sargent, the Chairman of the Commission. Of the epochal work of this Commission and Muir's relation to it, more later.

To Helen Muir

S.W. COR. LASALLE AND WASHINGTON STREETS
CHICAGO, *July 3d*, 1896

MY DEAR LITTLE HELEN:

I have enjoyed your sweet, bright, illustrated letters ever and ever so much; both the words and the pictures made me see everything at home as if I was there myself — the peaches, and the purring pussies, and the blue herons flying about, and all the people working and walking about and talking and guessing on the weather.

So many things have happened since I left home, and I have seen so many people and places and have traveled so fast and far, I have lost the measure of time, and it seems more than a year since I left home. Oh, dear! how tired I have been and excited and swirly! Sometimes my head felt so benumbed, I hardly knew where I was. And yet everything done seems to have been done for the best, and I believe God has been guiding us. . . .

I went to New York and then up the Hudson a hundred miles to see John Burroughs and Professor Osborn, to escape being sunstruck and choked in the horrid weather of the streets; and then, refreshed, I got back to New York and started for Boston and Cambridge and got through the Harvard business all right and caught a fast train . . . back to Portage in time for the funeral. Then I stopped three or four days to settle all the business and write to Scotland, and comfort Sarah and Annie and Mary; then I ran down a half-day to Madison, and went to Milwaukee and stayed a night with William Trout, with whom I used to live in a famous hollow in the Canada woods thirty years ago. Next day I went to Indianapolis and saw everybody there and stopped with them one night. Then came here last night and stopped with [A. H.] Sellers. I am now in his office awaiting the arrival of the Forestry Commission, with whom I expect to start West to-night at half-past ten o'clock. It is now about noon. I feel that this is the end of the strange lot of events I have been talking about, for when I reach the Rocky Mountains I'll feel at home. I saw a wonderful lot of squirrels at Osborn's, and Mrs. Osborn wants you and Wanda and Mamma to visit her and stay a long time.

Good-bye, darling, and give my love to Wanda and Mamma and Grandma and Maggie. Go over and comfort Maggie and tell Mamma to write to poor Sarah. Tell Mamma I spent a long evening with [Nicola] Tesla and I found him quite a wonderful and interesting fellow.

[JOHN MUIR]

To Wanda Muir

HOT SPRINGS, S.D.
July 5th, 1896

MY DEAR WANDA:

I am now fairly on my way West again, and a thousand miles nearer you than I was a few days ago. We got here this morning, after a long ride from Chicago. By *we* I mean Professors Sargent, Brewer, Hague, and General Abbot — all interesting wise men and grand company. It was dreadfully hot the day we left Chicago, but it rained before morning of the 4th, and so that day was dustless and cool, and the ride across Iowa was delightful. That State is very fertile and beautiful. The cornfields and wheatfields are boundless, or appear

299

so as we skim through them on the cars, and all are rich and bountiful-looking. Flowers in bloom line the roads, and tall grasses and bushes. The surface of the ground is rolling, with hills beyond hills, many of them crowned with trees. I never before knew that Iowa was so beautiful and inexhaustibly rich.

Nebraska is monotonously level like a green grassy sea — no hills or mountains in sight for hundreds of miles. Here, too, are cornfields without end and full of promise this year, after three years of famine from drouth.

South Dakota, by the way we came, is dry and desert-like until you get into the Black Hills. The latter get their name from the dark color they have in the distance from the pine forests that cover them. The pine of these woods is the ponderosa or yellow pine, the same as the one that grows in the Sierra, Oregon, Washington, Nevada, Utah, Colorado, Montana, Idaho, Wyoming, and all the West in general. No other pine in the world has so wide a range or is so hardy at all heights and under all circumstances and conditions of climate and soil. This is near its eastern limit, and here it is interesting to find that many plants of the Atlantic and Pacific slopes meet and grow well together. . . .

[JOHN MUIR]

TREES AND TRAVEL

To Helen and Wanda Muir

SYLVAN LAKE HOTEL
CUSTER, S.D., *July* 6, 1896

HELLO, MIDGE! HELLO, WANDA!

My!! if you could only come here when I call you how wonderful you would think this hollow in the rocky Black Hills is! It is wonderful even to me after seeing so many wild mountains — curious rocks rising alone or in clusters, gray and jagged and rounded in the midst of a forest of pines and spruces and poplars and birches, with a little lake in the middle and carpet of meadow gay with flowers. It is in the heart of the famous Black Hills where the Indians and Whites quarreled and fought so much. The whites wanted the gold in the rocks, and the Indians wanted the game — the deer and elk that used to abound here. As a grand deer pasture this was said to have been the best in America, and no wonder the Indians wanted to keep it, for wherever the white man goes the game vanishes.

We came here this forenoon from Hot Springs, fifty miles by rail and twelve by wagon. And most of the way was through woods fairly carpeted with beautiful flowers. A lovely red lily, *Lilium Pennsylvanicum*, was common, two kinds of spiræa and a beautiful wild rose in full bloom, anemones, calochortus, larkspur,

301

etc., etc., far beyond time to tell. But I must not fail to mention linnæa. How sweet the air is! I would like to stop a long time and have you and Mamma with me. What walks we would have!!

We leave to-night for Edgemont. Here are some mica flakes and a bit of spiræa I picked up in a walk with Professor Sargent.

Good-bye, my babes. Sometime I must bring you here. I send love and hope you are well.

JOHN MUIR

The following letter expresses Muir's stand in the matter of the recession of Yosemite Valley by the State of California to the Federal Government. The mismanagement of the Valley under ever-changing political appointees of the various Governors had become a national scandal, and Muir was determined that, in spite of some objectors, the Sierra Club should have an opportunity to express itself on the issue. The bill for recession was reported favorably in the California Assembly in February, but it encountered so much pettifogging and politically inspired opposition that it was not actually passed until 1905.

TREES AND TRAVEL

To Warren Olney, Sr.

MARTINEZ, *January* 18, 1897

MY DEAR OLNEY:

I think with you that a resolution like the one you offered the other day should be thoroughly studied and discussed before final action is taken and a close approximation made to unanimity, if possible. Still, I don't see that one or two objectors should have the right to kill all action of the Club in this or any other matter rightly belonging to it. Professor Davidson's objection is also held by Professor LeConte, or was, but how they can consistently sing praise to the Federal Government in the management of the National Parks, and at the same time regard the same management of Yosemite as degrading to the State, I can't see. For my part, I'm proud of California and prouder of Uncle Sam, for the U.S. is all of California and more. And as to our Secretary's objection, it seemed to me merely political, and if the Sierra Club is to be run by politicians, the sooner mountaineers get out of it the better. Fortunately, the matter is not of first importance, but now it has been raised, I shall insist on getting it squarely before the Club. I had given up the question as a bad job, but so many of our members have urged it lately I now regard its discussion as a duty of the Club.

JOHN MUIR

CHAPTER XVII

UNTO THE LAST

I

1897–1905

THOUGH little evidence of the fact appears in extant letters, the year 1897 was one of great importance in Muir's career. So significant, indeed, was his work in defending [1] the recommendations of the National Forest Commission of 1896 that we must reserve fuller discussion of it for a chapter on Muir's service to the nation. With the exception of his story of the dog Stickeen and a vivid description of an Alaska trip, appearing respectively in the August and September numbers of the "Century," nearly the entire output of his pen that year was devoted to the saving of the thirteen forest reservations proclaimed by President Cleveland on the basis of the Forest Commission's report.

During the month of August he joined Professor C. S. Sargent and Mr. William M. Canby on an expedition to study forest trees in the

[1] This service was specially recognized in 1897 by the University of Wisconsin, his *alma mater*, in the bestowal of an LL.D. degree.

Rocky Mountains and in Alaska. To this and other matters allusion is made in the following excerpt from a November letter to Professor Henry Fairfield Osborn.

I spent a short time [he writes] in the Rocky Mountain forests between Banff and Glacier with Professor Sargent and Mr. Canby, and then we went to Alaska, mostly by the same route you traveled. We were on the Queen and had your staterooms. The weather was not so fine as during your trip. The glorious color we so enjoyed on the upper deck was wanting, but the views of the noble peaks of the Fairweather Range were sublime. They were perfectly clear, and loomed in the azure, ice-laden and white, like very gods. Canby and Sargent were lost in admiration as if they had got into a perfectly new world, and so they had, old travelers though they are.

I've been writing about the forests, mostly, doing what little I can to save them. "Harper's Weekly" [1] and the "Atlantic Monthly" have published something; the latter published an article [2] last August. I sent another two weeks ago and am pegging away on three others for the same magazine on the national parks — Yellowstone, Yosemite, and Sequoia — and I want this winter to try some more Alaska. But I make slow, hard work of it — slow and hard as glaciers. . . . When are you coming again to our wild side of the continent and how goes your big book? I suppose it will be about as huge as Sargent's "Silva."

[1] "Forest Reservations and National Parks," June 5, 1897.
[2] "American Forests."

One of the pleasant by-products of Muir's spirited defense of the reservations was the beginning of a warm friendship with the late Walter Hines Page, then editor of the "Atlantic." The latter, like Robert Underwood Johnson, stimulated his literary productiveness and was largely responsible for his final choice of Houghton, Mifflin & Company as his publishers. Some years later, in 1905, Mr. and Mrs. Page paid a visit to Muir at his home in the Alhambra Valley. The articles contributed to the "Atlantic" during the nineties were in 1901 brought out in book form under the title of "Our National Parks."

Apropos of Muir's apologetic references to the fact that he found writing a slow, hard task, Page remarked: "I thank God that you do not write in glib, acrobatic fashion: anybody can do that. Half the people in the world are doing it all the time, to my infinite regret and confusion. . . . The two books on the Parks and on Alaska will not need any special season's sales, nor other accidental circumstances: they'll be Literature!" On another occasion, in October, 1897, Page writes: "Mr. John Burroughs has been spending a little while with me, and he talks about nothing else so earnestly as about you and your work. He declares in the most emphatic fashion that it will be a misfortune too great to estimate if you do not write up all those bags of notes which you have gathered. He encourages me, to put it in his own words, to 'keep firing at him, keep firing at him.'"

In February, 1898, Professor Sargent wrote Muir that he was in urgent need of the flowers of the red fir to be used for an illustrative plate in his "Silva." The following letter is in part a report on Muir's first futile effort to secure them. Ten days later, above Deer Park in the Tahoe region, he succeeded in finding and collecting specimens of both pistillate and staminate flowers, which up to that time, according to Sargent, "did not exist in any herbarium in this country or in Europe."

To Charles Sprague Sargent

MARTINEZ, *June* 7, 1898

MY DEAR PROFESSOR SARGENT:

Yesterday I returned from a week's trip to Shasta and the Scott Mountains for [*Abies*] *magnifica* flowers, but am again in bad luck. I searched the woods, wallowing through the snow nearly to the upper limit of the fir belt, but saw no flowers or buds that promised anything except on a few trees. I cut down six on Shasta and two on Scott Mountains west of Sissons. On one of the Shasta trees I found the staminate flowers just emerging from the scales, but not a single pistillate flower. I send the staminate, though hardly worth while. Last year's crop of cones was nearly all frost-killed and most of the leaf buds also, so there is little chance for flowers thereabouts this year.

Sonne writes that the Truckee Lumber Company is to begin cutting Magnifica in the Washoe Range ten miles east of Truckee on the 8th or 10th of this month, and he promises to be promptly on hand among the fresh-felled trees to get the flowers, while Miss Eastwood starts this evening for the Sierra summit above Truckee, and I have a friend in Yosemite watching the trees around the rim of the Valley, so we can hardly fail to get good flowers even in so bad a year as this is.

I have got through the first reading of your Pine volume.[1] It is bravely, sturdily, handsomely done. Grand old Ponderosa you have set forth in magnificent style, describing its many forms and allowing species-makers to name as many as they like, while showing their inseparable characters. But you should have mentioned the thick, scaly, uninflammable bark with which, like a wandering warrior of

[1] Volume XI of Sargent's *Silva*, devoted to the Coniferæ. The author's dedication reads, "To John Muir, lover and interpreter of nature, who best has told the story of the Sierra forests, this eleventh volume of THE SILVA OF NORTH AMERICA is gratefully dedicated."

King Arthur's time, it is clad, as accounting in great part for its wide distribution and endurance of extremes of climate. You seem to rank it above the sugar pine. But in youth and age, clothed with beauty and majesty, Lambertiana is easily King of all the world-wide realm of pines, while Ponderosa is the noble, unconquerable mailed knight without fear and without reproach.

By brave and mighty Proteus-Muggins [1] you have also done well, though you might have praised him a little more loudly for hearty endurance under manifold hardships, defying the salt blasts of the sea from Alaska to the California Golden Gate, and the frosts and fires of the Rocky Mountains — growing patiently in mossy bogs and on craggy mountain-tops — crouching low on glacier granite pavements, holding on by narrow cleavage joints, or waving tall and slender and graceful in flowery garden spots sheltered from every wind among columbines and lilies, etc. A line or two of sound sturdy Mother Earth poetry such as you ventured to give Ponderosa in no wise weakens or blurs the necessarily dry, stubbed, scientific description, and I'm sure Muggins deserves it. However, I'm not going fault-finding. It's a

[1] Probably *Pinus contorta* of the *Silva*, one of its variants being the Murray or Tamarac Pine of the High Sierra.

grand volume — a kingly Lambertiana job; and on many a mountain trees now seedlings will be giants and will wave their shining tassels two hundred feet in the sky ere another pine book will be made. So you may well sing your nunc dimittis, and so, in sooth, may I, since you have engraved my name on the head of it.

That Alleghany trip you so kindly offer is mighty tempting. It has stirred up wild lover's longings to renew my acquaintance with old forest friends and gain new ones under such incomparable auspices. I'm just dying to see basswood and shell-bark and liriodendron once more. When could you start, and when would you have me meet you? I think I might get away from here about the middle of July and go around by the Great Northern and lakes, stopping a few days on old familiar ground about the shores of Georgian Bay. I want to avoid cities and dinners as much as possible and travel light and free. If tree-lovers could only grow bark and bread on their bodies, how fine it would be, making even handbags useless!

Ever yours

JOHN MUIR

While trying to avoid people as much as possible and seeing only you and trees, I should, if I make this Eastern trip, want to call on Mrs.

Asa Gray, for I heartily love and admire Gray,
and in my mind his memory fades not at all.

The projected trip into the Alleghanies with
Sargent and Canby was undertaken during
September and October when the Southern
forests were in their autumn glory. Muir had
entered into the plan with great eagerness. "I
don't want to die," he wrote to Sargent in
June, "without once more saluting the grand,
godly, round-headed trees of the east side of
America that I first learned to love and beneath
which I used to weep for joy when nobody
knew me." The task of mapping a route was
assigned by Sargent to Mr. Canby on account
of his special acquaintance with the region.
"Dear old streak o' lightning on ice," the latter
wrote to Muir in July, "I was delighted to hear
from the glacial period once more and to know
that you were going to make your escape from
Purgatory and emerge into the heavenly forests of the Alleghanies. . . . Have you seen the
Luray Caverns or the Natural Bridge? If not,
do you care to? I should like to have you look
from the summit of Salt Pond Mountain in
Virginia and the Roan in North Carolina."

For a month or more the three of them
roamed through the Southern forests, Muir
being especially charmed by the regions about

311

Cranberry, Cloudland, and Grandfather Mountain, in North Carolina. From Roan Mountain to Lenoir, about seventy-five miles, they drove in a carriage — in Muir's judgment "the finest drive of its kind in America." In Tennessee, Georgia, and Alabama he crossed at various times his old trail of 1867.

On his return to Boston, he "spent a night at Page's home and visited Mrs. Gray and talked over old botanic times." On the first of November he is at "Four Brook Farm," R. W. Gilder's country-place at Tyringham in the Berkshire Hills, whence he writes to his daughter Wanda: "Tell mamma that I have enjoyed Mr. and Mrs. Gilder ever so much. On the way here, on the car, I was introduced to Joseph Choate, the great lawyer, and on Sunday Mr. Gilder and I drove over to his fine residence at Stockbridge to dinner, and I had a long talk with him about forests as well as glaciers. To-day we all go back to New York. This evening I dine with Johnson, and to-morrow I go up the Hudson to the Osborns'."

UNTO THE LAST

To Helen Muir

"WING-AND-WING"
GARRISONS-ON-HUDSON
November 4, 1898

MY DARLING HELEN:

This is a fine calm thoughtful morning, bracing and sparkling, just the least touch of hoarfrost, quickly melting where the sunbeams, streaming through between the trees, fall in yellow plashes and lances on the lawns. Every now and then a red or yellow leaf comes swirling down, though there is not the slightest breeze. Most of the hickories are leafless now, but the big buds on the ends of the twigs are full of baby leaves and flowers that are already planning and thinking about next summer. Many of the maples, too, and the dogwoods are showing leafless branches; but many along the sheltered ravines are still rejoicing in all their glory of color, and look like gigantic goldenrods. God's forests, my dear, are among the grandest of terrestrial things that you may look forward to. I have not heard from Professor Sargent since he left New York a week ago, and so I don't know whether he is ready to go to Florida, but I'll hear soon, and then I'll know nearly the time I'll get home. Anyhow, it won't be long.

I am enjoying a fine rest. I have "the blue

room" in this charming home, and it has the daintiest linen and embroidery I ever saw. The bed is so soft and fine I like to lie awake to enjoy it, instead of sleeping. A servant brings in a cup of coffee before I rise. This morning when I was sipping coffee in bed, a red squirrel looked in the window at me from a branch of a big tulip-tree, and seemed to be saying as he watched me. "Oh, John Muir! camping, tramping, tree-climbing scrambler! Churr, churr! why have you left us? Chip churr, who would have thought it?"

Five days after the date of the above letter he writes to his wife:

"DEAR LASSIE, it is settled that I go on a short visit to Florida with Sargent. . . . I leave here [Wing-and-Wing] to-morrow for New York, dine with Tesla and others, and then meet Sargent at Wilmington, Wednesday. I've had a fine rest in this charming home and feel ready for Florida, which is now cool and healthy. I'm glad to see the South again and may write about it."

The trip to Florida, replete with color and incident, is too full of particularity for recital here. A halt in Savannah, Georgia, stirred up old memories, for "here," he writes in a letter to his wife, "is where I spent a hungry, weary,

314

yet happy week camping in Bonaventure graveyard thirty-one years ago. Many changes, I'm told, have been made in its groves and avenues of late, and how many in my life!"

A dramatic occurrence was the finding at Archer of Mrs. Hodgson, who had nursed him back to health on his thousand-mile walk to the Gulf. The incident is told in the following excerpt from a letter to his wife under date of November 21, 1898:

The day before yesterday we stopped at Palatka on the famous St. Johns River, where I saw the most magnificent magnolias, some four feet in diameter and one hundred feet high, also the largest and most beautiful hickories and oaks. From there we went to Cedar Keys. Of course I inquired for the Hodgsons, at whose house I lay sick so long. Mr. Hodgson died long ago, also the eldest son, with whom I used to go boating, but Mrs. Hodgson and the rest of the family, two boys and three girls, are alive and well, and I saw them all to-day, except one of the boys. I found them at Archer, where I stopped four hours on my way from Cedar Keys. Mrs. Hodgson and the two eldest girls remembered me well. The house was pointed out to me, and I found the good old lady who nursed me in the garden. I asked her if she knew me. She answered no, and asked my name. I said Muir. "*John* Muir?" she almost screamed. "*My* California John Muir? My California John?" I said, "Why, yes, I promised to come back and visit you in about twenty-five years, and though a little late I've come." I stopped to dinner and we talked over old times in grand style, you may be sure.

The following letter, full of good-natured badinage and new plans for travel, was written soon after his return home in December:

To Charles Sprague Sargent

MARTINEZ, *December* 28, 1898

MY DEAR PROFESSOR SARGENT:

I'm glad you're miserable about not going to Mexico, for it shows that your heartwood is still honest and loving towards the grand trees down there, though football games and Connecticut turkey momentarily got the better of you. The grand Taxodiums were object enough for the trip, and I came pretty near making it alone — would certainly have done it had I not felt childishly lonesome and woe-begone after you left me. No wonder I looked like an inland coot to friend Mellichamp. But what would that sharp observer have said to the Canby huckleberry party gyrating lost in the Delaware woods, and splashing along the edge of the marshy bay "froggin' and crabbin'" with devout scientific solemnity! ! !

Mellichamp I liked ever so much, and blessed old Mohr more than ever. For these good men and many, many trees I have to thank you, and I do over and over again as the main blessings

of the passing year. And I have to thank you
also for Gray's writings — Essays, etc. —
which I have read with great interest. More
than ever I want to see Japan and eastern Asia.
I wonder if Canby could be converted to sufficient sanity to go with us on that glorious
dendrological trip. . . . Confound his Yankee
savings bank! He has done more than enough
in that line. It will soon be dark. Soon our
good botanical pegs will be straightened in a
box and planted, and it behooves us as reasonable naturalists to keep them tramping and
twinkling in the woods as long as possible. . . .

Wishing you and family and "Silva" happy
New Year, I am,

Ever yours

JOHN MUIR

There were not a few among Muir's literary
friends, men like Walter Hines Page and
Richard Watson Gilder, who as early as 1898
began to urge him to write his autobiography.
"I thank you for your kind suggestions about
'Recollections of a Naturalist,'" he replies to
Gilder in March, 1899. "Possibly I may try
something of the sort some of these days,
though my life on the whole has been level and
uneventful, and therefore hard to make a book
of that many would read. I am not anxious to

tell what I have done, but what Nature has done — an infinitely more important story."

In April, 1899, he accepted an invitation to join the Harriman Alaska Expedition. During the cruise a warm friendship sprang up between him and Mr. Harriman, who came to value highly not only his personal qualities, but also his sturdy independence. It was some years afterward, while he was the guest of Mr. Harriman at Pelican Lodge on Klamath Lake, that Muir was persuaded to dictate his memoirs to Mr. Harriman's private secretary. We owe it to the use of this expedient that Muir was enabled to complete at least a part of his autobiography before he passed on. The little book [1] written by Muir in appreciation of Mr. Harriman after his death sprang from memories of many kindnesses, and unheralded occasions too, when Mr. Harriman's influence turned the scales in favor of some important conservation measure dear to Muir's heart. Both held in warm regard Captain P. A. Doran, of the Elder, which in 1899 carried the expeditionary party. "I am deeply touched at your letter of the second just received," wrote Mr. Harriman to Muir on August 8, 1907, shortly after a tragedy of the sea in which Captain Doran perished. "We all grieved much over

[1] *Edward Henry Harriman*, by John Muir. 1916.

poor Doran. I had grown to look upon him as a real friend and knew him to be a true man. I am glad to have shared his friendship with you. I am fortunate in having many friends and am indeed proud to count you among the best. My troubles are not to be considered with yours and some others, for they are only passing and will be eventually cleared up and understood even by the 'some' to whom you refer. The responsibilities weigh most when such misfortunes occur as the loss of the poor passenger who passed on with brave Doran."

To Charles Sprague Sargent

MARTINEZ, *April* 30, 1899

MY DEAR PROFESSOR SARGENT:

You are no doubt right about the little Tahoe reservation — a scheme full of special personalities, pushed through by a lot of lawyers, etc., but the more we get the better anyhow. It is a natural park, and because of its beauty and accessibility is visited more than any other part of the Sierra except Yosemite.

All I know of the Rainier and Olympic reservations has come through the newspapers. The Olympic will surely be attacked again and again for its timber, but the interests of Seattle and Tacoma will probably save Rainier. I expect to find out something about them soon, as

I am going north from Seattle to Cook Inlet
and Kodiak for a couple of months with a
"scientific party." ... This section of the
coast is the only one I have not seen, and I'm
glad of the chance.

Good luck to you. I wish I were going to
those leafy woods instead of icy Alaska. Be
good to the trees, you tough, sturdy pair.
Don't frighten the much-enduring Cratæguses
and make them drop their spurs, and don't tell
them quite eternally that you are from Boston
and the Delaware Huckleberry Peninsula.

My love to Canby — keep his frisks within
bounds. Remember me to the Biltmore friends
and blessed Mohr and Mellichamp. And remember me also to the Messrs. Hickory and
Oak, and, oh, the magnolias in bloom! Heavens, how they glow and shine and invite a
fellow! Good-bye. I'll hope to see you in
August.

Ever yours

JOHN MUIR

To Walter Hines Page

[MARTINEZ, CALIFORNIA, May, 1899]

MY DEAR PAGE:

I send the article on Yosemite Park to-day
by registered mail. It is short, but perhaps
long enough for this sort of stuff. I have three

other articles on camping in the park, and on the trees and shrubs, gardens, etc., and on Sequoia Park, blocked out and more than half written. I wanted to complete these and get the book put together and off my hands this summer, and, now that I have all the material well in hand and on the move, I hate to leave it.

I start to-morrow on a two months' trip with Harriman's Alaska Expedition. John Burroughs and Professor [W. H.] Brewer and a whole lot of good naturalists are going. But I would not have gone, however tempting, were it not to visit the only part of the coast I have not seen and one of the scenes that I would have to visit sometime anyhow. This has been a barren year, and I am all the less willing to go, though the auspices are so good. I lost half the winter in a confounded fight with sheep and cattlemen and politicians on behalf of the forests. During the other half I was benumbed and interrupted by sickness in the family, while in word works, even at the best, as you know, I'm slow as a glacier. You'll get these papers, however, sometime, and they will be hammered into a book — if I live long enough.

I was very glad to get your letter, as it showed you were well enough to be at work again. With best wishes, I am,

Faithfully yours   J. M.

JOHN MUIR

To Mrs. Muir

VICTORIA, *June* 1, 1899

DEAR LOUIE:

We sail from here in about two hours, and I have just time to say another good-bye. The ship is furnished in fine style, and I find we are going just where I want to go — Yakutat, Prince William Sound, Cook Inlet, etc. I am on the Executive Committee, and of course have something to say as to routes, time to be spent at each point, etc. The company is very harmonious for scientists. Yesterday I tramped over Seattle with John Burroughs. At Portland the Mazamas were very demonstrative and kind. I hope you are all busy with the hay. Helen will keep it well tumbled and tramped with Keenie's help. I am making pleasant acquaintances. Give my love to Maggie. Good-bye. Ever your affectionate husband

JOHN MUIR

To Wanda and Helen Muir

FORT WRANGELL, *June* 5, [1899,] 7 A.M.

How are you all? We arrived here last evening. This is a lovely morning — water like glass. Looks like home. The flowers are in bloom, so are the forests. We leave in an hour for Juneau. The mountains are pure white. Went to church at Metlakatla, heard Duncan preach, and the Indians sing. Had fine ramble in the woods with Burroughs. He is ashore looking and listening for birds. The song sparrow, a little dun, speckledy muggins, sings best. Most of the passengers are looking at totem poles.

Have letters for me at Seattle. No use trying to forward them up here, as we don't know where we will touch on the way down home.

I hope you are all well and not too lonesome. Take good care of Stickeen and Tom. We landed at four places on the way up here. I was glad to see the woods in those new places.

Love to all. Ever your loving papa

J. M.

To Louie, Wanda, and Helen

JUNEAU, *June* 6, [1899,] 9 A.M.

Cold rainy day. We stop here only a few minutes, and I have only time to scribble love to my darlings. The green mountains rise into the gray cloudy sky four thousand feet, rich in trees and grass and flowers and wild goats.

We are all well and happy. Yesterday was bright and the mountains all the way up from Wrangell were passed in review, opening their snowy, icy recesses, and closing them, like turning over the leaves of a grand picture book. Everybody gazed at the grand glaciers and peaks, and we saw icebergs floating past for the first time on the trip.

We landed on two points on the way up and had rambles in the woods, and the naturalists set traps and caught five white-footed mice. We were in the woods I wandered in twenty years ago, and I had many questions to answer. Heaven bless you. We go next to Douglas Mine, then to Skagway, then to Glacier Bay.

Good-bye   JOHN MUIR

To Mrs. Muir and daughters

SITKA, ALASKA, *June* 10, 1899

DEAR LOUIE, WANDA, AND HELEN:

I wrote two days ago, and I suppose you will get this at the same time as the other. We had the Governor at dinner and a society affair afterward that looked queer in the wilderness. This eve we are to have a reception at the Governor's, and to-morrow we sail for Yakutat Bay, thence to Prince William Sound, Cook Inlet, etc. We were at the Hot Springs yesterday, fifteen miles from here amid lovely scenery.

The Topeka arrived last eve, and sails in an hour or so. I met Professor Moses and his wife on the wharf and then some Berkeley people besides; then the Raymond agent, who introduced a lot of people, to whom I lectured in the street. The thing was like a revival meeting. The weather is wondrous fine, and all goes well. I regret not having [had] a letter forwarded here, as I long for a word of your welfare. Heaven keep you, darlings. Ever yours

JOHN MUIR

To Mrs. Muir

SITKA, *June* 14, 1899

DEAR LOUIE AND BAIRNS:

We are just entering Sitka Harbor after a delightful sail down Peril Straits, and a perfectly glorious time in Glacier Bay — five days of the most splendid weather I ever saw in Alaska. I was out three days with Gilbert and Palache revisiting the glaciers of the upper end of the Bay. Great changes have taken place. The Pacific Glacier has melted back four miles and changed into three separate glaciers, each discharging bergs in grand style. One of them, unnamed and unexplored, I named last evening, in a lecture they made me give in the social hall, the Harriman Glacier, which was received with hearty cheers. After the lecture Mr. Harriman came to me and thanked me for the great honor I had done him. It is a very beautiful glacier, the front discharging bergs like the Muir — about three quarters of a mile wide on the sea wall.

Everybody was delighted with Glacier Bay and the grand Muir Glacier, watching the beautiful bergs born in thunder, parties scattered out in every direction in rowboats and steam and naphtha launches on every sort of quest. John Burroughs and Charlie Keeler climbed the mountain on the east side of Muir Glacier, three thousand feet, and obtained a grand view far back over the mountain to the glorious Fairweather Range. I tried hard to get out of lecturing, but was compelled to do it. All seemed pleased. Lectures every night. The company all good-natured and harmonious. Our next stop will be Yakutat.

I'm all sunburned by three bright days among the bergs. I often wish you could have been with us. You will see it all some day. Heaven bless you. Remember me to Maggie.

Good-bye

[JOHN MUIR]

To Mrs. Muir

OFF PRINCE WILLIAM SOUND
June 24, 1899

DEAR LOUIE AND DARLINGS:

We are just approaching Prince William Sound — the place above all others I have long wished to see. The snow and ice-laden mountains loom grandly in crowded ranks above the dark, heaving sea, and I can already trace the courses of some of the largest of the glaciers. It is 2 P.M., and in three or four hours we shall be at Orca, near the mouth of the bay, where I will mail this note.

We had a glorious view of the mountains and glaciers in sailing up the coast along the Fairweather Range from Sitka to Yakutat Bay. In Yakutat and Disenchantment Bays we spent four days, and I saw their three great glaciers discharging bergs and hundreds of others to best advantage. Also the loveliest flower gardens. Here are a few of the most beautiful of the rubuses. This charming plant covers acres like a carpet. One of the islands we landed on, in front of the largest thundering glacier, was so flower-covered that I could smell the fragrance from the boat among the bergs half a mile away.

I'm getting strong fast, and can walk and climb about as well as ever, and eat everything with prodigious appetite.

I hope to have a good view of the grand glaciers here, though some of the party are eager to push on to Cook Inlet. I think I'll have a chance to mail another letter ere we leave the Sound.

Love to all

J. M.

JOHN MUIR

To Wanda Muir

MY DEAR WANDA AND HELEN AND MAMMA:

We arrived here this cloudy, rainy, foggy morning after a glorious sail from Sand Harbor on Unga Island, one of the Shumagin group, all the way along the volcano-dotted coast of the Alaska Peninsula and Unimak Island. The volcanoes are about as thick as haycocks on our alfalfa field in a wet year, and the highest of them are smoking and steaming in grand style. Shishaldin is the handsomest volcanic cone I ever saw and it looked like this last evening. [Drawing.] I'll show you a better sketch in my

notebook when I get home. About nine thousand feet high, snow and ice on its slopes, hot and bare at the top. A few miles from Shishaldin there is a wild rugged old giant of a volcano that blew or burst its own head off a few years ago, and covered the sea with ashes and cinders and killed fish and raised a tidal wave that lashed the shores of San Francisco and even Martinez.

There is a ship, the Loredo, that is to sail in an hour, so I'm in a hurry, as usual. We are going to the Seal Islands and St. Lawrence Island from here, and a point or two on the Siberian coast — then home. We are taking on coal, and will leave in three or four hours. I hope fondly that you are all well. . . . I'll soon be back, my darlings. God bless you.

Good-bye

[JOHN MUIR]

"To the 'Big Four': the Misses Mary and Cornelia Harriman, and the Misses Elizabeth Averell and Dorothea Draper, who with Carol and Roland [Harriman], the 'Little Two,' kept us all young on the never-to-be-forgotten H.A.E." [1]

[MARTINEZ,] August 30, 1899

DEAR GIRLS:

I received your kind compound letter from the railroad washout with great pleasure, for it showed, as I fondly thought, that no wreck, washout, or crevasse of any sort will be likely to break or wash out the memories of our grand trip, or abate the friendliness that sprung up on

[1] Harriman Alaska Expedition.

the Elder among the wild scenery of Alaska
during these last two memorable months. No
doubt every one of the favored happy band
feels, as I do, that this was the grandest trip of
his life. To me it was peculiarly grateful and
interesting because nearly all my life I have
wandered and studied alone. On the Elder, I
found not only the fields I liked best to study,
but a hotel, a club, and a home, together with a
floating University in which I enjoyed the instruction and companionship of a lot of the
best fellows imaginable, culled and arranged
like a well-balanced bouquet, or like a band of
glaciers flowing smoothly together, each in its
own channel, or perhaps at times like a lot of
round boulders merrily swirling and chafing
against each other in a glacier pothole.

And what a glorious trip it was for you girls,
flying like birds from wilderness to wilderness,
the wildest and brightest of America, tasting
almost every science under the sun, with fine
breezy exercise, scrambles over mossy logs and
rocks in the spruce forests, walks on the crystal
prairies of the glaciers, on the flowery boggy
tundras, in the luxuriant wild gardens of
Kodiak and the islands of Bering Sea, and
plashing boat rides in the piping bracing winds,
all the while your eyes filled with magnificent
scenery — the Alexander Archipelago with its

thousand forested islands and calm mirror
waters, Glacier Bay, Fairweather Mountains,
Yakutat and Enchantment Bays, the St. Elias
Alps and glaciers and the glorious Prince William Sound, Cook Inlet, and the Aleutian Peninsula with its flowery, icy, smoky volcanoes,
the blooming banks and braes and mountains
of Unalaska, and Bering Sea with its seals and
Innuits, whales and whalers, etc., etc., etc.

It is not easy to stop writing under the exhilaration of such an excursion, so much pure
wildness with so much fine company. It is a
pity so rare a company should have to be
broken, never to be assembled again. But
many, no doubt, *will* meet again. On your side
of the continent perhaps half the number may
be got together. Already I have had two trips
with Merriam to the Sierra Sequoias and Coast
Redwoods, during which you may be sure the
H.A.E. was enjoyed over again. A few days
after I got home, Captain Doran paid me a
visit, most of which was spent in a hearty review of the trip. And last week Gannett came
up and spent a couple of days, during which we
went over all our enjoyments, science and fun,
mountain ranges, glaciers, etc., discussing
everything from earth sculpture to Cassiope
and rhododendron gardens — from Welsh rare-
bit and jam and cracker feasts to Nunatak. I

hope to have visits from Professor Gilbert and poet Charlie ere long, and Earlybird Ritter, and possibly I may see a whole lot more in the East this coming winter or next. Anyhow, remember me to all the Harrimans and Averells and every one of the party you chance to meet. Just to think of them!! Ridgway with wonderful bird eyes, all the birds of America in them; Funny Fisher ever flashing out wit; Perpendicular E., erect and majestic as a Thlinket totem pole; Old-sea-beach G., hunting upheavals, downheavals, sideheavals, and hanging valleys; the Artists reveling in color beauty like bees in flower-beds; Ama-a-merst tripping along shore like a sprightly sandpiper, pecking kelp-bearded boulders for a meal of fossil molluscs; Genius Kincaid among his beetles and butterflies and "red-tailed bumble-bees that sting awful hard"; Innuit Dall smoking and musing; flowery Trelease and Coville; and Seaweed Saunders; our grand big-game Doctor, and how many more! Blessed Brewer of a thousand speeches and stories and merry ha-has, and Genial John Burroughs, who growled at and scowled at good Bering Sea and me, but never at thee. I feel pretty sure that he is now all right at his beloved Slabsides and I have a good mind to tell his whole Bering story in his own sort of good-natured, gnarly, snarly, jungle, jangle rhyme.

There! But how unconscionably long the thing is! I must stop short. Remember your penitential promises. Kill as few of your fellow beings as possible and pursue some branch of natural history at least far enough to see Nature's harmony. Don't forget me. God bless you. Good-bye.

Ever your friend

JOHN MUIR

To Julia Merrill Moores

July 25, 1900

MY DEAR FRIENDS:

I scarce need say that I have been with you and mourned with you every day since your blessed sister was called away, and wished I could do something to help and comfort you. Before your letter came, I had already commenced to write the memorial words you ask for, and I'll send them soon.

Her beautiful, noble, helpful life on earth was complete, and had she lived a thousand years she would still have been mourned, the more the longer she stayed. Death is as natural as life, sorrow as joy. Through pain and death come all our blessings, life and immortality.

However clear our faith and hope and love, we must suffer — but with glorious compensation. While death separates, it unites, and the sense of loneliness grows less and less as we become accustomed to the new light, communing with those who have gone on ahead in spirit, and feeling their influence as if again present in the flesh. Your own experience tells you this, however. The Source of all Good turns even sorrow and seeming separation to our advantage, makes us better, drawing us closer together in love, enlarging, strengthening, brightening our views of the spirit world and our hopes of immortal union. Blessed it is to know and feel, even at this cost, that neither distance nor death can truly separate those who love.

My friends, whether living or dead, have always been with me in my so-called lonely wanderings, so kind and wonderful are God's compensations. Few, dear friends, have greater cause for sorrow, or greater cause for joy, than you have. Your sister lives in a thousand hearts, and her influence, pure as sunshine and dew, can never be lost. . . .

Read again and again those blessed words, ever old, ever new: "Who redeemeth thy life from destruction; who crowneth thee with loving kindness and tender mercy," who pities you "like as a father pitieth his children, for He knoweth our frame, He knoweth that we are dust. Man's days are as grass, as a flower of the field the wind passeth over it and it is gone, but the mercy of the Lord is from everlasting to everlasting."

In His strength we must live on, work on, doing the good that comes to heart and hand, looking forward to meeting in that City which the streams of the River of Life make glad.

Ever your loving friend   J. M.

To Walter Hines Page

MARTINEZ, *June* 12, 1900

MY DEAR MR. PAGE:

I sent by mail to-day manuscript of ice article for the Harriman book, the receipt of which please acknowledge, and as it is short I hope you will read it, not for wandering words and sentences out of plumb, but for the ice of it. Coming as you do from the unglacial South, it may "fill a long-felt want." And before you settle down too hopelessly far in book business take a trip to our western Iceland. Go to Glacier Bay and Yakutat and Prince William Sound and get some pure wildness into your inky life. Neglect not this glacial advice and glacial salvation this hot weather, and believe me

Faithfully yours   JOHN MUIR

Very many letters of appreciation were written to Muir by persons who were strangers to him, except in spirit. One such came during the autumn of 1900 from an American woman resident in Yokohama. "More than twenty years ago," said the writer, "when I was at my mountain home in Siskiyou County, California, I read a short sketch of your own, in which you pictured your sense of delight in listening to the wind, with its many voices, sweeping through the pines. That article made a lifelong impression on me, and shaped an inner perception for the wonders of Nature which has gladdened my entire life since. . . . It has always seemed that I must some time thank you."

To Mrs. Richard Swain

MARTINEZ, CALIFORNIA
October 21, 1900

MRS. RICHARD SWAIN:

That you have so long remembered that sketch of the wind-storm in the forest of the Yuba gives me pleasure and encouragement in the midst of this hard life work, for to me it is hard, far harder than tree or mountain climbing. When I began my wanderings in God's wilds, I never dreamed of writing a word for publication, and since beginning literary work it has never seemed possible that much good to others could come of it. Written descriptions of fire or bread are of but little use to the cold or starving. Descriptive writing amounts to little

more than "Hurrah, here's something! Come!"
When my friends urged me to begin, saying,
"We cannot all go to the woods and mountains; you are free and love wildness; go and
bring it to us," I used to reply that it was not
possible to see and enjoy for others any more
than to eat for them or warm for them. Nature's tables are spread and fires burning. You
must go warm yourselves and eat. But letters
like yours which occasionally come to me show
that even nature writing is not altogether useless.

Some time I hope to see Japan's mountains
and forests. The flora of Japan and Manchuria
is among the richest and most interesting on
the globe. With best wishes, I am

Very truly yours

J. M.

To Katherine Merrill Graydon

MARTINEZ, *October 22, 1900*

MY DEAR MISS GRAYDON:

... Of course you know you have my sympathy in your loneliness — loneliness not of
miles, but of loss — the departure from earth of
your great-aunt Kate, the pole-star and lode-
stone of your life and of how many other lives.
What she was to me and what I thought of her
I have written and sent to your Aunt Julia for a

memorial book[1] her many friends are preparing. A rare beloved soul sent of God, all her long life a pure blessing. Her work is done; and she has gone to the Better Land, and now you must get used to seeing her there and hold on to her as your guide as before. . . .

Wanda, as you know, is going to school, and expects soon to enter the University. She is a faithful, steady scholar, not in the least odd or brilliant, but earnest and unstoppable as an avalanche. She comes home every Friday or Saturday by the new railway that crosses the vineyards near the house. Muir Station is just above the Reid house. What sort of a scholar Helen will be I don't know. She is very happy and strong. My sister Sarah is now with us, making four Muirs here, just half the family. . . .

Ever your friend

JOHN MUIR

To Dr. C. Hart Merriam

MARTINEZ, CAL.

October 23, 1900

MY DEAR DR. MERRIAM:

I am very glad to get your kind letter bringing back our big little Sierra trip through the

---

[1] *The Man Shakespeare, and Other Essays.* By Catharine Merrill. The Bowen-Merrill Company, 1902.

midst of so many blessed chipmunks and trees. Many thanks for your care and kindness about the photographs and for the pile of interesting bird and beast Bulletins. No. 3[1] contains lots of masterly work and might be expanded into a grand book. This you should do, adding and modifying in accordance with the knowledge you have gathered during the last ten years. But alas! Here you are pegging and puttering with the concerns of others as if in length of life you expect to rival Sequoia. That stream and fountain[2] article, which like Tennyson's brook threatened to "go on forever," is at last done, and I am now among the Big Tree parks. Not the man with the hoe, but the poor toiler with the pen, deserves mile-long commiseration in prose and rhyme.

Give my kindest regards to Mrs. and Mr. Bailey, and tell them I'll go guide with them to Yosemite whenever they like unless I should happen to be hopelessly tied up in some way.

With pleasant recollections from Mrs. Muir and the girls, I am

Very truly yours   JOHN MUIR

[1] *North American Fauna*, No. 3 — Results of a Biological Survey of San Francisco Mountains and the Desert of the Little Colorado, Arizona, by C. Hart Merriam, September, 1900.

[2] "Fountains and Streams of the Yosemite National Park," *Atlantic*, April, 1901.

JOHN MUIR

To Mrs. Henry Fairfield Osborn

MARTINEZ, CALIFORNIA
November 18, 1900

MY DEAR MRS. OSBORN:

Nothing could be kinder than your invitation to Wing-and-Wing, and how gladly we would accept, you know. But grim Duty, like Bunyan's Apollyon, is now "straddling across the whole breadth of the way," crying "No." . . .

I am at work on the last of a series of park and forest articles to be collected and published in book form by Houghton, Mifflin & Company and which I hope to get off my hands soon. But there is endless work in sight ahead — Sierra and Alaska things to follow as fast as my slow, sadly interrupted pen can be spurred to go.

Yes, I know it is two years since I enjoyed the dainty chickaree room you so kindly call mine. Last summer as you know I was in Alaska. This year I was in the Sierra, going up by way of Lake Tahoe and down by Yosemite Valley, crossing the range four times along the headwaters of the Truckee, Carson, Mokelumne, Stanislaus, Calaveras, Walker, Tuolumne and Merced Rivers, revisiting old haunts, examining forests, and learning what I could about birds and mammals with Dr. Merriam

340

and his sister and Mr. Bailey — keen naturalists with infinite appetite for voles, marmots, squirrels, chipmunks, etc. We had a delightful time, of course, and in Yosemite I remembered your hoped-for visit to the grand Valley and wished you were with us. I'm sorry I missed Sir Michael Foster. Though prevented now, I hope ere long to see Wing-and-Wing in autumn glory. In the mean time and always

I am ever your friend

JOHN MUIR

To Walter Hines Page

MARTINEZ, CAL.
January 10, 1902

Big thanks, my dear Page, for your great letter. The strength and shove and hearty ringing inspiration of it is enough to make the very trees and rocks write. The Park book, the publishers tell me, is successful. To you and Sargent it owes its existence; for before I got your urgent and encouraging letters I never dreamed of writing such a book. As to plans for others, I am now at work on —

1. A small one, "Yosemite and Other Yosemites," which Johnson has been trying to get me to write a long time and which I hope to get off my hands this year. I'll first offer it to the Century Company, hoping they will bring it

out in good shape, give it a good push toward readers and offer fair compensation. . . .

2. The California tree and shrub book was suggested by Merriam last summer, but I have already written so fully on forest trees and their underbrush I'm not sure that I can make another useful book about them. Possibly a handy volume, with short telling descriptions and illustrations of each species, enabling the ordinary observer to know them at sight, might be welcomed. This if undertaken will probably be done season after next, and you shall have the first sight of it.

3. Next should come a mountaineering book — all about walking, climbing, and camping, with a lot of illustrative excursions.

4. Alaska — glaciers, forests, mountains, travels, etc.

5. A book of studies — the action of landscape-making forces, earth sculpture, distribution of plants and animals, etc. My main real book in which I'll have to ask my readers to cerebrate. Still I hope it may be made readable to a good many.

6. Possibly my autobiography which for ten years or more all sorts of people have been begging me to write. My life, however, has been so smooth and regular and reasonable, so free from blundering exciting adventures, the

story seems hardly worth while in the midst of so much that is infinitely more important. Still, if I should live long enough I may be tempted to try it. For I begin to see that such a book would offer fair opportunities here and there to say a good word for God.

The Harriman Alaska book is superb and I gladly congratulate you on the job. In none of the reviews I have seen does Dr. Merriam get half the credit due him as editor.

Hearty thanks for the two Mowbray volumes. I've read them every word. The more of such nature books the better. Good luck to you. May your shop grow like a sequoia and may I meet you with all your family on this side the continent amid its best beauty.

Ever faithfully yours
JOHN MUIR

To Dr. C. Hart Merriam
[*January*, 1902]

MY DEAR DR. MERRIAM:

I send these clippings to give a few hints as to the sheep and forests. Please return them. If you have a file of "The Forester" handy, you might turn to the February and July numbers of 1898, and the one of June, 1900, for solemn discussions of the "proper regulation" of sheep grazing.

343

With the patronage of the business in the hands of the Western politician, the so-called proper regulation of sheep grazing by the Forestry Department is as hopelessly vain as would be laws and regulations for the proper management of ocean currents and earthquakes.

The politicians, in the interest of wealthy mine, mill, sheep, and cattle owners, of course nominate superintendents and supervisors of reservations supposed to be harmlessly blind to their stealings. Only from the Military Department, free from political spoils poison, has any real good worth mention been gained for forests, and so, as far as I can see, it will be, no matter how well the Forestry Department may be organized, until the supervisors, superintendents, and rangers are brought under Civil Service Reform.   Ever yours

JOHN MUIR

To Charles Sprague Sargent

MARTINEZ, *September* 10, 1902

MY DEAR SARGENT:

What are you so wildly "quitting" about? I've faithfully answered all your letters, and as far as I know you are yourself the supreme quitter — Quitter gigantea — quitting Mexico, quitting a too trusting companion in swamps and sand dunes of Florida, etc., etc. Better quit quitting, though since giving the world so noble a book you must, I suppose, be allowed to do as you like until time and Siberia effect a cure.

I am and have been up to the eyes in work, insignificant though it be. Last spring had to describe the Colorado Grand Cañon — the toughest job I ever tackled, strenuous enough to disturb the equanimity of even a Boston man. Then I had to rush off to the Sierra with [the Sierra] Club outing. Then had to explore Kern River Cañon, etc. Now I'm at work on a little Yosemite book. Most of the material for it has been published already, but a new chapter or two will have to be written. Then there is the "Silva" review, the most formidable job of all, which all along I've been hoping some abler, better equipped fellow would take off my hands. Can't you at least give me some helpful suggestions as to the right size, shape, and composition of this review?

Of course I want to take that big tree trip with you next season, and yet I should hate mortally to leave either of these tasks unfinished. Glorious congratulations on the ending of your noble book!

Ever faithfully yours
JOHN MUIR

JOHN MUIR

To Mrs. Anna R. Dickey

DEAR MRS. DICKEY:

I was glad to get your letter. It so vividly recalled our memorable ramble, merry and nobly elevating, and solemn in the solemn aboriginal woods and gardens of the great mountains — commonplace, sublime, and divine. I seemed to hear your voice in your letter, and see you gliding, drifting, scrambling along the trails with all the gay good company, or seated around our many camp-fires in the great illuminated groves, etc., etc. — altogether a good trip in which everybody was a happy scholar at the feet of Nature, and all learned something direct from earth and sky, bird and beast, trees, flowers, and chanting winds and waters; hints, suggestions, little-great lessons of God's infinite power and glory and goodness. No wonder your youth is renewed and Donald goes to his studies right heartily.

To talk plants to those who love them must ever be easy and delightful. By the way, that little fairy, airy, white-flowered plant which covers sandy dry ground on the mountains like a mist, which I told you was a near relative to Eriogonum, but whose name I could never recall, is *Oxytheca spergulina*. There is another rather common species in the region we traveled, but this is the finest and most abundant.

I'm glad you found the mountain hemlock, the loveliest of conifers. You will find it described in both my books. It is abundant in Kings River Cañon, but not beside the trails. The "heather" you mention is no doubt Bryanthus or Cassiope. Next year you and Donald should make collections of at least the most interesting plants. A plant press, tell Donald, is lighter and better than a gun. So is a camera, and good photographs of trees and shrubs are much to be desired.

I have heard from all the girls. Their enthusiasm is still fresh, and they are already planning and plotting for next year's outing in the Yosemite, Tuolumne, and Mono regions. . . . Gannett stayed two days with us, and is now, I suppose at home. I was hoping you might have a day or two for a visit to our little valley. Next time you come to the city try to stop off at "Muir Station" on the Santa Fé. We are only an hour and a half from the city. I should greatly enjoy a visit at your Ojai home, as you well know, but when fate and work will let me I dinna ken. . . . Give my sincere regard to Donald.

Ever faithfully yours

JOHN MUIR

JOHN MUIR

To Robert Underwood Johnson

 MARTINEZ, *September* 15, 1902

DEAR MR. JOHNSON:

On my return from the Kern region I heard loud but vague rumors of the discovery of a giant sequoia in Converse Basin on Kings River, one hundred and fifty-three feet in circumference and fifty feet in diameter, to which I paid no attention, having heard hundreds of such "biggest-tree-in-the-world" rumors before. But at Fresno I met a surveyor who assured me that he had himself measured the tree and found it to be one hundred and fifty-three feet in circumference six feet above ground. So of course I went back up the mountains to see and measure for myself, carrying a steel tapeline.

At one foot above ground it is 108 feet in circumference
" four feet   "   "   " " 97 " 6 inches in "
" six   "   "   "   " " 93 "   " "

One of the largest and finest every way of living sequoias that have been measured. But none can say it is certainly *the largest*. The immensely larger dead one that I discovered twenty-seven years ago stands within a few miles of this new wonder, and I think I have in my notebooks measurements of living specimens as large as the new tree, or larger. I have

348

a photo of the tree and can get others, I think, from a photographer who has a studio in Converse Basin. I'll write a few pages on Big Trees in general if you like; also touching on the horrible destruction of the Kings River groves now going on fiercely about the mills.

As to the discovery of a region grander than Yosemite by the Kelly brothers in the Kings Cañon, it is nearly all pure bosh. I explored the Cañon long ago. It is very deep, but has no El Capitan or anything like it.

Ever yours faithfully

John Muir

To Henry Fairfield Osborn

Martinez, California
July 16, 1904

Dear Mr. Osborn:

In the big talus of letters, books, pamphlets, etc., accumulated on my desk during more than a year's absence, I found your Boone and Crockett address [1] and have heartily enjoyed it. It is an admirable plea for our poor horizontal fellow-mortals, so fast passing away in ruthless starvation and slaughter. Never before has the need for places of refuge and protection been greater. Fortunately, at the last

[1] "Preservation of the Wild Animals of North America," *Forest and Stream*, April 16, 1904, pp. 312–13.

hour, with utter extinction in sight, the Government has begun to act under pressure of public opinion, however slight. Therefore your address is timely and should be widely published. I have often written on the subject, but mostly with non-effect. The murder business and sport by saint and sinner alike has been pushed ruthlessly, merrily on, until at last protective measures are being called for, partly, I suppose, because the pleasure of killing is in danger of being lost from there being little or nothing left to kill, and partly, let us hope, from a dim glimmering recognition of the rights of animals and their kinship to ourselves.

How long it seems since my last visit to Wing-and-Wing! and how far we have been! I got home a few weeks ago from a trip more than a year long. I went with Professor Sargent and his son Robeson through Europe visiting the principal parks, gardens, art galleries, etc. From Berlin we went to St. Petersburg, thence to the Crimea, by Moscow, the Caucasus, across by Dariel Pass from Tiflis, and back to Moscow. Thence across Siberia, Manchuria, etc., to Japan and Shanghai.

At Shanghai left the Sargents and set out on a grand trip alone and free to India, Egypt, Ceylon, Australia, New Zealand. Thence by way of Port Darwin, Timor, through the Malay

Archipelago to Manila. Thence to Hong Kong again and Japan and home by Honolulu. Had perfectly glorious times in India, Australia, and New Zealand. The flora of Australia and New Zealand is so novel and exciting I had to begin botanical studies over again, working night and day with endless enthusiasm. And what wondrous beasts and birds, too, are there!

Do write and let me know how you all are. Remember me with kindest regards to Mrs. Osborn and the children and believe me ever

Faithfully yours

JOHN MUIR

II
1905–1914

The closing period of Muir's life began with a great triumph and a bitter sorrow — both in the same year. His hour of triumph came with the successful issue of a seventeen-year campaign to rescue his beloved Yosemite Valley from the hands of spoilers. His chief helpers were Mr. Johnson in the East and Mr. William E. Colby in the West. The latter had, under the auspices of the Sierra Club, organized and conducted for many years summer outings of large parties of Club members into the High Sierra. These outings, by their simple and healthful camping methods, by their easy mobility amid hundreds of miles of superb mountain scenery, and by the deep love of unspoiled nature which they awakened in thousands of hearts, not only achieved a national reputation, but trained battalions of eager defenders of our national playgrounds. No one was more rejoiced by the growing success of the outings than John Muir, and the evenings when he spoke at the High Sierra camp-fires are treasured memories in many hearts.

When the battle for the recession of the Yosemite Valley grew keen during January and February, 1905, Mr. Muir and Mr. Colby went to Sacramento in order to counteract by their personal presence the propaganda of falsehoods which an interested opposition was industriously spreading. The bill passed by a safe majority and the first of the two following letters celebrates the event; the second relates to the later acceptance of the Valley by Congress, to be administered thereafter as an integral part of the Yosemite National Park.

On the heels of this achievement came a devastating bereavement — the death of his wife. Earlier in the year his daughter Helen had been taken seriously ill, and when she became convalescent she had to be removed to the dry air of Arizona. While there with her, a telegram called him back to the bedside of his wife, in whose case a long-standing illness had suddenly become serious. She died on the sixth of August, 1905, and thereafter the old house on the hill was a shelter and a place of work from time to time, but never a home again. "Get out among the mountains and the trees, friend, as soon as you can," wrote Theodore Roosevelt. "They will do more for you than either man or woman could." But anxiety over the health of his daughter Helen bound him to the Arizona desert for varying periods of time. There he discovered remnants of a wonderful petrified forest, which he studied with great eagerness. He urged that it be preserved as a national monument, and it was set aside by Theodore Roosevelt in 1906 under the name of the Petrified Forest National Monument.

These years of grief and anxiety proved comparatively barren in literary work. But part of the time he probably was engaged upon a revised and enlarged edition of his "Mountains of California," which appeared in 1911 with an affectionate dedication to the memory of his wife. In some notes, written during 1908, for his autobiography, Muir alludes to this period of stress with a pathetic foreboding that he might not live long enough to gather a matured literary harvest from his numerous notebooks.

JOHN MUIR

The letters of the closing years of his life show an increasing sense of urgency regarding the unwritten books mentioned in his letter to Walter Hines Page, and he applied himself to literary work too unremittingly for the requirements of his health. Much of his writing during this period was done at the home of Mr. and Mrs. J. D. Hooker in Los Angeles and at the summer home of Mr. and Mrs. Henry Fairfield Osborn at Garrison's-on-the-Hudson. The last long journey, in which he realized the dreams of a lifetime, was undertaken during the summer of 1911. It was the trip to South America, to the Amazon — the goal which he had in view when he set out on his thousand-mile walk to the Gulf in 1867. His chief object was to see the araucaria forests of Brazil. This accomplished, he went from South America to South Africa in order to see the Baobab tree in its native habitat.

During these few later years of domestic troubles and anxieties [he wrote in 1911] but little writing or studying of any sort has been possible. But these, fortunately, are now beginning to abate, and I hope that something worth while may still be accomplished before the coming of life's night. I have written but three [1] books as yet, and a number of scientific and popular articles in magazines, news-

[1] *Mountains of California, Our National Parks,* and *My First Summer in the Sierra.*

papers, etc. In the beginning of my studies I never intended to write a word for the press. In my life of lonely wanderings I was pushed and pulled on and on through everything by unwavering never-ending love of God's earth plans and works, and eternal, immortal, all-embracing Beauty; and when importuned to "write, write, write, and give your treasures to the world," I have always said that I could not stop field work until too old to climb mountains; but now, at the age of seventy, I begin to see that if any of the material collected in notebooks, already sufficient for a dozen volumes, is to be arranged and published by me, I must make haste.

To Robert Underwood Johnson

MARTINEZ, *February* 24, [1905]

DEAR MR. JOHNSON:

I wish I could have seen you last night when you received my news of the Yosemite victory, which for so many years, as commanding general, you have bravely and incessantly fought for.

About two years ago public opinion, which had long been on our side, began to rise into effective action. On the way to Yosemite [in 1903] both the President [1] and our Governor [1] were won to our side, and since then the movement was like Yosemite avalanches. But though almost everybody was with us, so ac-

[1] President Theodore Roosevelt and Governor George C. Pardee.

tive was the opposition of those pecuniarily and politically interested, we might have failed to get the bill through the Senate but for the help of Mr. H——, though, of course, his name or his company were never in sight through all the fight. About the beginning of January I wrote to Mr. H——. He promptly telegraphed a favorable reply.

Wish you could have heard the oratory of the opposition — fluffy, nebulous, shrieking, howling, threatening like sand-storms and dust whirlwinds in the desert. Sometime I hope to tell you all about it.

I am now an experienced lobbyist; my political education is complete. Have attended Legislature, made speeches, explained, exhorted, persuaded every mother's son of the legislators, newspaper reporters, and everybody else who would listen to me. And now that the fight is finished and my education as a politician and lobbyist is finished, I am almost finished myself.

Now, ho! for righteous management.... Of course you'll have a long editorial in the "Century."

Faithfully yours

[JOHN MUIR]

UNTO THE LAST

To Robert Underwood Johnson

ADAMANA, ARIZONA
July 16, 1906

Yes, my dear Johnson, sound the loud timbrel and let every Yosemite tree and stream rejoice!

You may be sure I knew when the big bill passed. Getting Congress to accept the Valley brought on, strange to say, a desperate fight both in the House and Senate. Sometime I'll tell you all the story. You don't know how accomplished a lobbyist I've become under your guidance. The fight you planned by that famous Tuolumne camp-fire seventeen years ago is at last fairly, gloriously won, every enemy down derry down.

Write a good, long, strong, heart-warming letter to Colby. He is the only one of all the Club who stood by me in downright effective fighting.

I congratulate you on your successful management of Vesuvius, as Gilder says, and safe return with yourself and family in all its far-spreading branches in good health. Helen is now much better. Wanda was married last month, and I am absorbed in these enchanted carboniferous forests. Come and let me guide you through them and the great Cañon.

Ever yours   JOHN MUIR

357

JOHN MUIR

To Francis Fisher Browne [1]

325 WEST ADAMS STREET
LOS ANGELES, CALIFORNIA
June 1, 1910

MY DEAR MR. BROWNE:

Good luck and congratulations on the "Dial's" thirtieth anniversary, and so Scottishly and well I learned to know you two summers ago, with blessed John Burroughs & Co., that I seem to have known you always.

I was surprised to get a long letter from Miss Barrus written at Seattle, and in writing to Mr. Burroughs later I proposed to him that he follow to this side of the continent and build a new Slabsides "where rolls the Oregon," and write more bird and bee books instead of his new-fangled Catskill Silurian and Devonian geology on which he at present seems to have gane gite, clean gite, having apparently forgotten that there is a single bird or bee in the sky. I also proposed that in his ripe, mellow, autumnal age he go with me to the basin of the Amazon for new ideas, and also to South Africa and Madagascar, where he might see something that would bring his early bird and bee days to mind.

[1] Editor of *The Dial* from 1880 to his death in 1913. A tribute by Muir under the title "Browne the Beloved" appeared in *The Dial* during June, 1913.

UNTO THE LAST

I have been hidden down here in Los Angeles for a month or two and have managed to get off a little book to Houghton Mifflin, which they propose to bring out as soon as possible. It is entitled "My First Summer in the Sierra." I also have another book nearly ready, made up of a lot of animal stories for boys, drawn from my experiences as a boy in Scotland and in the wild oak openings of Wisconsin. I have also rewritten the autobiographical notes dictated at Harriman's Pelican Lodge on Klamath Lake two years ago, but that seems to be an endless job, and, if completed at all, will require many a year. Next month I mean to try to bring together a lot of Yosemite material into a handbook for travelers, which ought to have been written long ago.

So you see I am fairly busy, and precious few trips will I be able to make this summer, although I took Professor Osborn and family into the Yosemite for a few days, and Mr. Hooker and his party on a short trip to the Grand Cañon.

Are you coming West this year? It would be delightful to see you once more.

I often think of the misery of Mr. Burroughs and his physician, caused by our revels in Burns' poems, reciting verse about in the resonant board chamber whose walls transmitted every one of the blessed words to the sleepy and unwilling ears of John.... Fun to us, but death and broken slumbers to Oom John!

With all best wishes, my dear Browne, and many warmly cherished memories, I am

Ever faithfully your friend

JOHN MUIR

To Henry Fairfield Osborn

325 WEST ADAMS STREET
LOS ANGELES, CALIFORNIA
June 1, 1910

MY DEAR MR. OSBORN:

Many thanks for the copy you sent me of your long good manly letter to Mr. Robert J. Collier on the Hetch-Hetchy Yosemite Park. As I suppose you have seen by the newspapers, San Francisco will have until May 1, 1911, to show cause why Hetch-Hetchy Valley should not be eliminated from the permit which the Government has given the city to develop a water supply in Yosemite Park. Meantime the municipality is to have detailed surveys made of the Lake Eleanor watershed, of the Hetch-Hetchy, and other available sources, and furnish such data and information as may be directed by the board of army engineers appointed by the President to act in an advisory capacity with Secretary Ballinger. Mr. Ballinger said to the San Francisco proponents of the damming scheme, "I want to know what is necessary so far as the Hetch-Hetchy is concerned." He also said, "What this Government wants to know and the American people want to know is whether it is a matter of absolute necessity for the people of San Francisco to have this water supply. Otherwise it belongs to the people for the purpose of a national park for which it has been set aside." Ballinger suggested that the Lake Eleanor plans should be submitted to the engineers at once so that they could have them as a basis for ascertaining if the full development of that watershed is contemplated, and to make a report of its data to the engineers as its preparation proceeded so that they may be kept in immediate touch with what is being done. Of the outcome of this thorough examination of the scheme there can be no doubt, and it must surely put the question at rest for all time, at least as far as our great park is concerned, and perhaps all the other national parks.

I have been hidden down here in Los Angeles a month or two working hard on books. Two or three weeks ago I sent the manuscript of a small book to Houghton Mifflin Company, who expect to bring it out as soon as possible. It is entitled "My First Summer in the Sierra," written from notes made forty-one years ago. I have also nearly ready a lot of animal stories for a boys' book, drawn chiefly from my experiences as a boy in Scotland and in the wild oak openings of Wisconsin. I have also rewritten a lot of autobiographical notes dictated at Mr. Harriman's Pelican Lodge on Klamath Lake two years ago. Next month I hope to bring together a lot of Yosemite sketches for a sort of travelers' guidebook, which ought to have been written many years ago.

So you see, what with furnishing illustrations, reading proof, and getting this Yosemite guidebook off my hands, it will not be likely that I can find time for even a short visit to New York this summer. Possibly, however, I may be able to get away a few weeks in the autumn. Nothing, as you well know, would be more delightful than a visit to your blessed Garrison's-on-the-Hudson, and I am sure to make it some time ere long, unless my usual good luck should fail me utterly.

With warmest regards to Mrs. Osborn and Josephine and all the family, I am, my dear Mr. Osborn,

Ever faithfully your friend
JOHN MUIR

UNTO THE LAST

To Mrs. J. D. Hooker

MARTINEZ, *September* 15, 1910

DEAR MRS. HOOKER:

Be of good cheer, make the best of whatever befalls; keep as near to headquarters as you may, and you will surely triumph over the ills of life, its frets and cares, with all other vermin of either earth or sky.

I'm ashamed to have enjoyed my visit so much. A lone good soul can still work miracles, charm an outlandish, crooked, zigzag flat into a lofty inspiring Olympus.

Do you know these fine verses of Thoreau?

"I will not doubt for evermore,
  Nor falter from a steadfast faith,
For though the system be turned o'er,
  God takes not back the word which once he saith.

"I will, then, trust the love untold
  Which not my worth nor want has bought,
Which wooed me young and wooes me old,
  And to this evening hath me brought."

Ever your friend

JOHN MUIR

To Mrs. J. D. Hooker

MARTINEZ, *December* 17, 1910

DEAR MRS. HOOKER:

I'm glad you're at work on a book, for as far as I know, however high or low Fortune's winds

363

may blow o'er life's solemn main, there is nothing so saving as good hearty work. From a letter just received from the Lark I learn the good news that Mr. Hooker is also hard at work with his pen.

As for myself, I've been reading old musty dusty Yosemite notes until I'm tired and blinky blind, trying to arrange them in something like lateral, medial, and terminal moraines on my den floor. I never imagined I had accumulated so vast a number. The long trains and embankments and heaped-up piles are truly appalling. I thought that in a quiet day or two I might select all that would be required for a guidebook; but the stuff seems enough for a score of big jungle books, and it's very hard, I find, to steer through it on anything like a steady course in reasonable time. Therefore, I'm beginning to see that I'll have to pick out only a moderate-sized bagful for the book and abandon the bulk of it to waste away like a snowbank or grow into other forms as time and chance may determine.

So, after all, I may be able to fly south in a few days and alight in your fine cañon garret. Anyhow, with good will and good wishes, to you all, I am

Ever faithfully, affectionately

JOHN MUIR

UNTO THE LAST

To Mrs. J. D. Hooker

[*June* 26, 1911]

... I went to New Haven Tuesday morning, the 20th, was warmly welcomed and entertained by Professor Phelps and taken to the ball game in the afternoon. Though at first a little nervous, especially about the approaching honorary degree ceremony, I quickly caught the glow of the Yale enthusiasm. Never before have I seen or heard anything just like it. The alumni, assembled in classes from all the country, were arrayed in wildly colored uniforms, and the way they rejoiced and made merry, capered and danced, sang and yelled, marched and ran, doubled, quadrupled, octupled is utterly indescribable; autumn leaves in whirlwinds are staid and dignified in comparison.

Then came memorable Wednesday when we donned our radiant academic robes and marched to the great hall where the degrees were conferred, shining like crow blackbirds. I was given perhaps the best seat on the platform, and when my name was called I arose with a grand air, shook my massive academic plumes into finest fluting folds, as became the occasion, stepped forward in awful majesty and stood rigid and solemn like an ancient sequoia while the orator poured praise on the honored wanderer's head — and in this heroic attitude I

365

think I had better leave him. Here is what the orator said. Pass it on to Helen at Daggett.

My love to all who love you.

Faithfully, affectionately

JOHN MUIR

To John Burroughs

GARRISON, N.Y.
July 14, 1911

DEAR JOHN BURROUGHS:

When I was on the train passing your place I threw you a hearty salute across the river, but I don't suppose that you heard or felt it. I would have been with you long ago if I had not been loaded down with odds and ends of duties, book-making, book-selling at Boston, Yosemite and Park affairs at Washington, and making arrangements for getting off to South America, etc., etc. I have never worked harder in my life, although I have not very much to show for it. I have got a volume of my autobiography finished. Houghton Mifflin are to bring it out. They want to bring it out immediately, but I would like to have at least part of it run through some suitable magazine, and thus gain ten or twenty times more readers than would be likely to see it in a book.

I have been working for the last month or more on the Yosemite book, trying to finish it before leaving for the Amazon, but I am not suffering in a monstrous city. I am on the top of as green a hill as I have seen in all the State, with hermit thrushes, woodchucks, and warm hearts, something like those about yourself.

I am at a place that I suppose you know well, Professor Osborn's summer residence at Garrison's, opposite West Point. After Mrs. Harriman left for Arden I went down to the "Century" Editorial Rooms, where I was offered every facility for writing in Gilder's room, and tried to secure a boarding-place near Union Square, but the first day was so hot that it made my head swim, and I hastily made preparations for this comfortable home up on the hill here, where I will remain until perhaps the 15th of August, when I expect to sail.

Nothing would be more delightful than to go from one beautiful place to another and from one friend to another, but it is utterly impossible to visit a hundredth part of the friends who are begging me to go and see them and at the same time get any work done. I am now shut up in a magnificent room pegging away at that book, and working as hard as I ever did in my life. I do not know what has got into me, making so many books all at once. It is not natural. . . .

JOHN MUIR

With all good wishes to your big and happy family, I am ever

Faithfully your friend

JOHN MUIR

To Mrs. Henry Fairfield Osborn

PARA, BRAZIL,
August 29, 1911

DEAR MRS. OSBORN:

Here at last is The River and thanks to your and Mrs. Harriman's loving care I'm well and strong for all South American work in sight that looks like mine.

Arrived here last eve — after a pleasant voyage — a long charming slide all the way to the equator between beautiful water and beautiful sky.

Approaching Para, had a glorious view of fifty miles or so of forest on the right bank of the river. This alone is noble compensation for my long desired and waited-for Amazon journey, even should I see no more.

And it's delightful to contemplate your cool restful mountain trip which is really a part of this equator trip. The more I see of our goodly Godly star, the more plainly comes to sight and mind the truth that it is all one like a face, every feature radiating beauty on the others.

I expect to start up the river to Manaos in a

day or two on the Dennis. Will write again on
my return before going south — and will hope
to get a letter from you and Mr. Osborn, who
must be enjoying his well-earned rest. How
often I've wished him with me. I often think of
you and Josephine among the Avalanche Lake
clintonias and linnæas. And that lovely boy
at Castle Rock. Virginia played benevolent
mother delightfully and sent me off rejoicing.

My love to each and all; ever, dear friend
and friends,

Faithfully, gratefully
JOHN MUIR

To Mrs. J. D. Hooker

PARA, BRAZIL
September 19, 1911

... Of course you need absolute rest. Lie
down among the pines for a while, then get to
plain, pure, white love-work with Marian, to
help humanity and other mortals and the Lord
— heal the sick, cheer the sorrowful, break the
jaws of the wicked, etc. But this Amazon delta
sermon is growing too long. How glad I am
that Marian was not with me, on account of
yellow fever and the most rapidly deadly of the
malarial kinds so prevalent up the river.

Nevertheless, I've had a most glorious time

369

on this trip, dreamed of nearly half a century — have seen more than a thousand miles of the noblest of Earth's streams, and gained far more telling views of the wonderful forests than I ever hoped for. The Amazon, as you know, is immensely broad, but for hundreds of miles the steamer ran so close to the bossy leafy banks I could almost touch the out-reaching branches — fancy how I stared and sketched.

I was a week at Manaos on the Rio Negro tributary, wandered in the wonderful woods, got acquainted with the best of the citizens through Mr. Sanford, a graduate of Yale, was dined and guided and guarded and befriended in the most wonderful way, and had a grand telling time in general. I have no end of fine things for you in the way of new beauty. The only fevers I have had so far are burning enthusiasms, but there's no space for them in letters.

Here, however, is something that I must tell right now. Away up in that wild Manaos region in the very heart of the vast Amazon basin I found a little case of books in a lonely house. Glancing over the titles, none attracted me except a soiled volume at the end of one of the shelves, the blurred title of which I was unable to read, so I opened the glass door, opened the book, and out of it like magic jumped Kathar-, ine and Marian Hooker, apparently in the very flesh. The book, needless to say, was "Wayfarers in Italy." The joy-shock I must not try to tell in detail, for medical Marian might call the whole story an equatorial fever dream.

Dear, dear friend, again good-bye. Rest in God's peace.

Affectionately

JOHN MUIR

To Mrs. J. D. Hooker

PYRAMIDES HOTEL, MONTEVIDEO
Dooombor 6, 1911

MY DEAR FRIEND:

Your letter of October 4th from San Francisco was forwarded from Para to Buenos Aires and received there at the American Consulate. Your and Marian's letter, dated August 7th, wore received at Para, not having been quite in time to reach me before I sailed, but forwarded by Mrs. Osburn. I can't think how I could have failed to acknowledge them. I have them and others with me, and they have been read times numberless when I was feeling lonely on my strange wanderings in all sorts of places.

But I'm now done with this glorious continent, at least for the present, as far as hard journeys along rivers, across mountains and tablelands, and through strange forests are concerned. I've seen all I sought for, and far, far, far more. From Para I sailed to Rio de Janeiro and at the first eager gaze into its wonderful harbor saw that it was a glacier bay, as unchanged by weathering as any in Alaska, every rock in it and about it a glacial monument, though within 23° of the equator, and feathered with palms instead of spruces, while every mountain and bay all the way down the coast to the Rio Grande do Sul corroborates the strange icy story. From Rio I sailed to Santos, and thence struck inland and wandered most joyfully a thousand miles or so, mostly in the State of Parana, through millions of acres of the ancient tree I was so anxious to find, *Araucaria Brasiliensis*. Just think of the glow of my joy in these noble aboriginal forests — the face of every tree marked with the inherited experiences of millions of years. From Paranagua I sailed for Buenos Aires; crossed the Andes to Santiago, Chile; thence south four or five hundred miles; thence straight to the snow-line, and found a glorious forest of *Araucaria imbricata*, the strangest of the strange genus.

The day after to-morrow, December 8th, I intend to sail for Teneriffe on way to South Africa; then home some way or other. But I can give no address until I reach New York. I'm so glad your health is restored, and, now that you are free to obey your heart and have your brother's help and Marian's cosmic energy, your good-doing can have no end. I'm glad you are not going to sell the Los Angeles garret and garden. Why, I hardly know. Perhaps because I'm weary and lonesome, with a long hot journey ahead, and I feel as if I were again bidding you all good-bye. I think you may send me a word or two to Cape Town, care the American Consul. It would not be lost, for it would follow me.

It's perfectly marvelous how kind hundreds of people have been to this wanderer, and the new beauty stored up is far beyond telling. Give my love to Marian, Maude, and Ellie and all who love you. I wish you would write a line now and then to darling Helen. She has a little bungalow of her own now at 233 Formosa Avenue, Hollywood, California.

It's growing late, and I've miserable packing to do. Good night. And once more, dear, dear friend, good-bye.

JOHN MUIR

JOHN MUIR

To Mr. and Mrs. Henry Fairfield Osborn

NEAR ZANZIBAR
January 31, 1912

DEAR FRIENDS:

What a lot of wild water has been roaring between us since those blessed Castle Rock days! But, roll and roar as it might, you have never been out of heart-sight.

How often I've wished you with me on the best of my wanderings so full of good things guided by wonderful luck, or shall I reverently, thankfully say Providence? Anyhow, it seems that I've had the most fruitful time of my life on this pair of hot continents. But I must not try to write my gains, for they are utterly unletterable both in size and kind. I'll tell what I can when I see you, probably in three months or less. From Cape Town I went north to the Zambesi baobab forests and Victoria Falls, and thence down through a glacial wonderland to Beira, where I caught this steamer, and am on my way to Mombasa and the Nyanza Lake region. From Mombasa I intend starting homeward via Suez and Naples and New York, fondly hoping to find you well. In the meantime I'm sending lots of wireless, tireless love messages to each and every Osborn, for I am

Ever faithfully yours

JOHN MUIR

UNTO THE LAST

To Mrs. Anna R. Dickey

MARTINEZ
May 1, 1912

DEAR CHEERY, EXHILARATING MRS. DICKEY:

Your fine lost letter has reached me at last. I found it in the big talus-heap awaiting me here.

The bright, shining, faithful, hopeful way you bear your crushing burdens is purely divine, out of darkness cheering everybody else with noble godlike sympathy. I'm so glad you have a home with the birds in the evergreen oaks — the feathered folk singing for you and every leaf shining, reflecting God's love. Donald, too, is so brave and happy. With youth on his side and joyful work, he is sure to grow stronger and under every disadvantage do more as a naturalist than thousands of others with every resource of health and wealth and special training.

I'm in my old library den, the house desolate, nobody living in it save a hungry mouse or two.... [I hold] dearly cherished memories about it and the fine garden grounds full of trees and bushes and flowers that my wife and father-in-law and I planted — fine things from every land.

But there's no good bread hereabouts and no housekeeper, so I may never be able to make it a home, fated, perhaps, to wander until sundown. Anyhow, I've had a glorious life, and I'll never have the heart to complain. The roses now are overrunning all bounds in glory of full bloom, and the Lebanon and Himalaya cedars, and the palms and Australian trees and shrubs, and the oaks on the valley hills seem happier and more exuberant than ever.

The Chelan trip would be according to my own heart, but whether or no I can go I dinna ken. Only lots of hard pen work seems certain. Anywhere, anyhow, with love to Donald, I am,
Ever faithfully, affectionately yours
JOHN MUIR

To William E. Colby

and

Mr. and Mrs. Edward T. Parsons

1525 FORMOSA AVENUE
HOLLYWOOD, CALIFORNIA
June 24, 1912

DEAR MR. COLBY AND MR. AND MRS. PARSONS:
I thank you very much for your kind wishes to give me a pleasant Kern River trip, and am very sorry that work has been so unmercifully piled upon me that I find it impossible to escape from it, so I must just stay and work.

I heartily congratulate you and all your merry mountaineers on the magnificent trip that lies before you. As you know, I have seen something of nearly all the mountain-chains of the world, and have experienced their varied climates and attractions of forests and rivers, lakes and meadows, etc. In fact, I have seen a little of all the high places and low places of the continents, but no mountain-range seems to me so kind, so beautiful, or so fine in its sculpture as the Sierra Nevada. If you were as free as the winds are and the light to choose a camp-ground in any part of the globe, I could not direct you to a single place for your outing that, all things considered, is so attractive, so exhilarating and uplifting in every way as just the trip that you are now making. You are far happier than you know. Good luck to you all, and I shall hope to see you all on your return — boys and girls, with the sparkle and exhilaration of the mountains still in your eyes. With love and countless fondly cherished memories,

Ever faithfully yours

JOHN MUIR

Of course, in all your camp-fire preaching and praying you will never forget Hetch-Hetchy.

JOHN MUIR

To Howard Palmer

MARTINEZ, CAL.
December 12, 1912

MR. HOWARD PALMER
Secretary American Alpine Club
New London, Conn.

DEAR SIR:

At the National Parks conference in Yosemite Valley last October, called by the Honorable Secretary of the Interior, comparatively little of importance was considered. The great question was, "Shall automobiles be allowed to enter Yosemite?" It overshadowed all others, and a prodigious lot of gaseous commercial eloquence was spent upon it by auto-club delegates from near and far.

The principal objection urged against the puffing machines was that on the steep Yosemite grades they would cause serious accidents. The machine men roared in reply that far fewer park-going people would be killed or wounded by the auto-way than by the old prehistoric wagon-way. All signs indicate automobile victory, and doubtless, under certain precautionary restrictions, these useful, progressive, blunt-nosed mechanical beetles will hereafter be allowed to puff their way into all the parks and mingle their gas-breath with the breath of the pines and waterfalls, and, from the mountaineer's standpoint, with but little harm or good.

In getting ready for the Canal-celebration visitors the need of opening the Valley gates as wide as possible was duly considered, and the repair of roads and trails, hotel and camp building, the supply of cars and stages and arrangements in general for getting the hoped-for crowds safely into the Valley and out again. But the Yosemite Park was lost sight of, as if its thousand square miles of wonderful mountains, cañons, glaciers, forests, and songful falling rivers had no existence.

In the development of the Park a road is needed from the Valley along the upper cañon of the Merced, across to the head of Tuolumne Meadows, down the great Tuolumne Cañon to Hetch-Hetchy valley, and thence back to Yosemite by the Big Oak Flat road. Good walkers can go anywhere in these hospitable mountains without artificial ways. But most visitors have to be rolled on wheels with blankets and kitchen arrangements.

Of course the few mountaineers present got in a word now and then on the need of park protection from commercial invasion like that now threatening Hetch-Hetchy. In particular the Secretary of the American Civic Association and the Sierra Club spoke on the highest value of wild parks as places of recreation, Nature's cathedrals, where all may gain inspiration and strength and get nearer to God.

The great need of a landscape gardener to lay out the roads and direct the work of thinning out the heavy undergrowth was also urged.

With all good New Year wishes, I am
Faithfully yours
JOHN MUIR

To Asa K. McIlhaney

MARTINEZ, CALIFORNIA
January 10, 1913

MR. ASA K. MCILHANEY
Bath, Penn.

DEAR SIR:

I thank you for your fine letter, but in reply I can't tell which of all God's trees I like best, though I should write a big book trying to. Sight-seers often ask me which is best, the Grand Cañon of Arizona or Yosemite. I always reply that I know a show better than either of them — both of them.

Anglo-Saxon folk have inherited love for oaks and heathers. Of all I know of the world's two hundred and fifty oaks perhaps I like best the *macrocarpa, chrysolepis, lobata, Virginiana, agrifolia,* and *Michauxii.* Of the little heather folk my favorite is Cassiope; of the

380

trees of the family, the Menzies arbutus, one of the world's great trees. The hickory is a favorite genus — I like them all, the pecan the best. Of flower trees, magnolia and liriodendron and the wonderful baobab; of conifers, *Sequoia gigantea*, the noblest of the whole noble race, and sugar pine, king of pines, and silver firs, especially *magnifica*. The grand larch forests of the upper Missouri and of Manchuria and the glorious deodars of the Himalaya, araucarias of Brazil and Chile and Australia. The wonderful eucalyptus, two hundred species, the New Zealand metrosideros and agathis. The magnificent eriodendron of the Amazon and the palm and tree fern and tree grass forests, and in our own country the delightful linden and oxydendron and maples and so on, without end. I may as well stop here as anywhere.

Wishing you a happy New Year and good times in God's woods,

Faithfully yours

JOHN MUIR

JOHN MUIR

To Miss M. Merrill

MARTINEZ, CALIFORNIA
May 31, 1913

DEAR MINA MERRILL:

I am more delighted with your letter than I can tell — to see your handwriting once more and know that you still love me. For through all life's wanderings you have held a warm place in my heart, and I have never ceased to thank God for giving me the blessed Merrill family as lifelong friends. As to the Scotch way of bringing up children, to which you refer, I think it is often too severe or even cruel. And as I hate cruelty, I called attention to it in the boyhood book while at the same time pointing out the value of sound religious training with steady work and restraint.

I'm now at work on an Alaska book, and as soon as it is off my hands I mean to continue the autobiography from leaving the University to botanical excursions in the northern woods, around Indianapolis, and thence to Florida, Cuba, and California. This will be volume number two.

It is now seven years since my beloved wife vanished in the land of the leal. Both of my girls are happily married and have homes and children of their own. Wanda has three lively boys, Helen has two and is living at Daggett,

California. Wanda is living on the ranch in the old adobe, while I am alone in my library den in the big house on the hill where you and sister Kate found me on your memorable visit long ago.

As the shadows lengthen in life's afternoon, we cling all the more fondly to the friends of our youth. And it is with the warmest gratitude that I recall the kindness of all your family when I was lying in darkness. That Heaven may ever bless you, dear Mina, is the heart prayer of your

Affectionate friend

JOHN MUIR

To Mrs. Henry Fairfield Osborn

MARTINEZ
July 3, 1913

DEAR MRS. OSBORN:

Warm thanks, thanks, thanks for your July invitation to blessed Castle Rock. How it goes to my heart all of you must know, but wae's me! I see no way of escape from the work piled on me here — the gatherings of half a century of wilderness wanderings to be sorted and sifted into something like clear, useful form. Never mind — for, anywhere, everywhere in immortal soul sympathy, I'm always with my friends, let time and the seas and con-

383

tinents spread their years and miles as they may.

Ever gratefully, faithfully

JOHN MUIR

To Henry Fairfield Osborn

MARTINEZ
July 15, 1913

DEAR FRIEND OSBORN:

I had no thought of your leaving your own great work and many-fold duties to go before the House Committee on the everlasting Hetch-Hetchy fight, but only to write to members of Congress you might know, especially to President Wilson, a Princeton man. This is the twenty-third year of almost continual battle for preservation of Yosemite National Park, sadly interrupting my natural work. Our enemies now seem to be having most everything their own wicked way, working beneath obscuring tariff and bank clouds, spending millions of the people's money for selfish ends. Think of three or four ambitious, shifty traders and politicians calling themselves "The City of San Francisco," bargaining with the United States for half of the Yosemite Park like Yankee horse-traders, as if the grandest of all our mountain playgrounds, full of God's best gifts, the joy and admiration of the world, were of no more account than any of the long list of tinker tariff articles.

Where are you going this summer? Wish I could go with you. The pleasure of my long lovely Garrison-Hudson Castle Rock days grows only the clearer and dearer as the years flow by.

My love to you, dear friend, and to all who love you.

Ever gratefully, affectionately

JOHN MUIR

To Mr. and Mrs. Henry Fairfield Osborn

MARTINEZ
January 4, 1914

DEAR FRIENDS OSBORNS:

With all my heart I wish you a happy New Year. How hard you have fought in the good fight to save the Tuolumne Yosemite I well know. The battle has lasted twelve years, from Pinchot and Company to President Wilson, and the wrong has prevailed over the best aroused sentiment of the whole country.

That a lane lined with lies could be forced through the middle of the U.S. Congress is truly wonderful even in these confused political days — a devil's masterpiece of log-rolling road-making. But the approval of such a job by scholarly, virtuous, Princeton Wilson is the greatest wonder of all! Fortunately wrong cannot last; soon or late it must fall back home to Hades, while some compensating good must surely follow.

With the new year to new work right gladly we will go — you to your studies of God's langsyne people in their magnificent Wyoming-Idaho mausoleums, I to crystal ice.

So devoutly prays your grateful admiring friend   JOHN MUIR

To Andrew Carnegie

MARTINEZ, CALIFORNIA
January 22, 1914

Many thanks, dear Mr. Carnegie, for your admirable "Apprenticeship." To how many fine godly men and women has our stormy, craggy, glacier-sculptured little Scotland given birth, influencing for good every country under the sun! Our immortal poet while yet a boy wished that for poor auld Scotland's sake he might "sing a sang at least." And what a song you have sung with your ringing, clanging hammers and furnace fires, blowing and flaming like volcanoes — a truly wonderful Caledonian performance. But far more wonderful is your coming forth out of that tremendous titanic iron and dollar work with a heart in sympathy with all humanity.

UNTO THE LAST

Like John Wesley, who took the world for his parish, you are teaching and preaching over all the world in your own Scotch way, with heroic benevolence putting to use the mine and mill wealth won from the iron hills. What wonderful burdens you have carried all your long life, and seemingly so easily and naturally, going right ahead on your course, steady as a star! How strong you must be and happy in doing so much good, in being able to illustrate so nobly the national character founded on God's immutable righteousness that makes Scotland loved at home, revered abroad! Everybody blessed with a drop of Scotch blood must be proud of you and bid you godspeed.

Your devoted admirer

JOHN MUIR

To Dr. C. Hart Merriam

MARTINEZ, CALIFORNIA
February 11, 1914

DEAR DR. MERRIAM:

I was very glad to hear from you once more last month, for, as you say, I haven't heard from you for an age. I fully intended to grope my way to Lagunitas in the fall before last, but it is such ancient history that I have only very dim recollections of the difficulty that hindered me from making the trip. I hope, however, to

387

have better luck next spring for I am really anxious to see you all once more.

I congratulate Dorothy on her engagement to marry Henry Abbot. If he is at all like his blessed old grandfather he must prove a glorious prize in life's lottery. I have been intimately acquainted with General Abbot ever since we camped together for months on the Forestry Commission, towards the end of President Cleveland's second administration.

Wanda, her husband, and three boys are quite well, living on the ranch here, in the old adobe, while I am living alone in the big house on the hill.

After living a year or two in Los Angeles, Helen with her two fine boys and her husband returned to the alfalfa ranch on the edge of the Mojave Desert near Daggett, on the Santa Fé Railway. They are all in fine health and will be glad to get word from you.

Our winter here has been one of the stormiest and foggiest I have ever experienced, and unfortunately I caught the grippe. The last two weeks, however, the weather has been quite bright and sunny and I hope soon to be as well as ever and get to work again.

That a few ruthless ambitious politicians should have been able to run a tunnel lined with all sorts of untruthful bewildering statements through both houses of Congress for Hetch-Hetchy is wonderful, but that the President should have signed the Raker Bill is most wonderful of all. As you say, it is a monumental mistake, but it is more, it is a monumental crime.

I have not heard a word yet from the Baileys. Hoping that they are well and looking forward with pleasure to seeing you all soon in California, I am as ever

Faithfully yours JOHN MUIR

Despite his hopeful allusion to the grippe which he had caught early in the winter of 1914, the disease made farther and farther inroads upon his vitality. Yet he worked away steadily at the task of completing his Alaska book. During the closing months he had the aid of Mrs. Marion Randall Parsons, at whose home the transcription of his Alaska journals had been begun in November, 1910. Unfortunately the Hetch-Hetchy conspiracy became acute again, and the book, barely begun, had to be laid aside that he might save, if possible, his beloved "Tuolumne Yosemite." "We may lose this particular fight," he wrote to William E. Colby, "but truth and right must prevail at last. Anyhow we must be true to ourselves and the Lord."

This particular battle, indeed, was lost because the park invaders had finally got into office a Secretary of the Interior who had previously been on San Francisco's payroll as an attorney to promote the desired Hetch-Hetchy legislation; also, because various other politicians of easy convictions on such fundamental questions of public policy as this had been won over to a concerted drive to accomplish the "grab" during a special summer session when no effective representation of opposing organizations could be secured. So flagrant was the performance in every aspect of it that Senator John D. Works of California afterwards introduced in the Senate a bill to repeal the Hetch-Hetchy legislation and in his vigorous remarks accompanying the same set forth the points on which he justified his action. But the fate of the Valley was sealed.

John Muir turned sadly but courageously to his note-books and memories of the great glacier-ploughed wilderness of Alaska. Shortly before Christmas, 1914, he set his house in order as if he had a presentiment that he was leaving it for the last time, and went to pay a holiday visit to the home of his younger daughter at Daggett. Upon his arrival there he was smitten with pneumonia and was rushed to a hospital in Los Angeles, where all his wander-

ings ended on Christmas Eve. Spread about
him on the bed, when the end came, were
manuscript sheets of his last book — "Travels
in Alaska" — to which he was bravely strug-
gling to give the last touches before the coming
of "the long sleep."

CHAPTER XVIII

HIS PUBLIC SERVICE

/ "THE last rays of the setting sun are shining into our window at the Palace Hotel and perhaps it is the last sunset we shall ever see in this city of the Golden Gate. I could not think ' of leaving the Pacific Coast without saying good-bye to you who so much love all the world about here. California, you may say, has made you, and you in return have made California, and you are both richer for having made each other." The concluding sentence of this parting message of former travel companions, sent to John Muir in 1879 when he was exploring the glaciers of Alaska, has grown truer each succeeding decade since then.

Intimately as his name was already identified with the natural beauty of California in 1879, the service which Muir was ultimately to render to the nation was only beginning at that time. Then there was only one national park, that of the Yellowstone, and no national forest reserves at all. Amid such a wealth of beautiful forests and wildernesses as our nation then possessed it required a very uncommon lover of nature and of humanity to advocate provision against a day of need. But that friend of generations unborn arose in the person of John Muir. Before he or any one had ever heard of national parks the idea of preserving some sections of our natural flora in their unspoiled wildness arose spontaneously in his mind.

It was a lovely carex meadow beside Fountain Lake, on his father's first Wisconsin farm, that gave him the germinal idea of a park in which plant societies were to be protected in their natural state. During the middle sixties, as he was about to leave his boyhood home forever, he found unbearable the thought of leaving this precious meadow unprotected, and offered to purchase it from his brother-in-law on condition that cattle and hogs be kept securely fenced out. Early correspondence shows that he pressed the matter repeatedly, but his relative treated the request as a sentimental dream, and ultimately the meadow was trampled out of existence. More than thirty years later, at a notable meeting of the Sierra Club in 1895, he for the first time made public this natural park dream of his boyhood. It was the national park idea in miniature, and the proposal was made before even the Yellowstone National Park had been established.

This was the type of man who during the

decade between 1879 and 1889 wrote for "Scribner's Monthly" and the "Century Magazine" a series of articles the like of which had never been written on American forests and scenery. Such were Muir's articles entitled "In the Heart of the California Alps," "Wild Sheep of the Sierra," "Coniferous Forests of the Sierra Nevada," and "Bee-Pastures of California." There was also the volume, edited by him, entitled "Picturesque California," with numerous articles by himself. The remarkably large correspondence which came to him as a result of this literary activity shows how deep was its educative effect upon the public mind.

Then came the eventful summer of 1889, during which he took Robert Underwood Johnson, one of the editors of the "Century," camping about Yosemite and on the Tuolumne Meadows, where, as Muir says, he showed him how uncountable sheep had eaten and trampled out of existence the wonderful flower gardens of the seventies. We have elsewhere shown how the two then and there determined to make a move for the establishment of what is now the Yosemite National Park, and to make its area sufficiently comprehensive to include all the headwaters of the Merced and the Tuolumne. This was during President Harrison's administration, and, fortunately for the project, John W. Noble, a faithful and far-sighted servant of the American people, was then Secretary of the Interior.

One may imagine with what fervor Muir threw himself into that campaign. The series of articles on the Yosemite region which he now wrote for the "Century" are among the best things he has ever done. Public-spirited men all over the country rallied to the support of the National Park movement, and on the first of October, 1890, the Yosemite National Park bill went through Congress, though bitterly contested by all kinds of selfishness and pettifoggery. A troop of cavalry immediately came to guard the new park; the "hoofed locusts" were expelled, and the flowers and undergrowth gradually returned to the meadows and forests.

The following year (1891) Congress passed an act empowering the President to create forest reserves. This was the initial step toward a rational forest conservation policy, and President Harrison was the first to establish forest reserves — to the extent of somewhat more than thirteen million acres. We cannot stop to go into the opening phases of this new movement, but the measure in which the country is indebted to John Muir also for this public benefit may be gathered from letters of introduction to scientists abroad which influential friends gave to Muir in 1893 when he was contemplating extensive travels in Europe. "It gives me great pleasure," wrote one of them, "to introduce to you Mr. John Muir, whose successful struggle for the reservation of about one-half of the western side of the Sierra Nevada has made him so well known to the friends of the forest in this country."

During his struggle for the forest reservations and for the establishment of the Yosemite National Park Muir had the effective coöperation of a considerable body of public-spirited citizens of California, who in 1892 were organized into the Sierra Club, in part, at least, for the purpose of assisting in creating public sentiment and in making it effective. During its long and distinguished public service this organization never swerved from one of its main purposes, "to enlist the support and coöperation of the people and the government in preserving the forests and other features of the Sierra Nevada Mountains," and when that thrilling volume of Muir's, "My First Summer in the Sierra," appeared in 1911, it was found to be dedicated "To the Sierra Club of California, Faithful Defender of the People's Playgrounds."

The assistance of this Club proved invalu-

able when Muir's greatest opportunity for
public service came in 1896. It was then that
our Federal Government began to realize at
last the imperative necessity of doing something at once to check the appalling waste of
our forest resources. Among the causes which
led up to this development of conscience was
the report of Edward A. Bowers, Inspector of
the Public Land Service. He estimated the
value of timber stolen from the public lands
during six years in the eighties at thirty-seven
million dollars. To this had to be added the
vastly greater loss annually inflicted upon the
public domain by sheepmen and prospectors,
who regularly set fire to the forests in autumn,
the former to secure open pasturage for their
flocks, the latter to lay bare the outcrops of
mineral-bearing rocks. But the most conse-
quential awakening of the public mind followed
the appearance of Muir's "Mountains of
California" In 1894. All readers of it knew
immediately that the trees had found a defender whose knowledge, enthusiasm, and gift
of expression made his pen more powerful than
a regiment of swords. Here at last was a man
who had no axes to grind by the measures he
advocated and thousands of new conservation
recruits heard the call and enlisted under his
leadership. One remarkable thing about the

numerous appreciative letters he received is the variety of persons, high and low, from whom they came.

The reader will recall that, as early as 1876, Muir had proposed the appointment of a national commission to inquire into the fearful wastage of forests, to take a survey of existing forest lands in public ownership, and to recommend measures for their conservation. Twenty years later, in June, 1896, Congress at last took the required action by appropriating twenty-five thousand dollars "to enable the Secretary of the Interior to meet the expenses of an investigation and report by the National Academy of Sciences on the inauguration of a national forestry policy for the forested lands of the United States." In pursuance of this act Wolcott Gibbs, President of the National Academy of Sciences, appointed as members of this Commission Charles S. Sargent, Director of the Arnold Arboretum; General Henry L. Abbot, of the United States Engineer Corps; Professor William H. Brewer of Yale University; Alexander Agassiz; Arnold Hague of the United States Geological Survey; and Gifford Pinchot, practical forester. It should be said to the credit of these men that they all accepted this appointment on the understanding that they were to serve without pay.

It is not surprising, in view of the circumstances, that Charles S. Sargent, the Chairman of the newly appointed Commission, immediately invited John Muir to accompany the party on a tour of investigation, and it was fortunate, as it turned out afterwards, that he went as a free lance and not as an official member of the party. During the summer of 1896, this Commission visited nearly all of the great forest areas of the West and the Northwest, and letters written to him later by individual members testify to the invaluable character of Muir's personal contribution to its work.

A report, made early in 1897, embodied the preliminary findings and recommendations of the Commission, and on Washington's Birthday of that year President Cleveland created thirteen forest reservations, comprising more than twenty-one million acres. This action of the President created a rogues' panic among the mining, stock, and lumber companies of the Northwest, who were fattening on the public domain. Through their subservient representatives in Congress they moved unitedly and with great alacrity against the reservations. In less than a week after the President's proclamation they had secured in the United States Senate, without opposition, the passage of an amendment to the Sundry Civil Bill whereby "all the lands set apart and reserved by Executive orders of February 22, 1897," were "restored to the public domain ... the same as if said Executive orders and proclamations had not been made." To the lasting credit of California let it be said that the California reservations were expressly exempted from the provisions of this nullifying amendment at the request of the California Senators, Perkins and White, behind whom was the public sentiment of the State, enlightened by John Muir and many like-minded friends.

The great battle between the public interest and selfish special interests, or between "landscape righteousness and the devil," as Muir used to say, was now joined for a fight to the finish. The general public as yet knew little about the value of forests as conservers and regulators of water-flow in streams. They knew even less about their effect upon rainfall, climate, and public welfare, and the day when forest reserves would be needed to meet the failing timber supply seemed far, far off.

But there is nothing like a great conflict between public and private interests to create an atmosphere in which enlightening discussion can do its work, and no one knew this better than John Muir. "This forest battle," he wrote, "is part of the eternal conflict between right and wrong. . . . The sooner it is stirred up and debated before the people the better, for thus the light will be let into it." When traveling with the Forestry Commission he had on one occasion seen an apparently well-behaved horse suddenly take a fit of bucking, kicking, and biting that made every one run for safety. Its strange actions were a mystery until a yellow jacket emerged from its ear!

Muir seized the occurrence for an explanation of the sudden and insanely violent outcry against forest reservations. "One man," he said, "with a thousand-dollar yellow jacket in his ear will make more bewildering noise and do more effective kicking and fighting on certain public measures than a million working men minding their own business, and whose cash interests are not visibly involved. But as soon as the light comes the awakened million creates a public opinion that overcomes wrong however cunningly veiled."

He was not mistaken, as we shall see, though for a time wrong seemed triumphant. The amendment nullifying the forest reservations died through lack of President Cleveland's signature. But in the extra session, which followed the inauguration of President McKinley, a bill was passed in June, 1897, that

restored to the public domain, until March 1,
1898, all the forest reservations created by
Cleveland, excepting those of California. This
interval, of course, was used shamelessly by
all greedy forest-grabbers, while Congress was
holding the door open! Emboldened by success, certain lumbermen even tried to secure
Congressional authority to cut the wonderful
sequoia grove in the General Grant National
Park.

But John Muir's Scotch fighting blood was
up now. Besides, his friends, East and West,
were calling for the aid of his eagle's quill to
enlighten the citizens of our country on the
issues involved in the conflict. "No man in the
world can place the forests' claim before them
so clearly and forcibly as your own dear self,"
wrote his friend Charles Sprague Sargent,
Chairman of the Commission now under fire.
"No one knows so well as you the value of our
forests — that their use for lumber is but a
small part of the value." He proposed that
Muir write syndicate letters for the public
press. "There is no one in the United States,"
he wrote, "who can do this in such a telling
way as you can, and in writing these letters you
will perform a patriotic service."

Meanwhile the public press was becoming
interested in the issue. To a request from the

editor of "Harper's Weekly" Muir responded with an article entitled "Forest Reservations and National Parks," which appeared opportunely in June, 1897. The late Walter Hines Page, then editor of the "Atlantic Monthly," opened to him its pages for the telling contribution entitled "The American Forests." In both these articles Muir's style rose to the impassioned oratory of a Hebrew prophet arraigning wickedness in high places, and preaching the sacred duty of so using the country we live in that we may not leave it ravished by greed and ruined by ignorance, but may pass it on to future generations undiminished in richness and beauty.

Unsparingly he exposed to public scorn the methods by which the government was being defrauded. One typical illustration must suffice. "It was the practice of one lumber company," he writes, "to hire the entire crew of every vessel which might happen to touch at any port in the redwood belt, to enter one hundred and sixty acres each and immediately deed the land to the company, in consideration of the company's paying all expenses and giving the jolly sailors fifty dollars apiece for their trouble."

This was the type of undesirable citizens who, through their representatives in Congress, raised the hue and cry that poor settlers, looking for homesteads, were being driven into more hopeless poverty by the forest reservations — a piece of sophistry through which Muir's trenchant language cut like a Damascus blade.

The outcries we hear against forest reservations [he wrote] come mostly from thieves who are wealthy and steal timber by wholesale. They have so long been allowed to steal and destroy in peace that any impediment to forest robbery is denounced as a cruel and irreligious interference with "vested rights," likely to endanger the repose of all ungodly welfare. Gold, gold, gold! How strong a voice that metal has! . . . Even in Congress, a sizable chunk of gold, carefully concealed will outtalk and outfight all the nation on a subject like forestry . . . in which the money interests of only a few are conspicuously involved. Under these circumstances the bawling, blethering oratorical stuff drowns the voice of God himself . . . Honest citizens see that only the rights of the government are being trampled, not those of the settlers. Merely what belongs to all alike is reserved, and every acre that is left should be held together under the federal government as a basis for a general policy of administration for the public good. The people will not always be deceived by selfish opposition, whether from lumber and mining corporations or from sheepmen and prospectors, however cunningly brought forward underneath fables of gold.

He concluded this article with a remarkable peroration which no tree-lover could read without feeling, like the audiences that heard the philippics of Demosthenes, that something must be done immediately.

Any fool [he wrote] can destroy trees. They cannot run away; and if they could, they would still be destroyed — chased and hunted down as long as fun or a dollar could be got out of their bark hides, branching horns, or magnificent bole backbones. Few that fell trees plant them; nor would planting avail much towards getting back anything like the noble primeval forests. During a man's life only saplings can be grown, in the place of the old trees — tens of centuries old — that have been destroyed. It took more than three thousand years to make some of the trees in these Western woods — trees that are still standing in perfect strength and beauty, waving and singing in the mighty forests of the Sierra. Through all the wonderful, eventful centuries since Christ's time — and long before that — God has cared for these trees, saved them from drought, disease, avalanches, and a thousand straining, leveling tempests and floods; but He cannot save them from fools — only Uncle Sam can do that.

The period of nine months during which the Cleveland reservations had been suspended came to an end on the first of March, 1898. Enemies of the reservation policy again started a move in the Senate to annul them all. "In the excitement and din of this confounded [Spanish-American] War, the silent trees stand a poor show for justice," wrote Muir to his friend C. S. Sargent, who was sounding the alarm. Meanwhile Muir was conducting a surprisingly active campaign by post and telegraph, and through the Sierra Club. At last his efforts began to take effect and his confidence in the power of light to conquer darkness was justified. "You have evidently put in some good work," wrote Sargent, who was keeping closely in touch with the situation. "On Saturday all the members of the Public Lands Committee of the House agreed to oppose the Senate amendment wiping out the reservations." A large surviving correspondence shows how he continued to keep a strong hand on the helm. On the eighth of July the same friend, who was more than doing his own part, wrote, "Thank Heaven! the forest reservations are safe . . . for another year." As subsequent events have shown, they have been safe ever since. One gets directly at the cause of this gratifying result in a sentence from a letter of John F. Lacey, who was then Chairman of the Public Lands Committee of the House. In discussing the conflicting testimony of those who were urging various policies of concession toward cattle and sheep men in the administration of the reserves he said, "Mr. Muir's judgment will probably be better than that of any one of them."

HIS PUBLIC SERVICE

We have been able to indicate only in the briefest possible manner the decisive part that Muir played in the establishment and defence of the thirty-nine million acres of forest reserves made during the Harrison and Cleveland administrations. But even this bare glimpse of the inside history of that great struggle reveals the magnitude of the service John Muir rendered the nation in those critical times.

There were not lacking those who charged him with being an advocate of conservatism without use. But this criticism came from interested persons — abusers, not legitimate users — and is wholly false.

The United States Government [he said] has always been proud of the welcome it has extended to good men of every nation seeking freedom and homes and bread. Let them be welcomed still as nature welcomes them, to the woods as well as the prairies and plains. . . The ground will be glad to feed them, and the pines will come down from the mountains for their homes as willingly as the cedars came from Lebanon for Solomon's temple. Nor will the woods be the worse for this use, or their benign influences be diminished any more than the sun is diminished by shining. Mere destroyers, however, tree-killers, spreading death and confusion in the fairest groves and gardens ever planted, let the government hasten to cast them out and make an end of them. For it must be told again and again, and be burningly borne in mind, that just now,

407

JOHN MUIR

while protective measures are being deliberated languidly, destruction and use are speeding on faster and farther every day. The axe and saw are insanely busy, chips are flying thick as snowflakes, and every summer thousands of acres of priceless forests, with their underbrush, soil, springs, climate, scenery, and religion, are vanishing away in clouds of smoke, while, except in the national parks, not one forest guard is employed.

Stripped of metaphor, this moving appeal of John Muir to Uncle Sam was an appeal to the intelligence of the American people, and they did not disappoint his faith in their competence to deal justly and farsightedly with this problem. Great as was the achievement of rescuing in eight years more than thirty-nine million acres of forest from deliberate destruction by sheeping, lumbering, and burning, it was only an earnest of what awakened public opinion was prepared to do when it should find the right representative to carry it into force. That event occurred when Theodore Roosevelt came to the Presidency of the United States, and it is the writer's privilege to supply a bit of unwritten history on the manner in which Muir's informed enthusiasm and Roosevelt's courage and love of action were brought into coöperation for the country's good. In March, 1903, Dr. Chester Rowell, a Senator of the California Legislature, wrote to Muir confidentially as follows: "From private advices from Washington I learn that President Roosevelt is desirous of taking a trip into the High Sierra during his visit to California, and has expressed a wish to go with you practically alone. . . . If he attempts anything of the kind, he wishes it to be entirely unknown, carried out with great secrecy so that the crowds will not follow or annoy him, and he suggested that he could foot it and rough it with you or anybody else."

John Muir had already engaged passage for Europe in order to visit, with Professor Sargent, the forests of Japan, Russia, and Manchuria, and felt constrained to decline. But upon the urgent solicitation of President Benjamin Ide Wheeler, and following the receipt of a friendly letter from President Roosevelt, he postponed his sailing date, writing to Professor Sargent, "An influential man from Washington wants to make a trip into the Sierra with me, and I might be able to *do some forest good* in freely talking around the campfire."

By arrangement Muir joined the President at Raymond on Friday, the fifteenth of May, and at the Mariposa Big Trees the two inexorably separated themselves from the company and disappeared in the woods until the following Monday. Needless to say this was not what the disappointed politicians would have chosen, but their chagrin fortunately was as dust in the balance against the good of the forests.

In spite of efforts to keep secret the President's proposed trip to Yosemite, he had been met at Raymond by a big crowd. Emerging from his car in rough camp costume, he said: "Ladies and Gentlemen: I did not realize that I was to meet you to-day, still less to address an audience like this! I had only come prepared to go into Yosemite with John Muir, so I must ask you to excuse my costume." This statement was met by the audience with cries of "It is all right!" And it was all right. For three glorious days Theodore Roosevelt and John Muir were off together in Yosemite woods and on Yosemite trails. Just how much was planned by them, in those days together, for the future welfare of this nation we probably never shall fully know, for death has sealed the closed accounts of both. But I am fortunately able to throw some direct light upon the attendant circumstances and results of the trip.

While I was in correspondence with Theodore Roosevelt in 1916 over a book I had published on the Old Testament, he wrote, "Isn't there some chance of your getting to this side of the continent before you write your book on Muir?

Then you'll come out here to Sagamore Hill;
and I'll tell you all about the trip, and give you
one very amusing instance of his quaint and
most unworldly forgetfulness."

In November of the same year it was my
privilege to go for a memorable visit to Sagamore Hill, and while Colonel Roosevelt and I
were pacing briskly back and forth in his library, over lion skins and other trophies, he told
about the trip with John Muir, and the impression which his deep solicitude over the destruction of our great forests and scenery had made
upon his mind. Roosevelt had shown himself a
friend of the forests before this camping trip
with Muir, but he came away with a greatly
quickened conviction that vigorous action must
be taken speedily, ere it should be too late.
Muir's accounts of the wanton forest-destruc-
tion he had witnessed, and the frauds that had
been perpetrated against the government in the
acquisition of redwood forests, were not without effect upon Roosevelt's statesmanship, as
we shall see. Nor must we, in assessing the near
and distant public benefits of this trip, overlook
the fact that it was the beginning of a lifelong friendship between these two men. By a
strange fatality Muir's own letter accounts of
what occurred on the trip went from hand to
hand until they were lost. There survives a

411

passage in a letter to his wife in which he writes:
"I had a perfectly glorious time with the President and the mountains. I never before had
a more interesting, hearty, and manly companion." To his friend Merriam he wrote:
"Camping with the President was a memorable
experience. I fairly fell in love with him."
Roosevelt, John Muir, the Big Trees, and the
lofty summits that make our "Range of
Light"! — who could think of an association of
men and objects more elementally great and
more fittingly allied for the public good? In a
stenographically reported address delivered by
Roosevelt at Sacramento immediately after his
return from the mountains, we have a hint of
what the communion of these two greatest outdoor men of our time was going to mean for the
good of the country.

I have just come from a four days' rest in Yosemite [he said], and I wish to say a word to you here
in the capital city of California about certain of
your great natural resources, your forests and your
water supply coming from the streams that find
their sources among the forests of the mountains.
... No small part of the prosperity of California in
the hotter and drier agricultural regions depends
upon the preservation of her water supply; and the
water supply cannot be preserved unless the forests
are preserved. As regards some of the trees, I want
them preserved because they are the only things of

their kind in the world. Lying out at night under those giant sequoias was lying in a temple built by no hand of man, a temple grander than any human architect could by any possibility build, and I hope for the preservation of the groves of giant trees simply because it would be a shame to our civilization to let them disappear. They are monuments in themselves.

I ask for the preservation of other forests on grounds of wise and far-sighted economic policy. I do not ask that lumbering be stopped . . . only that the forests be so used that not only shall we here, this generation, get the benefit for the next few years, but that our children and our children's children shall get the benefit. In California I am impressed by how great the State is, but I am even more impressed by the immensely greater greatness that lies in the future, and I ask that your marvelous natural resources be handed on unimpaired to your posterity. We are not building this country of ours for a day. It is to last through the ages.

Let us now recall Muir's modest excuse for postponing a world tour in order to go alone into the mountains with Theodore Roosevelt — that he "might be able to do some forest good in freely talking around the camp-fire." It was in the glow of those camp-fires that Muir's enlightened enthusiasm and Roosevelt's courage were fused into action for the public good. The magnitude of the result was astonishing and one for which this country can never be sufficiently grateful. When Roosevelt came

to the White House in 1901, the total National
Forest area amounted to 46,153,119 acres, and
we have already seen what a battle it cost Muir
and his friends to prevent enemies in Congress
from securing the annulment of Cleveland's
twenty-five million acres of forest reserves.
When he left the White House, in the spring of
1909, he had set aside more than one hundred
and forty-eight million acres of additional
National Forests — more than three times as
much as Harrison, Cleveland, and McKinley
combined! Similarly the number of National
Parks was doubled during his administration.

But the Monuments and Antiquities Act,
passed by Congress during Roosevelt's administration, gave him a new, unique opportunity. During the last three years of his presidency he created by proclamation sixteen
National Monuments. Among them was the
Grand Cañon of the Colorado with an area of
806,400 acres. Efforts had been made, ever
since the days of Benjamin Harrison, to have
the Grand Cañon set aside as a national
park, but selfish opposition always carried the
day. Sargent and Johnson and Page had repeatedly appealed to Muir to write a description of the Cañon. "It is absolutely necessary," wrote Page in 1898, "that this great
region as well as the Yosemite should be de-

scribed by you, else you will not do the task that God sent you to do." When in 1902 his masterly description did appear, it led to renewed, but equally futile, efforts to have this wonder of earth sculpture included among our national playgrounds. Then Muir passed on to Roosevelt the suggestion that he proclaim the Cañon a national monument. A monument under ground was a new idea, but there was in it nothing inconsistent with the Monuments and Antiquities Act, and so Roosevelt, with his characteristic dash, in January, 1908, declared the whole eight hundred thousand acres of the Cañon a National Monument and the whole nation smiled and applauded. Subsequently Congress, somewhat grudgingly, changed its status to that of a national park, thus realizing the purpose for which Roosevelt's proclamation reserved it at the critical time.

The share of John Muir in the splendid achievements of these Rooseveltian years would be difficult to determine precisely, for his part was that of inspiration and advice — elements as imponderable as sunlight, but as all-pervasively powerful between friends as the pull of gravity across stellar spaces. And fast friends they remained to the end, as is shown by the letters that passed between them. Neither of them could feel or act again as if.

they had not talked "forest good" together beside Yosemite camp-fires. "I wish I could see you in person," wrote Roosevelt in 1907 at the end of a letter about national park matters. "I wish I could see you in person; and how I do wish I were again with you camping out under those great sequoias, or in the snow under the silver firs!"

In 1908 occurred an event that threw a deep shadow of care and worry and heart-breaking work across the last six years of Muir's life — years that otherwise would have gone into books which perforce have been left forever unwritten. We refer to the granting of a permit by James R. Garfield, then Secretary of the Interior, to the city of San Francisco to invade the Yosemite National Park in order to convert the beautiful Hetch-Hetchy Valley into a reservoir. In Muir's opinion it was the greatest breach of sound conservation principles in a whole century of improvidence, and in the dark and devious manner of its final accomplishment a good many things still wait to be brought to light. The following letter to Theodore Roosevelt, then serving his second term in the White House, is a frank presentation of the issues involved.

HIS PUBLIC SERVICE

To Theodore Roosevelt

[MARTINEZ, CALIFORNIA
April 21, 1908]

DEAR MR. PRESIDENT:

I am anxious that the Yosemite National
Park may be saved from all sorts of commercialism and marks of man's work other than the
roads, hotels, etc., required to make its wonders
and blessings available. For as far as I have
seen there is not in all the wonderful Sierra, or
indeed in the world, another so grand and wonderful and useful a block of Nature's mountain
handiwork.

There is now under consideration, as doubtless you well know, an application of San Francisco supervisors for the use of the Hetch-
Hetchy Valley and Lake Eleanor as storage
reservoirs for a city water supply. This application should, I think, be denied, especially
the Hetch-Hetchy part, for this Valley, as you
will see by the inclosed description, is a counter-
part of Yosemite, and one of the most sublime
and beautiful and important features of the
Park, and to dam and submerge it would be
hardly less destructive and deplorable in its effect on the Park in general than would be the
damming of Yosemite itself. For its falls and
groves and delightful camp-grounds are sur-

passed or equaled only in Yosemite, and furthermore it is the hall of entrance to the grand
Tuolumne Cañon, which opens a wonderful way
to the magnificent Tuolumne Meadows, the fo-
cus of pleasure travel in the Park and the grand
central camp-ground. If Hetch-Hetchy should
be submerged, as proposed, to a depth of one
hundred and seventy-five feet, not only would
the Meadows be made utterly inaccessible
along the Tuolumne, but this glorious cañon
way to the High Sierra would be blocked.

I am heartily in favor of a Sierra or even a
Tuolumne water supply for San Francisco, but
all the water required can be obtained from
sources outside the Park, leaving the twin
valleys, Hetch-Hetchy and Yosemite, to the
use they were intended for when the Park was
established. For every argument advanced for
making one into a reservoir would apply with
equal force to the other, excepting the cost of
the required dam.

The few promoters of the present scheme are
not unknown around the boundaries of the
Park, for some of them have been trying to
break through for years. However able they
may be as capitalists, engineers, lawyers, or
even philanthropists, none of the statements
they have made descriptive of Hetch-Hetchy
dammed or undammed is true. but they all

show forth the proud sort of confidence that comes of a good, sound, substantial, irrefragable ignorance.

For example, the capitalist Mr. James D. Phelan says, "There are a thousand places in the Sierra equally as beautiful as Hetch-Hetchy: it is inaccessible nine months of the year, and is an unlivable place the other three months because of mosquitoes." On the contrary, there is not another of its kind in all the Park excepting Yosemite. It is accessible all the year, and is not more mosquitoful than Yosemite. "The conversion of Hetch-Hetchy into a reservoir will simply mean a lake instead of a meadow." But Hetch-Hetchy is not a meadow: it is a Yosemite Valley. . . . These sacred mountain temples are the holiest ground that the heart of man has consecrated, and it behooves us all faithfully to do our part in seeing that our wild mountain parks are passed on unspoiled to those who come after us, for they are national properties in which every man has a right and interest.

I pray therefore that the people of California be granted time to be heard before this reservoir question is decided, for I believe that as soon as light is cast upon it, nine tenths or more of even the citizens of San Francisco would be opposed to it. And what the public opinion of the world would be may be guessed by the case of the Niagara Falls.

Faithfully and devotedly yours

JOHN MUIR

O for a tranquil camp hour with you like those beneath the sequoias in memorable 1903!

Muir did not know at the time, and it was a discouraging shock to discover the fact, that Chief Forester Gifford Pinchot had on May 28, 1906, written a letter to a San Francisco city official not only suggesting, but urging, that San Francisco "make provision for a water supply from the Yosemite National Park." In the work of accomplishing this scheme, he declared, "I will stand ready to render any assistance in my power." Six months later he wrote again to the same official, saying: "I cannot, of course, attempt to forecast the action of the new Secretary of the Interior [Mr. Garfield] on the San Francisco watershed question, but my advice to you is to assume that his attitude will be favorable, and to make the necessary preparations to set the case before him. I had supposed from an item in the paper that the city had definitely given up the Lake Eleanor plan and had purchased one of the other systems."

It was not surprising that his forecast of an action, which he already stood pledged to further with any means in his power, although he knew other sources to be available, proved correct. Neither Mr. Pinchot nor Mr. Garfield had so much as seen the Valley, and the language of the latter's permit shows that his decision was reached on partisan misrepresentations of its character which were later disproved in public hearings when the San Francisco authorities, unable to proceed with the revocable Garfield permit, applied to Congress for a confirmation of it through an exchange of lands. To take one of the two greatest wonders of the Yosemite National Park and hand it over, as the New York "Independent" justly observed, "without even the excuse of a real necessity, to the nearest hungry municipality that asks for it, is nothing less than conservation buried and staked to the ground. Such guardianship of our national resources would make every national park the back-yard annex of a neighboring city."

Muir's letter to Roosevelt showed him that his official advisers were thinking more of political favor than of the integrity of the people's playground; that, in short, a mistake had been made; and he wrote Muir that he would endeavor to have the project confined to

Lake Eleanor. But his administration came to an end without definite steps taken in the matter one way or another. President Taft, however, and Secretary Ballinger directed the city and county of San Francisco, in 1910, "to show why the Hetch-Hetchy Valley should not be eliminated from the Garfield permit." President Taft also directed the War Department to appoint an Advisory Board of Army Engineers to assist the Secretary of the Interior in passing upon the matters submitted to the Interior Department under the order to show cause.

In March, 1911, Secretary Ballinger was succeeded by Walter L. Fisher, during whose official term the city authorities requested and obtained five separate continuances, apparently in the hope that a change of administration would give them the desired political pull at Washington. Meantime the Advisory Board of Army Engineers reported: "The Board is of the opinion that there are several sources of water supply that could be obtained and used by the City of San Francisco and adjacent communities to supplement the near-by supplies as the necessity develops. From any one of these sources the water is sufficient in quantity and is, or can be made suitable in quality, while the engineering difficulties are not insurmountable. The determining factor is principally one of cost."

Under policies of National Park protection now generally acknowledged to be binding upon those who are charged to administer them for the public good, the finding of the army engineers should have made it impossible to destroy the Hetch-Hetchy Valley for a mere commercial difference in the cost of securing a supply of water from any one of several other adequate sources. But, as Muir states in one of his letters, "the wrong prevailed over the best aroused sentiment of the entire country."

The compensating good which he felt sure would arise, even out of this tragic sacrifice, must be sought in the consolidation of public sentiment against any possible repetition of such a raid. In this determined public sentiment, aroused by Muir's leadership in the long fight, his spirit still is watching over the people's playgrounds.

THE END

INDEX

Abbot, General, Henry L., of the National Forestry Commission, ii, 299, 388, 398.
Abbot, Henry, ii, 388.
Advisory Board of Army Engineers, its report on water supply of San Francisco, ii, 422, 423.
Africa, visited by Muir, ii, 354, 374.
Agassiz, Louis, his statement, "a physical fact is as sacred as a moral principle," i, 146; in the Yosemite, 230; influence of, on Muir, 253; on Muir's studies, 342; his opinion of Muir, ii, 292, 293; of the National Forestry Commission, 398.
Alaska, Muir goes to, ii, 123; letters to the "Evening Bulletin" on, 123; Muir leaves on second trip to, 137; account of Muir's second trip to, 138, 61; Muir's third trip to, 245; description of trip to, in the "Century," 304; studying forest trees in, 305; Harriman Expedition to, 318, 320–33.
Alaska Commercial Company, ii, 168, 169.
Alhambra Valley, ii, 99, 99 n., 130.
Alleghanies, the, trip to, ii, 311.
Allen, Mr., ascends Mount Hamilton with Muir, ii, 71.
Amazon, the, Muir's plan to float down, on raft, i, 173, 174; visited by Muir, ii, 354, 370.

"American Forests," ii, 305, 403.
Andrews, E. C., tribute to Muir, i, 359.
Animals, Muir's observation of, i, 40–42; Muir's interest in, 42–44; the mechanistic interpreters of, 42, 43.
Araucaria forests of Brazil, ii, 354, 372.
Armes, Professor William Dallam, and the Sierra Club, ii, 256.
Athenæ Literary and Debating Society, i, 115.
"Atlantic Monthly," articles of Muir published in, ii, 305, 306, 339, 403.
Audubon, John James, naturalist, i, 36.
Auroral display, ii, 154, 155.
Australia, visited by Muir, ii, 350.
Autobiography, of Muir, quoted, i, 119–29, 159–50, 180–200, 207, 208; ii, 193, 194, 204–00, 248–51, 296; taken down from dictation by direction of E. H. Harriman, 120, 318; Muir urged to write, 317; referred to by Muir, 359, 362, 366, 382.
Averell, Elizabeth, ii, 329.
Avery, Benjamin P., takes over editorial direction of the "Overland Monthly," i, 317; ii, 4; Minister to China, 5: death, 5.

Badè, W. F., on visit at Sagamore Hill, ii, 410, 411.

INDEX

Ballinger, Richard A.; Secretary of the Interior, ii, 361, 422.

Baobab trees, ii, 354, 374.

Baptism, Muir's views of, i, 217.

Bear, visits camp at Bridal Veil Meadows, i, 186; attack on sheep made by, 199.

Beardslee, Commander, ii, 152.

Bears, raid provisions, ii, 28.

"Bee-Pastures of California," ii, 394.

Bering Sea, formation of, ii, 173.

Bering Strait, formation of, ii, 173.

Berlin, visited by Muir, ii, 350.

Bible, Daniel Muir's idea of, 18–22; Muir's familiarity with, 26, 27; Daniel Muir's insistence on the word of, 71–74; Muir's changing views of, 145–48.

Bidwell, Annie E. K., quoted on Muir, ii, 72.

Bidwell, General John, visited by Muir, ii, 72.

Bidwell, General John and Mrs., letters to, ii, 73, 87, 242.

Bierce, Ambrose, contributor to the "Overland Monthly," ii, 4.

Black, Mr., ii, 21, 22.

Black, Mrs., ii, 29.

Black Hills, South Dakota, ii, 300, 301.

Black's Hotel, Yosemite, i, 241, 299, 314, 315, 365; ii, 236.

Blake, William Phipps, mistakenly credited with being the originator of the erosian theory, i, 308 n., 356.

Blakley, Hamilton, husband of Mary Muir, i, 7.

Bloody Cañon, i, 233.

Boise, James R., Professor of Greek, University of Michigan, i, 114.

Boling, Captain, enters Hetch-Hetchy, i, 310.

Boone and Crockett Club, addresses vote of thanks to President Harrison and Secretary Noble, ii, 258.

Boston, i, references to, 228, 256, 261; Muir in, ii, 266, 298, 312.

Boston Society of Natural History, i, 326.

Botany, Muir's first lesson in, i, 95; Muir's enthusiasm for study of, 95–97; practicing, in Wisconsin River valley, 97–113; trip to Canada in interest of, 117–51.

Bowers, Edward A., his services to the cause of forest conservation, ii, 257 n.; Inspector of the Public Land Service, 397.

Boyce, Colonel, ii, 132.

Bradley, Cornelius Beach, and the Sierra Club, ii, 256.

Brawley, Mr., ascends Mount Hamilton with Muir, ii, 71.

Brazil, visited by Muir, ii, 354.

Bremer, Mount, ii, 41.

Brewer, Professor William H., assistant of Whitney, i, 275; of the National Forestry Commission, ii, 299, 398; on the Harriman Alaska Expedition, 321, 332.

Bridal Veil Fall, i, 185.

Broderick, Mount, i, 275.

Brown, Grace Blakley, daughter of Mary Muir, i, 5.

Brown, John, author of "Rab and His Friends," ii, 272, 273.

Browne, Francis Fisher, editor of "The Dial," letter to, ii, 358–60.

"Browne the Beloved," ii, 358 n.

426

INDEX

Burns, Robert, quoted, ii, 285; reciting his verses, 359.

Burroughs, John, discussion about animals with Muir, i, 42; sees Muir in New York, ii, 264; refuses to go to Europe with Muir, 265; visited by Muir, 298; his words about Muir, 306; on the Harriman Alaska Expedition, 321–23, 326, 332; Muir proposes that he go to South America, 358; and Burns's poems, 359; letter to, ii, 366.

Butler, Professor James Davie, of University of Wisconsin, i, 81; Muir writes to, about finding Calypso, 121; sends letter of introduction to Muir, 154; reference to, 220; letter to, ii, 231.

Butterflies, collected for Edwards by Muir, i, 263, 264, 383.

"Byways of Yosemite Travel," ii, 10.

Cable, George W., letter from, ii, 285, 286.

California, State of, systematic geological survey of, begun, i, 274; political factions in, ii, 37; and Muir, what they did for each other, 392; forest reservations of, exempted from nullifying amendment, 400.

California State Geological Survey, i, 302, 303.

Calminetti Bill, ii, 257.

Calypso borealis, discovery of, in Canadian swamp, i, 120, 121.

Cambridge, visited by Muir, ii, 270, 298.

Campbell, Mrs., of Highland Scotch farm in Canada, i, 123, 124.

Campbell, Alexander and William, i, 123–25.

Canada, sojourn of Muir in, 1864–1866, i, 117–51.

Canby, William M., makes expedition to study forest trees in Rocky Mountains and Alaska, ii, 304, 305; makes trip with Muir and Sargent into the Alleghanies, 311, 312.

Carlyle, Jeanie Welch, her grave, ii, 277.

Carmany, John H., spent thirty thousand dollars on the "Overland Monthly," i, 317; ii, 4; gives up the "Overland," 5.

Carmelita, Mrs. Carr's Southern home, ii, 60.

Carnegie, Andrew, his accomplishment, ii, 386, 387.

Carr, Professor Ezra Slocum, of University of Wisconsin, i, 80, 81; appointed to professorship in University of California, 202; invites Muir to visit him, 202; work accomplished by, 236; visited by Emerson, 258; a calm thinker, 321; death of son, 399; elected State Superintendent of Public Instruction, ii, 37.

Carr, Jeanne C., becomes acquainted with Muir, i, 80, 138; reports on Muir's inventions, 81; value of her friendship to Muir, 138–44, 205, 227, 334, 336, 340, 387; ii, 26; on Muir's "good demon," i, 157; removal to California, 202; abets Muir in plan for South American trip, 203; on hordes that

427

INDEX

visit the Yosemite, 221; favors American colonization scheme, 234, 239; sends greeting to Muir, 240; visited by Emerson, 258; prophecy of, 261; introduces Henry Edwards, 262; tries to bring Muir into "waiting society," 265, 293; her views of glaciers, 266; Muir sends article to, 269; letter to, on the Sequoias, 270–73; mediates for publication of Muir's "Yosemite Valley in Flood," 317; sends writings of Muir to Emerson for publication, 317; estimates Muir's literary power accurately, 317, 318; comes to the Yosemite, 322; ii, 28; urges Muir to publish his own discoveries, i, 323; Muir to have ramble with, 324; her plan for study of Coast Range, 338, 339; mediates between Muir and Agassiz, 342; introduces William Keith and Irwin to Muir, 343; Muir consults with, on literary matters, 368; death of son, 399; "Sierra Studies" largely due to, ii, 5, 6; Deputy State Superintendent of Public Instruction, 37; death of second son, 66; her home, Carmelita, the literary center of Southern California, 66, 67, 197; interested in marriage of Muir, 100, 123; letters to, of the year 1865, i, 139; of the year 1869, 205; of the year 1870, 213, 218–39, 270; of the year 1871, 242, 249, 266, 291–302; of the year 1872, 260, 318, 328 31, 334–37, 339, 344–52, 354; of the year 1873, 381–84, 386–94; of the year 1874, ii, 10–33, 37; of

the year 1875, 50–55; of the year 1877, 67–72.

Cedar Keys, Florida, i, 170–72.

"Century," articles by Muir in, ii, 234, 304, 394, 395.

Chadbourne, Paul O., Chancellor of University of Wisconsin, i, 138.

Chicago World's Fair, ii, 261–63.

Chico, Rancho, of General John Bidwell, ii, 72.

Child-beating, i, 57.

Chilwell, Mr., accompanies Muir on Yosemite trip, i, 177; learns to shoot, 182–85; adventure with bear, 186; practises shooting, 187, 188; acts as driver of jackrabbits, 188; tries owl flesh, 188, 189; eats himself sick, 189.

China, visited by Muir, ii, 350, 351.

Choate, Joseph, meeting with Muir, ii, 312.

Civilization, and Nature, compared, i, 325, 342.

Clark, Galen, Yosemite pioneer, i, 185, 186, 256; accompanies Muir on Kings River Excursion, 386–390; seen after years, ii, 236.

Clemens, S. L., contributor to the "Overland Monthly," ii, 4.

Cleveland, President, appoints commission to report on condition of national forest areas, ii, 60; thirteen forest reservations proclaimed by, 304, 399; fails to sign amendment nullifying forest reservation, 401.

Clocks, invented by Muir, i, 59–62, 74, 75, 81, 86.

INDEX

Cloud, Jack ("McLeod"), i, 172.

Cloud's Rest, excursion to, i, 368–71.

Coast and Geodetic Survey, ii, 49.

Coast Range, the, Mrs. Carr's plan for study of, i, 338, 339.

Colby, William E., i, 359; assists Muir in securing cession of Yosemite Valley to Federal Government, ii, 351, 352, 357; summer outings to High Sierra organized and conducted by, 351; letter to, 376.

Colleges, called "old grannies," i, 333.

Collier, Robert J., letter of Osborn to, on the Hetch-Hetchy Yosemite Park, ii, 360.

Colonization scheme, i, 233–35.

Colorado Grand Cañon, ii, 345.

Comb, William, ii, 274.

Concord, Muir at, i, 261; ii, 266.

Cougar, Dr. E. M., fellow student of Muir, ii, 67; visited by Muir, 68, 69.

"Coniferous Forests of the Sierra Nevada," ii, 394.

Connel, John ("Smoky Jack"), sheep-man, i, 100, 101.

Converse, Charles, ii, 58.

Converse Basin, ii, 348.

Copley Medal, ii, 283.

Corliss, Doctor, missionary, ii, 152.

Corwin, the, United States Revenue steamer, ii, 161; goes in search of DeLong and the Jeannette, 161–63; account of the expedition, 163–91; makes landing on Wrangell Land, 187.

Coulterville, i, 182.

Cowper, William, i, 301.

Crane's Flat, i, 243, 244; ii, 25.

Crawfordjohn, Lanarkshire, early home of Daniel Muir, i, 5–7.

Creation, a common conception of, i, 166, 167.

Crittenden, Colonel, ii, 156.

"Cruise of the Corwin, The," ii, 162, 163.

Cuba, Muir botanizes in, i, 173.

Daggett, Kate N., letter to, i, 372.

Dana, Charles A., of the New York "Sun," ii, 270.

Dana, Mount, i, 233.

Darwin, Charles, his "Origin of Species," i, 145; read by Muir, 240, 297; a great man, 335.

Davel Brae school, the, i, 27, 32.

Davidson, Professor, on the issue of the recession of the Yosemite Valley to the Federal Government, ii, 303.

Dawson Glacier, ii, 158; first called Young Glacier.

Deady, Judge, ii, 148.

Death, Muir's conception of, i, 164, 165; ii, 333–35.

Death song of Indians, ii, 21, 22.

Degrees conferred on Muir, ii, 295, 296, 298, 304 n., 365.

Delaney, Pat, i, 195, 202, 235; ii, 19.

DeLong, Commander, relief expedition in search of, ii, 161; first news that he had failed to touch Herald Island or Wrangell Land, 163.

Dewing (J.) Company, ii, 218.

Diablo, Mount, ascent of, ii, 90, 94.

"Dial, The," tribute to F. F. Browne in, ii, 358.

Dick, Robert, geologist, ii, 283.

429

INDEX

Dick, Thomas, his "The Christian Philosopher," i, 72.
Dick, Mr., teacher, ii, 280.
Dickey, Mrs. Anna R., letters to, ii, 346, 375.
Doran, Captain P. A., of the Elder, ii, 318, 319; visits Muir, 331.
Douglas, David, and Muir, ii, 272, 273, 277.
Douglas squirrel, companion of Sequoia, i, 271.
Draper, Dorothea, ii, 329.
Dumfries, visited by Muir, ii, 280.
Dunbar, Scotland, i, 8, 13; Davel Brae school at, 26, 27, 31, 32; grammar school of, 27, 28; the country about, 30–35; romantic associations of, 34; visited by Muir, 273–80; field of the battle of, 278.
Duncan, William, ii, 212.
Dwinell, Doctor I. E., clergyman, ii, 135.

Eagle Rock, fall of, i, 327.
"Early-rising machine," i, 59–62, 74.
Earthquakes, experienced by Muir, i, 325–29.
Eastwood, Miss, ii, 308.
Edinburgh, visited by Muir, ii, 272–75.
"Edward Henry Harriman," ii, 318.
Edwards, Henry, introduced by Mrs. Carr, i, 262; Muir collects butterflies for, 263, 264, 292, 383; names butterfly for Muir, 264 n.; allusion to, ii, 13.
Edwards Collection, the, i, 264 n.
Egleston, Mr., i, 190.
Egypt, visited by Muir, ii, 350.

El Capitan, i, 311.
Elder, the, Captain Doran of, ii, 318, 319; on board, 329–32.
Eleanor, Lake, ii, 360, 361, 417, 422.
Eliot, C. W., ii, 271; salutation of, in conferring honorary degree from Harvard on Muir, 296 n.
Emerson, Edward Waldo, Muir dines with, ii, 268.
Emerson, Ralph Waldo, meeting with Muir, i, 252–57; influence of, on Muir, 253; visits the Carrs, 258; corresponds with Muir, 258–60; sends books to Muir, 258–60; Muir at grave of, 261; ii, 267; material of Muir sent to, for publication, 317; prophesies that Muir will visit the Atlantic coast, 319; Muir dines with his son, ii, 266; Muir visits his home, 268; tries to get Muir for teaching, 292.
Emerson, Mount, i, 389.
Engelmann, Doctor, i, 343.
Ennis, Samuel, buys Fountain Lake farm, i, 50 n.
Ennis Lake. See Fountain Lake.
Erigeron Muirii, ii, 191.
Erosion, caused by ice and by water, compared, i, 355, 356. See Glacial erosion, Glaciers.
Erwin, Louisiana, marries John Strentzel, ii, 99.
Esquimo village, population of, dead of starvation, ii, 184.
"Evening Bulletin," of San Francisco, letters of Muir in, ii, 32, 36, 51, 62, 71, 98, 123, 125, 163, 174, 190.
"Explorations in the Great Tuolumne Cañon," i, 396.

430

INDEX

INDEX

Gilbert, Charles, introduced to Muir, ii, 127, 332.

Gilder, Richard Watson, meets Muir, ii, 264; Muir at his country-place, 312; urges Muir to write his autobiography, 317.

Gilder, Mrs. R. W., ii, 312.

"Gilderoy," ballad, i, 11.

Gilderoy, David. See Gilrye.

Gilderoy (Gildroy, Gilroy), James, maternal great-grandfather of John Muir, i, 12.

Gilderoy, John, son of James, i, 12.

Gilderoys, the, old Scottish stock, 11.

Gilroy, Susan, cousin of Muir, ii, 280.

Gilroy. See Gilderoy.

Gilrye, Ann, daughter of David and Margaret Hay Gilrye, i, 14; marriage to Daniel Muir, 15. See Muir, Ann Gilrye.

Gilrye, David, son of James Gilderoy, i, 12; the "grandfather Gilrye" of Muir's boyhood, 12; settles at Dunbar, 12, 13; marries Margaret Hay, 13; children of, 14; Muir's earliest teacher and guide, 26; death, 37; prophecy of, 40; farewell gift of, 78.

Gilrye, David, brother of Ann Gilrye, i, 15.

Gilrye, Margaret, daughter of David and Margaret Hay Gilrye, aunt of Muir, 14; married to James Rae, 15.

Gilrye, Margaret Hay, maternal grandmother of Muir, 13; children of, 14; death, 37.

Gist, Governor W. H., i, 77.

Glacial erosion, as origin of Yosemite, Muir's early advocacy of, i, 278–95; Muir urged by Professor Runkle to write out his theory of, 295; Muir considers writing out his theory of, 296, 297; Muir continues his study of, 298–308; publication of Muir's first article on, 308, 316; W. P. Blake mistakenly credited with being the originator of theory of, 308 n.; Muir states his intention to write a book on, 314, 315; a rock due to, ii, 11, 12. See Glaciers.

Glacier, Dawes, ii, 158; Harriman, ii, 325; Lyell, i, 230, 350; Merced, i, 285, 286; Muir, ii, 124, 160, 246–51, 326; Red Mountain, i, 350; Ribbon, i, 304–06; Young, ii, 158.

Glacier Bay, ii, 123, 124, 160, 246, 247.

Glacier Point, i, 283, 284, 329, 330, 368.

Glaciers, existence of living, in the Sierra Nevada, i, 230; two views of, 266; what they accomplished, 266 68; Whitney's disbelief in origin of Yosemite as due to, 276, 277; residual, in the High Sierras, 286; Muir discovers traces of, in the Yosemite Valley, 289–91; summary of Muir's studies in, up to 1871, 302–08; living, in Sierra Nevada, first published announcement made of, 323; living, in Sierra Nevada, Muir's first full account of discovery of, 344–52; traces of, in Nevada, ii, 104, 105, 107, 114; in Alaska, 123, 124, 126; up Holkham Bay (Sumdum), 158, 159; at head of Taylor

432

INDEX

Bay, 160; traces of, at Unalaska Harbor, 166, 167; action of, in Arctic lands, 165–67, 173, 181, 183; on Mount Rainier, 232; action of, in and about New York, 266; action of, at Rio de Janeiro, 372. *See* Glacial erosion.

Glenora Peak, S. Hall Young's rescue from death on, ii, 124.

God, Daniel Muir's idea of, i, 18–22; John Muir's idea of, 166, 332, 333; a common conception of, 166.

"God's First Temples," ii, 58, 59.

"Gold-Hunters," ii, 233.

Goodrich, Mrs., i, 104.

Grand Cañon of the Colorado, created a National Monument by President Roosevelt, ii, 414, 415.

Grasshoppers, the embroidery left by, ii, 14–16.

Gray, Asa, Muir warm friend of, i, 146, 335; influence of, on Muir, 253; meeting with Muir, 337, 366; asks that Muir send him plants, 342; Muir describes excursion to Cloud's Rest to, 368–71, the "angular factiness of his pursuits," 369; plants sent to, 379–81; guest at Rancho Chico, ii, 72; on Mount Shasta expedition, 80–84; and Muir's collection of Arctic plants, 191; death, 242; memories of, 243; tries to get Muir for Harvard, 292; his writings read by Muir, 317.

Gray, Mrs. Asa, ii, 311; Muir visits, 312.

Gray Herbarium at Harvard University, plants from Her-

ald Island and Wrangell Land in, ii, 191.

Graydon, Katharine Merrill, correspondence with Muir, ii, 126–30, 133–35; death of great-aunt, 337.

Graydon, Mary Merrill, letter to, ii, 258–60.

Greenbaum, Mr., agent of the Alaska Commercial Company, ii, 168.

Greenwood, Grace. *See* Lippincott.

Griswold, M. S., gives Muir first lesson in botany, i, 95.

Hague, Professor, of the National Forestry Commission, ii, 299, 398.

Half Dome, i, 275.

Hamilton, Mount, ii, 71.

Hang-nest, the, i, 247, 248.

"Harper's Weekly," article of Muir published in, ii, 305, 403.

Harriman, Carol and Roland, ii, 329.

Harriman, E. H., Muir's boyhood memoirs taken down by direction of, ii, 120, 318; friendship with, 318.

Harriman, the Misses Mary and Cornelia, ii, 329.

Harriman Alaska Expedition, joined by Muir, ii, 318, 320–33.

Harriman Glacier, ii, 329.

Harrison, Benjamin, President, ii, 414; established first forest reserves under Act of March 3, 1891, 257, 395.

Harte, Francis Bret, withdraws from editorial direction of the "Overland Monthly," i, 317; ii, 4; contributor to the "Overland Monthly," 4.

Harvard University, gives de-

INDEX

gree to Muir, i, 253; Gray
Herbarium at, ii, 191; Gray
suggests that Muir come to,
292; awards honorary degree
to Muir, 295, 296, 298.

Havana, i, 173.

Hawaii, visited by Muir, ii,
351.

Hawthorne, Nathaniel, on the
spirituality of locomotive
railroad travel, i, 235, 368;
his grave, ii, 267; Muir visits
his homes at Concord, 268.

Hay, James and Hardy, ii, 284,
285.

Hay, Margaret, maternal
grandmother of John Muir,
i, 13. *See* Gilrye, Margaret
Hay.

Hayden, Doctor F. V., in charge
of United States Geological
and Geographical Survey of
the Territories, ii, 80.

Hazel Green, ii, 25.

Hepburn, G. Buchanan, on excursion with Muir, ii, 41; his
death, 41 *n.*

Herald Island, ii, 163; plants
from, 191.

Herbarium, from Canada, i,
117; from Arctic lands, ii,
191.

Hetch-Hetchy Valley, i, 300;
Muir makes first expedition
to, 310–13; a lake bottom
filled with sand and moraine
matter, 354; revisited, ii,
289, 290; and the question of
San Francisco's water supply,
360, 361, 384, 389; permis-
sion granted that it be
converted into a reservoir,
416–23.

'Hetch-Hetchy Valley," i,
396.

Hickory Hill farm, bought by
Daniel Muir, i, 9; sale of, 22;

purchase of, 51; digging of
well on, 52; Muir's farewell
visit to, 156, 158.

Higgs, Sarah, paternal grandmother of Muir, i, 4–6.

High, James L., fellow student
of Muir, i, 114.

High Sierra, the, residual glaciers in, i, 286.

Hodgson, Mr., his family
nurse Muir, i, 170; spot
where his house stood, 170,
171; his family in after years,
ii, 315; death of, 315.

Hodgson, Mrs., nurses Muir, i,
170; found in after years, ii,
315.

Hoffman, Charles F., assistant
of Whitney, i, 275.

Hoffman, Mount, i, 198, 290,
292, 351, 352.

Holkham Bay, glaciers in, ii,
158; Tracy Arm of, 159.

"Hollow," the, near Meaford,
description of the people of, i,
129; Muir's sojourn at, 129–
51; burning of factory at,
149; reference to, ii, 298.

Holman, Doctor, ii, 168.

Honolulu, i, 223.

Hooker, Sir Joseph Dalton,
English botanist, Muir warm
friend of, i, 146; guest at
Rancho Chico, ii, 72; on
Mount Shasta expedition,
80–84; discovers *Linnæa borealis*, 81, 82; visited by
Muir at Sunningdale, 282,
283; praises "Mountains of
California," 289; home of, in
Los Angeles, some of Muir's
writing done at, 354; Muir
goes to the Grand Cañon
with, 359.

Hooker, Mrs. J. D., ii, 282,
354; letters to, 363–66, 369.

Hooker, Katharine and Marian,

434

INDEX

INDEX

355–57; suggests initiation of project for establishment of Yosemite National Park, 234, 394; assists Muir in an effort to secure enlargement of the Sequoia National Park, 253; urges Muir to get a supporting organization on the Pacific Coast, 255; Muir with, in New York, 264; with Muir at Emerson's home, 269; much devoted to Muir, 271; stimulated Muir's literary productiveness, 306; assists Muir in securing cession of Yosemite Valley to Federal Government, 351; urges Muir to write a description of the Grand Cañon of the Colorado, 414.

Johnson, Mrs. R. U., ii, 264.

Jordan, Professor David Starr, introduced to Muir, ii, 127; gives name of Ouzel Basin to glacier channel, 130; introduces Muir as "author of the Muir Glacier," 259.

Kalmia, i, 377, 378.

Kaweah grove, efforts to secure inclusion of, in Sequoia National Park, ii, 253.

Keeler, Charlie, ii, 326.

Keith, William, artist, i, 322; ii, 219, 245; beginning of Muir's friendship with, i, 343; with Muir in the Yosemite, ii, 51, 53.

Kellogg, Albert, botanist of the California Academy of Sciences, i, 322; on Kings River trip, 386; injustice done to, ii, 70; death, 242; memories, 243.

Kennedy, Sallie, letter to, ii, 73.

Kern River Cañon, ii, 345.

Keyes, Judge, ii, 268, 269.

King, Clarence, assistant of Whitney, i, 275; his opinion of the origin of the Yosemite, 276, 277, 357, 358; not the originator of the glacial erosion theory as regards the Yosemite, 277 *n.*, 356; carries butterflies to Edwards, 292; refuses to accept theory of living glaciers, 353; his supposed ascent of Mount Whitney, 394; ascends Mount Whitney, 396; discovered glaciers on Shasta, ii, 30.

Kings River, excursions to, i, 385–94; ii, 82, 85, 88; region, efforts to secure inclusion of, in Sequoia National Park, 253.

Kings River Cañon, ii, 252, 253.

Klawak, ii, 153, 154.

Kneeland, Professor Samuel, prepares paper on erosion theory, i, 309; reads extracts from Muir's letters, 316, 345.

Knox, Mr., i, 324.

Koshoto, Chief of the Hoonas, ii, 152.

Lacey, John F., Chairman of the Public Lands Committee of the House, ii, 406.

Lakes, along the Yosemite streams, i, 355.

Lammermoor, Bride of, the castle of, ii, 278.

Lamon, James C., visits Yosemite in winter, i, 204; his Yosemite claim, 225; in Thérèse Yelverton's novel, 279; his grave, ii, 53.

Lamon, John, the earliest inhabitant of the Yosemite, i, 365; his sheep corral, 365, 366.

INDEX

Manchuria, visited by Muir, ii, 350.

Manila, visited by Muir, ii, 351.

Manufacture, articles of, to be pure works of God, i, 374.

Maple sugar, the making of, i, 128.

Maps, outline glacier, i, 320.

Mariposa Sequoia Grove, the, i, 187.

Mariposa trail, the, i, 186.

Marysville Buttes, ii, 76.

Marysville flood, the, ii, 43.

Mather, Jane, ii, 280.

Matthews, Nathan, Mayor of Boston, ii, 270.

McChesney, Alice, i, 372; ii, 33–36.

McChesney, J. B., i, 227; consulted by Muir, 265; letters to, 366, 371, 375; Muir's friendship for, 371, 372; Muir takes room in house of, 399; with Muir in the Yosemite, ii, 51.

McChesney, Mrs. J. B., i, 399.

McCloud River, the, ii, 39, 40.

McClure, Mount, glacier, i, 348–50.

McGwinn, Howard, owner of Muir house tract of Fountain Lake farm, i, 50 n.

McIlhaney, Asa K., letter to, ii, 380.

McKinley, William, President, ii, 401.

Meaford, Canada, the "Hollow" near, i, 129–51.

Mechanical contrivances of Muir, i, 59–62, 74, 78–81, 86, 88, 89, 131, 148, 149, 153, 210.

Melville, playmate of Muir, ii, 273.

Merced basin, i, 203.

Merced Glacier, the, i, 285, 286.

Merced Lake, ii, 28.

Merced River, the, i, 285, 286; in the valley of, ii, 18; a sail down, 90, 93.

Merriam, Doctor C. Hart, ii, 331, 340, 342, 343; letters to, 338, 343, 387.

Merriam, Clinton L., letter to, i, 302–08.

Merrill, Catharine, Muir describes Fountain Lake to, i, 160–62; sympathetic letter of Muir to, 231–33; Muir describes glacier to, 288–91.

Merrill, Mina, letter to, ii, 382.

Mice, field, the embroidery left by, ii, 16, 17.

Michigan, University, i, 96.

Miller, Hugh, ii, 272, 273.

Miller, Joaquin, contributor to the "Overland Monthly," ii, 4.

Moderation, an attribute of Nature, i, 319.

Mono Lake, i, 233, 284.

Monuments and Antiquities Act, ii, 414, 415.

Moore, J. P., i, 335, 336.

Moore, Mrs. J. P., i, 335, 336.

Moores, Charles W., son of Julia Merrill Moores, i, 117.

Moores, Janet Douglass, correspondence with, ii, 213–18.

Moores, Julia Merrill, early Indianapolis friend of Muir, i, 117; ii, 213; her daughter, 213; death of sister, 333–35.

Moores, Merrill, accompanies Muir on walk, i, 160; visits Muir in the Yosemite, 338; sister of, ii, 213; elected member of Congress, 213.

Moraines, Muir's study of, in Sierra Nevada, i, 344–52; outlines of, marked by fir forests, i, 353, 355. *See* Glaciers.

Morrill Act, the, i, 91, 92.

438

INDEX

Morris, Major, Treasury agent, ii, 143, 148.

Morrison, Mr., ii, 148.

Moses, Professor and Mrs., ii, 324.

Mount Bremer, ii, 41.

Mount Broderick, i, 275.

Mount Dana, i, 233.

Mount Diablo, ii, 90, 94.

Mount Emerson, i, 389.

Mount Florence, i, 280 n.

Mount Hamilton, ii, 71.

Mount Hoffman, i, 198, 290, 292, 351, 352.

Mount Humphreys, i, 388.

Mount Lyell, i, 230, 350.

Mount McClure, i, 348–50.

Mount Rainier, ii, 219, 229, 232.

Mount Shasta, ii, 29–41, 49, 51, 72–84.

Mount Whitney, i, 392–90.

Mountain Models, i, 320.

"Mountain Sculpture," ii, 4.

"Mountains of California," published, ii, 288; its reception, 288, 289; at work on enlarged edition of, 353; public mind awakened by, 397.

Muir, Ann Gilrye, mother of John Muir, wife of Daniel Muir, i, 15; characterization of, 16; had kinship of soul with her son, John, 16–18; had concern for her son's spiritual welfare, 17; death, 25; emigrates to America, 38; writes to son, 83; letter to, 314; son has premonition of her death, ii, 296.

Muir, Anna, sister of John, i, 16; letter to, 136.

Muir, Daniel, father of John Muir, birth, i, 4, 5; early life, 5–8; Dunbar days, 8; emigrates to America, 8, 9, 36, 37; his religious activity, 9, 10; characterized by his son, 10;

his first wife, 15; marries Ann Gilrye, 15; attitude toward scientific study of son, 18, 19; his ideas of God and nature, 19–22; decides to sell farm, 22; goes on evangelistic trips, 23–25; death, 25; ii, 206, 208; settles at Fountain Lake, i, 38; severity of his discipline and farm régime, 44, 47–50, 59; religiousness in household of, 59–63; takes up vegetarianism, 71; in Biblical argument with his son, 71–74; hostile to harmony between nature and revelation, 72–74; sends his son ten dollars, 83; Muir's premonition of his death, ii, 204–06; last meeting with his son, 206–08; account of his death, 208–10.

Muir, Daniel, brother of John, i, 16; at the "Hollow," 129, 130, 132; at home again, 136.

Muir, David Gilrye, brother of John, i, 16; urged by his brother to restrain father, 23–25; letters to, 23, 208, 216; goes with father to America, 36, 37; at work on farm, 59; drives John to station, 78; illness of wife, 208, 209, ii, 195.

Muir, Helen, daughter of Muir, letters to, ii, 275, 283, 297, 301, 313, 322; illness of, 352, 353, 357; bungalow of, 373; her home, 382, 388.

Muir, Joanna, sister of John, i, 16; letter to, 136.

Muir, John, grandfather of John Muir, i, 4–6.

Muir, John, a curious sketch of his ancestry, i, 3; his ancestry, 4–16; his sketch of his father's life, 5–11; heather in, 6, 272; birth, 16, 26; had kin-

439

INDEX

Henry Edwards, 262; collects butterflies for Edwards, 263, 264, 292; urged to come out of his solitude, 265, 293; his view of glaciers, a form of terrestrial love, 266; letter on the things accomplished by glaciers, 266–68; sends article to Mrs. Carr, 269; letter on the Sequoias, 270–73; as to the time when he began to advocate the glacial erosion theory of the origin of the Yosemite, 278–86; his rejection of Whitney's theory of the origin of the Yosemite, 287; on the frightful tendencies of a "Christian" school, 288, 289; discovers dead glacier in the Yosemite Valley, 289–91; continues his glacial investigations, 294; urged by Runkle to write out his glacial theory, 295; considers his financial situation, 296; considers writing out his theory, 296, 297; continues his study of glacial erosion, 298–308; his "Yosemite Glaciers" published in New York "Tribune," 308, 316; disapproves of Professor Kneeland's paper, 309; makes first expedition to Hetch-Hetchy, 310–13; states intention of writing a book containing his erosion theory, 314, 315; writes various articles on the Yosemite, 316, 317; his literary power accurately estimated by Mrs. Carr, 317, 318; on Ruskin's attributes of Nature, 319; his unconditional surrender to Nature, 320; gets in touch with Emily Pelton again, 321; undying loyalty and devotion a trait of, 322; his friendship for Keith, 322; LeConte makes first published announcement of his discovery of living glaciers in Sierra Nevada, 323; urged to publish his own discoveries, 323; engagements of, 324; compares Nature and civilization, 325; his opinion of men, 325, 371, 373, 374; enjoys earthquakes, 325–29; knows not what to write, 336; meeting with Asa Gray, 337; visited by Merrill Moores, 338; Mrs. Carr's plan for his study of the Coast Range, 338, 339; his glow at turning to the mountains, 341; nurses disappointment over Gray, 342; wins approval from Agassiz, 342; and John Torrey, 343; beginning of his friendship with William Keith, 343; his first full account of discovery of living glaciers in Sierra Nevada, 344–52; his "Living Glaciers of California," 352; was the first who demonstrated the part that ice played in the making of Yosemite, 356, 357, 361; his "Studies in the Sierra," 358; E. C. Andrews's tribute to, 359; did not take up question of the pre-glacial Yosemite, 360, 361; evaluation of study of the Yosemite, 361, 362; enjoyed deeper satisfactions of the soul, 362, 363; legends about, 364; his cabins, 364–66; climbs Glacier Point in the snow, 367, 368; meeting with Sill, 368; excursion to Cloud's Rest, 368–71; letter of acknowledgment for pre-

442

sent of lamp, 372–74; critique
of dualism and artificiality
of Ruskin's nature philosophy, 374–78; a letter on
plants sent to Gray, 379–81;
on the shortcomings of words,
382; list of writings to be sent
to Mrs. Carr, 383, 384; hopes
to put his mountain studies
in permanent form, 385;
makes excursion to Kings
River, 385–94; his ascent of
Mount Whitney, 395; never
left his name in the wilderness, 396; enters Tuolumne
Cañon, 397; projected writings of, 396, 398; developed
muscle sense, 397, 398;.
takes room in home of J. B.
McChesney, 399.
"The strangle Oakland
epoch" in his life, ii, 3; contributions to the "Overland
Monthly," 4, 5; his "Sierra
Studies" in large measure due
to Mrs. Carr, 5, 6; his distaste
for the mechanics of writing,
6, 7; his dislike for the solitariness of writing, 7, 8; chafed at
being among men, 8; as a contributor to the "Overland" T–9; publishes
articles, 9, 10; goes for his
health to the Yosemite, 10;
his joy at returning to the
mountains, 10–13; traces
embroidery left in sand, 13–
17; catches eternal harmonies of Nature, 17; in the
Valley of the Merced, 18; in
the Valley of the Tuolumne,
19–21; on a night-tramp in
the mountains, 21–26; prepares to leave the Yosemite
forever, 26–29; his purpose
in life "to entice people to
look at Nature's loveliness,"
29; ascends Mount Shasta,

29–36; letters in "Evening
Bulletin," 32, 36, 51, 62, 71,
98, 123, 125, 163, 174, 190;
his fondness for children, 33;
around Shasta, 37–41; studies
sheep on Mount Brewer, 41;
climbs Douglas spruce in
order to enjoy storm, 41,
42; enjoyed storms, 42–46;
sometimes apologizes for the
life he leads, 13–15; in a
storm on Mount Shasta, 49–
51, 84; has deepening interest
in trees, 51, 52, 54, 56; glad to
be free from problems of life,
54; tries to arouse sentiment
against forest devastation,
58, 59; lectures, 60, 61, 71;
on blessings of domestic life,
62; enjoys writing his first
book, 63; his preference for
quills, 64, 65; visits Utah,
65–67; goes to Los Angeles,
67, 68; visits Congar, 69;
Shasta with Hooker and
Gray, 72, 80–84; descends
Sacramento River in skiff,
73–80; discovers *Linnœa
borealis*, 81, 82; on Thanksgiving dinners, 83, 85, 86; ac-
count of wanderings of wanderings, 87–90, 94, 95; his gains
from wanderings, 91; joins
survey bound for Nevada, 97,
101; guest in Strentzel household, 100; his account of
Nevada trip, 101–16; has
lodgings with Isaac Upham,
117; difference between his
spoken and written words,
119, 120; brilliancy of his conversation, 120; his boyhood
memoirs taken down by di-
rection of E. H. Harriman,
120, 318; Miss Strentzel an
attraction to, 121, 122; becomes engaged to Miss Strent-

zel, 123; goes to Alaska, 123;
with S. Hall Young, 123, 124;
looked upon as mysterious
being by the Indians, 124;
scares Indians by fire on
mountain, 124; his gains in
Alaska, 126; correspondence
with Katharine Merrill
Graydon, 126–30, 133–35;
marriage announced, 131;
as an arguer, 132; wedding,
135; home of, 136; leaves on
second Alaska trip, 137; his
second trip to Alaska, 138–
61; daughter born to, 161;
joins Arctic relief expedition,
161; his account of the expedition to Wrangell Land,
163–91; on Wrangell Land,
163; his collection of plants
gathered in Arctic lands,
191; happy in the enjoyments
of home, 192; his earnings
from magazine articles, 193;
his summary of the years,
1881–1891, 193, 194; takes
wife to Yosemite Valley,
194; second daughter born
to, 195; Helen Hunt Jackson
applies to, for itinerary, 196–
98; his answer to Helen Hunt
Jackson's letter, 198–202;
his letter to Helen Hunt
Jackson answered, 202, 203;
his premonition of Daniel
Muir's death, 204–06; last
meeting with his father, 206–
08; his account of Daniel
Muir's death, 208–10; re-
visits old scenes and people,
210–13; correspondence with
Janet Moores, 213–18; un-
dertakes to edit and contribute to "Picturesque California," 218; feels the strain
of care and worry, 218–20;
experience with a reporter,

221–24; passages for "Picturesque California," 226–
30; meeting with Robert Underwood Johnson, 233; takes
Johnson through the Yosemite, 234–36; writes articles
for the "Century," 234; in-
itiates project of establishment of Yosemite National
Park, 234; on the Yosemite
Park project, 237–42, 244;
memories of Torrey, Gray,
Kellogg, and Parry, 242,
243; his third trip to Alaska,
245.
Advocates enlargement of
Sequoia National Park, 253,
254; president of Sierra
Club, 256; meeting with J. W.
Riley, 259; goes East on
way to Scotland, 261; visits
Chicago World's Fair, 261–
63; in New York, 265, 266;
in Boston, 266, 269; visits
Concord, 266–69; visits Cambridge, 270; visits Manchester, 271; at Edinburgh, 272–
73; at Dunbar, 273–80; at
various places in Scotland,
280, 281, 283; visits Sir
Joseph Hooker, 282, 283;
visits Ireland, 283; his
"Mountains of California,"
288, 289; revisits Hetch-
Hetchy, 289, 290; attempts
to secure him as teacher,
291–93; visits Yosemite
Valley, 294, 295; awarded
honorary degree by Harvard,
295, 296, 298; has premonition of his mother's death,
296; accompanies unofficially
the Forestry Commission,
297–302, 399; his Eastern experiences, 298, 299; defends
recommendations of Forest
Commission, 304; joins Sar-

444

INDEX

gent and Canby on expedition to Rocky Mountains and Alaska to study forest trees, 304, 305; degree conferred upon, by University of Wisconsin, 304 *n.*; on his difficulty of writing, 306; discovers flowers of red fir, 307, 308; makes trip into the Alleghanies, 311, 312; with the Osborns, 312–14; goes with Sargent to Florida, 313–16; urged to write his autobiography, 317; joins Harriman Alaska Expedition, 318, 320, 321; his account of the Expedition, 322–33; receives letters of appreciation, 336–38; receives invitation to visit the Osborns, 340; literary plans, 341 43; on killing of wild animals, 349, 350; visits foreign lands, 350, 351; his work in securing union of Yosemite Valley with Yosemite National Park, 351, 352, 355–57; death of wife, 352, 353; discovers petrified forest, 353; doubts being able to accomplish literary plans, 353–55; visits South America, 354, 369–73; visits South Africa, 354, 374; rewrites autobiographical notes, 359, 362; at work on Yosemite notes, 364; degrees conferred on by Yale, 365; has finished a volume of his autobiography, 366; his preference among trees, 380, 381; death, 390, 391.

And California, what they did for each other, 392; the idea of national reserves conceived by, 392, 393; his services in the cause

of forest reservations, 395, 396; effect of his "Mountains of California" in awakening the public mind, 397; understands outcry against forest reservations, 401; urged to write syndicate letters on forest reserves, 402; writes articles for forest reservation, 403–05, 407, 408; his efforts for forest reservation successful, 406; in the High Sierra with President Roosevelt, 408–13; friendship with President Roosevelt, 411, 415, 416; results of his trip with President Roosevelt, 414; urged to write a description of the Grand Cañon of the Colorado, 414; writes description, 415; suggests to President that he proclaim the Grand Cañon a national monument, 415; letter to President Roosevelt on the Hetch-Hetchy Valley question, 417–20; effect of his letter, 421.

Muir, Mrs. John (*see* Louie Wanda Strentzel) daughter born to, ii, 161; second daughter born to, 195; concerned for her husband's health, 220; a stimulating and appreciative helper of her husband, 221; death, 352, 353; letters to, 138–57, 163–91, 208–13, 221–31, 235, 246, 261–83, 322–33.

Muir, Margaret, sister of John, i, 16.

Muir, Mary, aunt of John, i, 4, 5, 7.

Muir, Mary, sister of John, i, 16; letter to, 136.

Muir, Sarah, sister of John, i, 16; goes with father to America, 37; marries David M.

INDEX

The Secret Marriage," i, 278 n.
"Old Log Schoolhouse," juvenile poem of Muir, i, 65–68.
Olmsted, Frederick Law, ii, 263.
Olney, Warren, Sr., and the Sierra Club, ii, 256; letter to, 303.
Osborn, Professor Henry Fairfield, visited by Muir, ii, 266, 298, 312–14; letters to, 349, 360, 374, 384–86; some of Muir's writing done at home of, 354, 367; Muir goes to Yosemite with, 359.
Osborn, Mrs. H. F., ii, 299; letters to, 340, 368, 374, 383.
"Our National Parks," ii, 306.
"Our New Arctic Territory," ii, 187.
Ouzel Basin, ii, 130.
Over-industry, vice of, i, 48–50.
"Overland Monthly," the, editorial direction of, i, 317; ii, 3, 4; a costly magazine, i, 317; ii, 4; Muir publishes "Yosemite Valley in Flood" and "Twenty Hill Hollow" in, i, 317; "Living Glaciers of California" published in, 352; "Studies in the Sierra" published in, 358, 396; ii, 4; Muir writes occasionally for, i, 385; "Hetch-Hetchy Valley" and "Explorations in the Great Tuolumne Cañon published in, 396; contributors to, ii, 4; abandoned, 5; "Wild Wool" in, 41; "A Flood-Storm in the Sierra" in, 44, 45.

Pacheco Pass, the, i, 179, 180.
Page, Walter Hines, friendship with Muir, ii, 306; stimu-

lated Muir's literary productiveness, 306; Muir at his home, 312; urges Muir to write his autobiography, 317; letters to, 320, 335, 341; opens pages of "Atlantic Monthly" for "The American Forests," 403; urges Muir to write a description of the Grand Cañon of the Colorado, 414.
Page, Mrs., W. H., ii, 306.
Palmer, Howard, letter to, ii, 378.
Palmetto, the, Muir enraptured with, i, 169.
Panama, Isthmus of, trip across, i, 176.
Para, Brazil, visited by Muir, ii, 368–71.
Pardee, Governor George C., ii, 355.
Paregoy, Mr., i, 330.
Parkinson, John D., tutor, i, 89.
Parkman, Francis, ii, 270.
Parks. See National parks.
Parry, Charles C., i, 343; death, ii, 242; memories of, 243.
Parsons, Captain, of the Island Belle, i, 172–74.
Parsons, Mr. and Mrs. Edward J., letter to, ii, 376.
Parsons, Marion Randall, ii, 389.
Parsons, Mr., superintendent of Central Park, ii, 270.
Pelton, Emily, letters of Muir to, descriptive of botanical tour, i, 97–106; Muir again gets in touch with, 321; comes to the Yosemite Valley, 322; ii, 28; letter to, i, 323; Muir calls on, ii, 29, 40, 44.
Pelton family, i, 82.

447

INDEX

Perkins, Senator, of California, ii, 400.

Peters' Colonization Company, ii, 99.

Petrified forest, remnants of, discovered by Muir, ii, 353.

Petrified Forest National Monument, ii, 353.

Phelan, James D., his ignorance about the Hetch-Hetchy Valley, ii, 419.

Phelps, Professor, ii, 365.

"Picturesque California," ii, 218–30, 394.

Pinchot, Gifford, ii, 265; of the National Forestry Commission, 398; suggests that San Francisco take its water supply from the Yosemite National Park, 420, 421.

Pine, sugar, ii, 52; white, 115; foxtail, 116; yellow, 116, 300.

Piper, A. D., promoter of American colonization scheme, i, 233.

Pixley, Frank, ii, 236.

Plant-stem register, invention of Muir, i, 88.

Pohono, i, 228, 229.

Ponderosa, ii, 300, 308.

Prairie du Chien, i, 82, 83.

Proteus-Muggins, ii, 309.

Puget Sound, masts sent from, ii, 227.

Purns, Agnes, ii, 279.

Rabe, Carl, i, 396.

Rae, James, husband of Margaret Gilrye, i, 15.

Rail-splitting, i, 46.

Rainier, Mount, ascended by Muir, ii, 219, 229, 232.

Ramsay, Dean, "Reminiscences of Scottish Life and Character," ii, 272.

Range of Light, the, i, 201.

Rapelye, Mrs., i, 228.

Ravens, ii, 251.

Red fir, flowers of, discovered by Muir, ii, 307, 308.

Red Mountain glacier, i, 350.

Redding, Cyrus, his play, "A Wife and not a Wife," 278 n.

Redwood, the, ii, 51, 68.

Reid (Harry Fielding) and Cushing party, in Alaska, ii, 247.

Reid, Harvey, fellow student of Muir, i, 85.

Religiousness, in household of Daniel Muir, i, 59–63; if warped, may cause harm, 62.

Repose, an attribute of Nature, i, 319.

Ribbon glacier, i, 304–06.

Riley, Henry, ii, 259.

Riley, James Whitcomb, meeting with Muir, ii, 259.

Rio de Janeiro, its harbor a glacial bay, ii, 372.

"Rival of the Yosemite, A," ii, 254.

River, a dead, ii, 43.

Rocky Mountains, studying forest trees in, ii, 304, 305.

Rodgers, August F., Assistant of United States Coast and Geodetic Survey, ii, 97.

Roosevelt, Theodore, services rendered by, to cause of forests and parks, ii, 254; inspires, signs, and transmits resolution of Boone and Crockett Club, 258; counsels Muir, 353; sets aside petrified forest, 353; supported transference of Yosemite Valley to Federal Government, 355; in the High Sierra with Muir, 408–13; friendship with Muir, 411, 415, 416; results of his trip with Muir, 414; letter of Muir to, on Hetch-Hetchy question, 417–20;

448

INDEX

INDEX

INDEX

Soda Springs, ii, 230.

Sonne, Mr., ii, 308.

South America, Muir plans to visit, i, 173, 203; colonization scheme, 233; visited by Muir, ii, 354, 368–73.

South Dakota, character of the State, ii, 300.

Spanish-American War, ii, 405.

Stebbins, Dr., i, 382, 383.

"Steep Trails," ii, 49, 66.

Stein, Philip, impressions of Muir, i, 89.

Sterling, Professor John W., of University of Wisconsin, i, 91, 138, 139.

Stewart, George W., his "Mount Whitney Club Journal," i, 394.

Stickeen, the dog, on canoe trip, ii, 157, 160; his antecedents, 160 n.; Muir repeats story of, 265, 270, 271; story of, appears in the "Century," 304.

"Stickeen," ii, 42, 304.

Stirling, visited by Muir, ii, 280.

Stoddard, Charles Warren, i, 231, 367.

Storms, Muir's enjoyment of, ii, 42–46.

Strentzel, Dr. John, career, ii, 00; death, 252.

Strentzel, Mrs. John, ii, 252.

Strentzel, Louie Wanda, daughter of John Strentzel, ii, 100; an attraction to Muir, 121, 122; becomes engaged to Muir, 123; engagement announced, 131; wedding, 135. See Muir, Mrs. John.

Strentzel, Dr., Mrs. John, and Miss, letters to, ii, 94, 101–19.

"Studies in the Formation of Mountains in the Sierra Nevada," ii, 9, 10.

"Studies in the Sierra," i, 358, 359, 396; ii, 4, 5, 9, 63.

Styles, Mr., of "Forest and Stream," ii, 270.

Sugar pine, the, ii, 52.

Sunset, a mountain, i, 369, 370.

Swain, Mrs. Richard, letter to, ii, 336.

Swett, Helen, ii, 90, ill, 116, 118.

Swett, John, with Muir in the Yosemite, ii, 51, 54; Muir at home of, 67, 68; sickness in family of, 116; on Muir's writing, 120.

Swett, Mrs. John, letter from, ii, 131–33.

Taft, William H., President, ii, 422.

Tahoe reservation, ii, 319.

Taylor, J. G., impressions of Muir, i, 89.

Taylor Bay, ii, 159, 160.

Tenaya Cañon, climb through, i, 368, 369.

Tenaya Lake, i, 232, 299, 300.

Tesla, Nicola, ii, 299, 314.

Thanksgiving dinners, ii, 83, 85, 86.

Thayer, James Bradley, meeting with Muir, i, 254; his "A Western journey with Mr. Emerson," 254 n.

Thecla Muiri, i, 264 n.

Thermometer invented by Muir, i, 75, 76.

Thomson, William, his "Orpheus Caledonius," i, 12.

Thoreau, Henry David, his "Maine Woods," i, 223; Muir at his grave, ii, 267; Muir visits his residence, 268; verses of, quoted, 363.

"Thousand-Mile Walk to the Gulf, A," i, 157, 164.

Thurso, ii, 283.

Torrey, John, i, 230; and Muir,

451

INDEX

343; death, 242; memories, 243.

Toyatte, death of, ii, 148, 152, 153.

"Travels in Alaska," ii, 123, 390, 391.

"Treasures of Yosemite, The," in the "Century," ii, 234.

Trees, become of interest to Muir, ii, 51, 52; in Rocky Mountains and Alaska, expedition to study, 304, 305; Muir's preference among, 380, 381. *See* Sequoias.

Trout, Harriet, of the "Hollow," i, 129, 150.

Trout, Mary, of the "Hollow," i, 129, 150.

Trout, William H., of the "Hollow," i, 129; his account of Muir's sojourn at the Hollow, 130–33; last letter of Muir to, 150, 151; visited by Muir, ii, 298.

Truman, Ben, ii, 236.

Tule grove, efforts to secure inclusion of, in Sequoia National Park, ii, 253.

Tuolumne Cañon, i, 311, 397; ii, 244, 418.

Tuolumne Meadows, i, 232; ii, 244, 418.

Tuolumne River, the, in the valley of, ii, 19–21.

Tuolumne Yosemite, the, i, 310; ii, 358, 389. *See* Hetch-Hetchy.

Twain, Mark. *See* Clemens.

"Twenty Hill Hollow," i, 317.

Tyndall, John, in the Yosemite, i, 230; read by Muir, 240; Muir receives book of, 297; a great man, 335, 367.

University degrees conferred on Muir, ii, 295, 296, 298, 304 n., 365.

Upham, Isaac, Muir has lodgings with, ii, 117.

Utah, visited by Muir, ii, 65–67.

Vancouver Island, ii, 139–48.

Vanderbilt, Mr., ii, 150, 151.

Vandever, General William, member of Congress, ii, 234.

Varnel, Mr., i, 76.

Victoria, ii, 142–47.

Vigilance, whaler, ii, 178.

Vroman, Charles E., his account of Muir, i, 89–91.

Walden Pond, ii, 268.

"Water Ouzel," ii, 127.

Waterston, Mrs. Robert C., visits the Yosemite, i, 225, 228; on Muir's letters, 225.

Watson, Frank E., of the American Museum of Natural History, i, 264 n.

Well-digging, i, 52, 53.

Wesley, John, ii, 387.

Wheeler, Benjamin Ide, ii, 409.

Whipping, a Scotch fashion, i, 47.

White, Senator, of California, ii, 400.

White Pine, ii, 115.

White Pine mining region, ii, 112.

Whitehead, James, buys Fountain Lake farm, i, 50 n., 135.

Whitney, Mount, i, 392–96.

Whitney, Josiah D., on the Yosemite, i, 215; State Geologist of California, 274; made Professor of Geology at Harvard University, 275; publishes books on the Yosemite, 275; his theory of the origin of the Yosemite, 275–77, 287; his "Yosemite Guide-Book," 275, 277, 282;

INDEX

in Thérèse Yelverton's novel, 279, 282; scorns Muir's theory of origin of the Yosemite, 287, 288; repudiates former statement, 302; beginning of the end of his theory, 309; his impressions of the Sierra Nevada, 312; refuses to accept theory of living glaciers, 353, 355, 356; and King's views of the Yosemite, 357; statement on entrance of Tuolumne Cañon disproved, 397.

Wild animals, preservation of, ii, 349–51.

"Wild Sheep in California," ii, 10.

"Wild Sheep of the Sierra," ii, 394.

"Wild Wool," ii, 41.

Williams, Sam, editor of San Francisco "Evening Bulletin," ii, 125.

Willymott, William, his "Selections from the Colloquies of Corderius," i, 28.

Wilson, Alexander, ornithologist, i, 36.

Wilson, Emily Pelton. *See* Pelton, Emily.

Wilson, President Woodrow, ii, 384, 388, 389.

"Wind Storm in the Forest of the Yuba, A," ii, 42.

Wirad, Mr., machine-shop of, i, 82.

Wisconsin, the Muirs settle in, i, 38; schooling in, 65.

Wisconsin, University of, Muir student at, i, 82, 84, 85, 88–95; crisis at, 91, 93; reorganized, 92; Muir takes farewell of, 113; invites Muir to return as free student, 139; confers degree upon Muir, ii, 304 n.

Wisconsin Agricultural Society, i, 79–81.

Wisconsin River valley, botanical tour down, i, 97–106; description of excursion in, 109–12.

Wisconsin State Agricultural Fair, i, 76, 79.

Wolves, adventure with, in Canadian woods, i, 122; adventure with, on Muir Glacier, ii, 248–50.

Works, Senator John D., ii, 390.

Wrangell Land, one of the objectives of relief expedition, ii, 162; difficulty of approaching, 186; the Corwin makes landing on, 187; plants from, 191.

Writing, the mechanics and solitariness of, irksome to Muir, ii, 6–8.

Yale, confers honorary degree on Muir, ii, 365.

Yellow pine, ii, 116, 300.

Yelverton, Thérèse, her novel, "Zanita, a Tale of the Yosemite," i, 225, 228, 278–85; in the Yosemite, 228, 233, 236; her perils in the snow, 238, her disputed marriage rights, 278 n., 278 n.; envies Muir's calmness of heart, 362, 363.

Yelverton, William Charles, Viscount Avonmore, i, 278 n.

"Yosemite, The," i, 386.

Yosemite Bay, ii, 159.

Yosemite Creek, i, 304–07.

Yosemite Falls, upper, i, 249–51.

Yosemite fountains, ii, 244.

"Yosemite Glaciers," i, 308, 316.

Yosemite National Park, es-

453

S. Clara Co ✠